BEST

NONFICTION

Advanced Level

7 Selections for Young People

with Lessons for Teaching the Basic Elements of Nonfiction

Christine Lund Orciuch

Theodore Knight, Ph.D.

JAMESTOWN PUBLISHERS

a division of NTC/CONTEMPORARY PUBLISHING GROUP
Lincolnwood, Illinois USA

Cover Design: Steve Straus
Interior Design: Steve Straus
Cover Illustration: Dennis Lyall
Interior Illustrations:
Unit 1: © Ken Dequaine/The Picture Cube, Inc. (page x)
Unit 2: © Richard During/Tony Stone Images (page 28); Mount Rainier illustration
by Harold Smelcer. First appeared in *Smithsonian* magazine, July 1996. Reprinted by
permission of Harold Smelcer. All rights reserved. (pages 58-59)
Unit 3: CATHY © 1995 Cathy Guisewite. Reprinted with permission of Universal
Press Syndicate. All rights reserved. (page 64)
Unit 4: © David Weintraub (page 96)
Unit 5: Culver Pictures (page 134)
Unit 6: Culver Pictures (page 172)
Unit 7: Walter Bennett/Time Magazine, © Time Inc. (page 206)

ISBN: 0-89061-901-8 (hardbound)
ISBN: 0-89061-884-4 (softbound)

Published by Jamestown Publishers,
a division of NTC/Contemporary Publishing Group, Inc.
4255 West Touhy Avenue, Lincolnwood (Chicago), Illinois 60646-1975, U.S.A.
© 1998 NTC/Contemporary Publishing Group, Inc.

8 9 0 QB 0 9 8 7 6 5 4 3 2 1

ACKNOWLEDGMENTS

Acknowledgment is gratefully made to the following publishers, authors, and agents for permission to reprint these works. Every effort has been made to determine copyright owners. In the case of any omissions, the Publisher will be pleased to make suitable acknowledgments in future editions.

"Blue Winds Dancing" by Thomas S. Whitecloud is reprinted with the permission of Scribner, a Division of Simon & Schuster from *Scribner's Magazine*, Vol. III, Number 2, February 1938. Copyright 1938 by Charles Scribner's Sons; copyright renewed © 1966.

"Mount Rainier: Washington's Tranquil Threat" by Jon Krakauer. First appeared in *Smithsonian* magazine, July 1996, Volume 27, Number 4. Reprinted by permission of the author, Jon Krakauer. All rights reserved.

"Remember Who You Are" speech given by Cathy Guisewite from *Hold Fast Your Dreams: Twenty Commencement Speeches*, Scholastic, Inc. Copyright © 1996. Published by permission of Cathy Guisewite. All rights reserved.

"Sojourners Who Came to Stay" by Donald Dale Jackson. First appeared in *Smithsonian* magazine, February 1991, Volume 21, Number 11. Reprinted by permission of the author, Donald Dale Jackson. All rights reserved.

"Mark Twain: The Early Years" by Skip Press from *The Importance of Mark Twain*. Copyright © 1994 by Lucent Books, Inc. Reprinted by permission of Lucent Books, Inc., P.O. Box 289011, San Diego, CA 92198-9011.

"Letter from Birmingham Jail" by Martin Luther King, Jr. Reprinted by arrangement with The Heirs to the Estate of Martin Luther King, Jr., c/o Writer's House, Inc., as agent for the proprietor. Copyright 1963 by Coretta Scott King.

CONTENTS

TO THE STUDENT

Nonfiction is literature about real people, places, and events—unlike fiction, which comes mostly from a writer's imagination. When you read magazine or newspaper articles, history books, instructional manuals or guides, biographies and autobiographies, and diaries or journals, you are reading nonfiction. The life story of Martin Luther King, Jr.; a science article about the latest research into heart disease; or a cookbook about desserts are other examples of nonfiction. To many people good nonfiction is as interesting as, or even more interesting than, fiction.

Writers of nonfiction examine real people, events, and experiences in order to understand them. Like all writers, nonfiction writers try to communicate their thoughts, feelings, and ideas about a subject. They may want to explain the reason for certain events; to describe an interesting person, place, or incident; or to persuade an audience to follow a particular course of action. An author's purpose in writing shapes his or her work.

People read nonfiction to gain understanding. They may be curious about a subject—the person, event, or idea—that the writer has chosen to write about. To keep the interest of their readers, writers must not only organize the information but also choose what facts to include and emphasize. In this book you will learn skills that will help you analyze how writers develop and organize their material to create lively, interesting works of nonfiction. By understanding how good writers communicate and by studying the works of good nonfiction writers, you can learn techniques to improve your own writing.

Each unit in this book contains a nonfiction selection and lessons that teach concepts and skills that will help you interpret the selection and understand the particular techniques the author uses to accomplish his or her purpose. Each unit also includes writing exercises that provide an opportunity to use what you learn in the lessons in your own writing.

UNIT FORMAT AND ACTIVITIES

- Each unit begins with a photograph or an illustration depicting someone or something connected with the selection. The photograph or illustration will help you make some predictions about the selection.

- The Introduction begins with background information about the selection and its author. Important literary concepts and skills are then presented, and you are given an opportunity to begin to develop these concepts and skills in your own writing. Finally, there are questions for you to consider as you read. These questions will help you focus on the concepts and skills presented in the unit's lessons.

- The selection makes up the next section. It may be a complete work, such as an essay or an article, or an excerpt from a biography, autobiography, or diary.

- Following each selection are questions that test your comprehension of the events and other elements of the selection as well as your critical-thinking skills. Your answers to these questions and to other exercises in the unit should be recorded in a personal literature notebook. Check your answers with your teacher.

- Your teacher may provide you with charts to record your progress in developing your comprehension skills: The Comprehension Skills Graph *records* your scores and the Comprehension Skills Profile *analyzes* your scores—providing you with information about the skills on which you need to focus. You can talk with your teacher about ways to work on those comprehension skills.

- The next section begins with a discussion of the literary concept that is the unit's focus. This is followed by three lessons, each of which illustrates a technique the author uses to develop that concept. For example, you will see how an author of a persuasive essay develops rational arguments, supports those arguments, and uses emotional appeals to persuade his audience to understand and accept his motives and actions.

- Short-answer exercises test your understanding of the author's techniques as illustrated by short excerpts from the selection. You can check your answers to the exercises with your teacher and determine what you need to review.
- Each lesson also includes a writing exercise that guides you in creating your own original nonfiction work using the techniques you have just studied.
- Discussion guides and a final writing activity round out each unit in the book. These activities will help sharpen your reading, thinking, speaking, and writing skills.

Reading the selections in this book will enable you to recognize and appreciate the skills it takes to write interesting nonfiction. When you understand what makes good nonfiction, you become a better reader. The writing exercises and assignments will help you become a better writer by giving you practice in using the authors' techniques to make your own nonfiction writing interesting.

UNIT 1

Style, Use of Language, and Comparison

Blue Winds Dancing

by Thomas S. Whitecloud

INTRODUCTION

BUILDING BACKGROUND

Thomas Whitecloud says, "Those are never lonely who love the snow and the pines." This photo was taken in northern Wisconsin in February. Places like this are truly "home" to Whitecloud.

Although Thomas S. Whitecloud is better known as a physician than a writer, his essay "Blue Winds Dancing" is well known for its powerful theme and its graceful, almost lyrical, style. "Blue Winds Dancing," written in Whitecloud's senior year at college, won first prize in a Phi Beta Kappa essay contest in 1938. It describes his thoughts as he travels from California to his home in Wisconsin.

In 1938, when Whitecloud wrote this essay, the United States, along with most of the world, was still in the grips of the Great Depression (1929–1939). By 1933 almost half of the banks in the United States had failed, and 25–30 percent of the work force was unemployed. The national spirit was broken. People had less to spend, and the demand for new goods dropped. As a result, production dropped and unemployment rose. The downward spiral of the economy continued.

In addition to living in these hard economic times, Native Americans were experiencing great difficulties trying to live in an America that was mostly white. In his essay Whitecloud expresses the difficulty he has assimilating the ways of the white world and still retaining his own tribal culture. His world is closely related to nature. To Whitecloud and other Native Americans, the white world is artificial, with little connection to the natural environment or tribal beliefs.

ABOUT THE AUTHOR

Thomas St. Germain Whitecloud was born in 1914 in New York City. His father was Chippewa, and his mother was white. The elder Whitecloud graduated from Yale Law School but decided not to practice. The Whiteclouds later divorced, and Thomas's father returned to the Lac du Flambeau Reservation in Wisconsin. Although the boy lived with his mother, he spent much of his childhood with his father on the reservation. During his troubled childhood he was expelled from several public schools and federal Indian schools. After settling down during high school, Whitecloud decided upon medicine as his career. He graduated from the University of Redlands in California and attended Tulane University Medical School, where he received his M.D. degree.

Whitecloud worked as a physician with the Indian Service in Montana and Minnesota before entering private practice in Texas. For more than seven years he not only ran the county hospital but also served as deputy sheriff, health officer, and county coroner. He served as a consultant to the Department of Health, Education, and Welfare; founded the Three Feathers Society, an Indian corresponding group; and helped establish the American Association of Indian Physicians. During his later years Whitecloud wrote and lectured extensively. At his death in 1972, he left a number of works as unfinished manuscripts.

ABOUT THE LESSONS

The lessons that follow "Blue Winds Dancing" focus on the author's style and use of language and comparison.

When you read nonfiction, you typically pay close attention to *what* the author is saying. Yet *how* the author says it may be important as well. Whitecloud's essay is well known, not only because of its powerful theme, but also because of its elegant style and use of descriptive language. As you will see, Whitecloud creates vivid images to help express his views of the white world and his Native American roots. Whitecloud's use of comparison to help express his views will be examined also.

WRITING: DESCRIBING A PERSONAL EXPERIENCE

At the end of this unit, you will write a vivid description of a personal experience you have had in your life. The suggestions below will help you get started:

- Think of two or three experiences that you have had in your life. They could be as simple as a walk in the woods or as serious as an experience that profoundly changed your life. You may have had an experience that taught you a lesson about the importance of family, honesty, or friendship. Perhaps, while taking a walk in the woods or on a beach, you came to an important decision or reflected on an important event. Perhaps you have some particular memories of your first day at junior high or senior high school.
- Copy the graphic organizer on the next page onto a sheet of paper.
- In the first column of the organizer, list the two or three experiences you've thought of. For each experience think of pictures, or images, that come to mind as you recall that experience. In the second column, list words or phrases that describe each image. Try to recall what you saw, heard, smelled, tasted, or touched.

  If, for example, one experience you thought of was your first day of high school, write that down in the first column. In the second column, write down words that describe the images you have of that first day. You might write, "Huge halls, long and crowded corridors, echoing footsteps, gray lockers, smell of food from the cafeteria, my heart pounding."

- Finally, in the third column write down why that particular experience is important to you. You might write that the experience was a step toward becoming an adult, or perhaps you felt it was a new beginning.

Event or Experience	Image	Importance

AS YOU READ Think about the following questions as you read the essay. They will help you see why "Blue Winds Dancing" is well known, not only for its powerful theme, but also because of its author's style of writing.

- How does the author help you share with him the sights and sounds of his home in Wisconsin?
- How does the author express his feelings to the reader about life in the white world and life in his Indian world?

Blue Winds Dancing

by Thomas S. Whitecloud

There is a moon out tonight. Moon and stars and clouds tipped
with moonlight. And there is a fall wind blowing in my heart.
Ever since this evening, when against a fading sky I saw geese
wedge southward. They were going home. . . . Now I try to
study, but against the pages I see them again, driving southward.
Going home.

Across the valley there are heavy mountains holding up the
night sky, and beyond the mountains there is home. Home, and
peace, and the beat of drums, and blue winds dancing over snow
fields. The Indian lodge will fill with my people, and our gods
will come and sit among them. I should be there then. I should
be at home.

But home is beyond the mountains, and I am here. Here
where fall hides in the valleys and winter never comes down
from the mountains. Here where all the trees grow in rows; the
palms stand stiffly by the roadsides, and in the groves the orange
trees line in military rows, and endlessly bear fruit. Beautiful,
yes; there is always beauty in order, in rows of growing things!
But it is the beauty of captivity. A pine fighting for existence on
a windy knoll is much more beautiful.

In my Wisconsin, the leaves change before the snows come.
In the air there is the smell of wild rice and venison cooking;

and when the winds come whispering through the forests, they carry the smell of rotting leaves. In the evenings, the loon calls, lonely; and birds sing their last songs before leaving. Bears dig roots and eat late fall berries, fattening for their long winter sleep. Later, when the first snows fall, one awakens in the morning to find the world white and beautiful and clean. Then one can look back over his trail and see the tracks following. In the woods there are tracks of deer and snowshoe rabbits and long streaks where partridges slide to alight. Chipmunks make tiny footprints on the limbs; and one can hear squirrels busy in hollow trees, sorting acorns. Soft lake waves wash the shores, and sunsets burst each evening over the lakes and make them look as if they were afire.

That land which is my home! Beautiful, calm—where there is no hurry to get anywhere, no driving to keep up in a race that knows no ending and no goal. No classes where men talk and talk, and then stop now and then to hear their own words come back to them from the students. No constant peering into the maelstrom[1] of one's mind; no worries about grades and honors; no hysterical preparing for life until that life is half over; no anxiety about one's place in the thing they call Society.

I hear again the ring of axes in deep woods, the crunch of snow beneath my feet. I feel again the smooth velvet of ghost-birch bark. I hear the rhythm of the drums. . . . I am tired. I am weary of trying to keep up this bluff of being civilized. Being civilized means trying to do everything you don't want to, never doing anything you want to. It means dancing to the strings of custom and tradition; it means living in houses and never knowing or caring who is next door. These civilized white men want us to be like them— always dissatisfied, getting a hill and wanting a mountain.

Then again, maybe I am not tired. Maybe I'm licked. Maybe I am just not smart enough to grasp these things that go to make up civilization. Maybe I am just too lazy to think hard enough to keep up.

Still, I know my people have many things that civilization has taken from the whites. They know how to give—how to tear

[1] a powerful, often violent, whirlpool that draws in objects around it

one's piece of meat in two and share it with one's brother. They know how to sing—how to make each man his own songs and sing them; for their music they do not have to listen to other men singing over a radio. They know how to make things with their hands—how to shape beads into design and make a thing of beauty from a piece of birch bark.

But we are inferior. It is terrible to have to feel inferior, to have to read reports of intelligence tests and learn that one's race is behind. It is terrible to sit in classes and hear men tell you that your people worship sticks of wood—that your gods are all false, that the Manitou[2] forgot your people and did not write them a book.

I am tired. I want to walk again among the ghost-birches. I want to see the leaves turn in autumn, the smoke rise from the lodgehouses, and to feel the blue winds. I want to hear the drums; I want to hear the drums and feel the blue whispering winds.

There is a train wailing into the night. The trains go across the mountains. It would be easy to catch a freight. They will say he has gone back to the blanket; I don't care. The dance at Christmas. . . .

A bunch of bums warming at a tiny fire talk politics and women and joke about the Relief and the WPA[3] and smoke cigarettes. These men in caps and overcoats and dirty overalls living on the outskirts of civilization are free, but they pay the price of being free in civilization. They are outcasts. I remember a sociology professor lecturing on adjustment to society; hobos and prostitutes and criminals are individuals who never adjusted, he said. He could learn a lot if he came and listened to a bunch of bums talk. He would learn that work and a woman and a place to hang his hat are all the ordinary man wants. These are all he wants, but other men are not content to let him want only these. He must be taught to want radios and automobiles and a new suit every spring. Progress would stop if he did not want these things. I listen to hear if there is any talk of com-

[2] Great Spirit; the reference to the book not written is a comparison to the Bible

[3] Works Projects Administration, a work program created in 1935 by the federal government to create jobs for the vast number of unemployed

munism or socialism in the hobo jungles. There is none. At best there is a sort of disgusted philosophy about life. They seem to think there should be a better distribution of wealth, or more work, or something. But they are not rabid about it. The radicals live in the cities.

I find a fellow headed for Albuquerque, and talk road-talk with him. "It is hard to ride fruit cars. Bums break in. Better to wait for a cattle car going back to the Middle West, and ride that." We catch the next east-bound and walk the tops until we find a cattle car. Inside, we crouch near the forward wall, huddle, and try to sleep. I feel peaceful and content at last. I am going home. The cattle car rocks. I sleep.

Morning and the desert. Noon and the Salton Sea, lying more lifeless than a mirage under a somber sun in a pale sky. Skeleton mountains rearing on the skyline, thrusting out of the desert floor, all rock and shadow and edges. Desert. Good country for an Indian reservation. . . .

Yuma and the muddy Colorado. Night again, and I wait shivering for the dawn.

Phoenix. Pima country. Mountains that look like cardboard sets on a forgotten stage. Tucson. Papago country. Giant cacti that look like petrified hitchhikers along the highways. Apache country. At El Paso my road-buddy decides to go on to Houston. I leave him and head north to the mesa country. Las Cruces and the terrible Organ Mountains, jagged peaks that instill fear and wondering. Albuquerque. Pueblos along the Rio Grande. On the boardwalk there are some Indian women in colored sashes selling bits of pottery. The stone age offering its art to the twentieth century. They hold up a piece and fix the tourists with black eyes until, embarrassed, he buys or turns away. I feel suddenly angry that my people should have to do such things for a living. . . .

Santa Fe trains are fast, and they keep them pretty clean of bums. I decide to hurry and ride passenger coal tenders. Hide in the dark, judge the speed of the train as it leaves, and then dash out, and catch it. I hug the cold steel wall of the tender and think of the roaring fire in the engine ahead and of the passengers back in the dining car reading their papers over hot coffee.

Beneath me there is a blur of rails. Death would come quick if my hands should freeze and I fall. Up over the Sangre De Cristo range, around cliffs and through canyons to Denver. Bitter cold here, and I must watch out for Denver Bob. He is a railroad bull who has thrown bums from fast freights. I miss him. It is too cold, I suppose. On north to the Sioux country.

Small towns lit for the coming Christmas. On the streets of one I see a beam-shouldered young farmer gazing into a window filled with shining silver toasters. He is tall and wears a blue shirt, buttoned, with no tie. His young wife by his side looks at him hopefully. He wants decorations for his place to hang his hat to please his woman. . . .

Northward again. Minnesota, and great white fields of snow, frozen lakes, and dawn running into dusk without noon. Long forests wearing white. Bitter cold, and one night the northern lights. I am nearing home.

I reach Woodruff at midnight. Suddenly I am afraid, now that I am but twenty miles from home. Afraid of what my father will say, afraid of being looked on as a stranger by my own people. I sit by a fire and think about myself and all the other young Indians. We just don't seem to fit in anywhere—certainly not among the whites, and not among the older people. I think again about the learned sociology professor and his professing. So many things seem to be clear now that I am away from school and do not have to worry about some man's opinion of my ideas. It is easy to think while looking at dancing flames.

Morning. I spend the day cleaning up and buying some presents for my family with what is left of my money. Nothing much, but a gift is a gift, if a man buys it with his last quarter. I wait until evening, then start up the track toward home.

Christmas Eve comes in on a north wind. Snow clouds hang over the pines, and the night comes early. Walking along the railroad bed, I feel the calm peace of snowbound forests on either side of me. I take my time; I am back in a world where time does not mean so much now. I am alone; alone but not nearly so lonely as I was back on the campus at school. Those are never lonely who love the snow and the pines; never lonely when the pines are wearing white shawls and snow crunches coldly underfoot. In the woods I know there are the tracks of deer and rabbit; I know that if I leave the rails and go into the woods, I shall find them. I walk along feeling glad because my legs are light and my feet seem to know that they are home. A deer comes out of the woods just ahead of me and stands silhouetted on the rails. The North, I feel, has welcomed me home. I watch him and am glad that I do not wish for a gun. He goes into the woods quietly, leaving only the design of his tracks in the snow. I walk on. Now and then I pass a field, white under the night sky, with houses at the far end. Smoke comes from the chimneys of the houses, and I try to tell what sort of wood each is burning by the smoke; some burn pine, others aspen, others tamarack. There is one from which comes black coal smoke that rises lazily and drifts out over the tops of the trees. I like to watch houses and try to imagine what might be happening in them.

Just as a light snow begins to fall, I cross the reservation boundary; somehow it seems as though I have stepped into another world. Deep woods in a white-and-black winter night. A faint trail leading to the village.

The railroad on which I stand comes from a city sprawled by a lake—a city with a million people who walk around without seeing one another; a city sucking the life from all the country around; a city with stores and police and intellectuals and criminals and movies and apartment houses; a city with its politics and libraries and zoos.

Laughing, I go into the woods. As I cross a frozen lake, I begin to hear the drums. Soft in the night the drums beat. It is like the pulse beat of the world. The white line of the lake ends at a black forest, and above the trees the blue winds are dancing.

I come to the outlying houses of the village. Simple box houses, etched black in the night. From one or two windows soft lamp light falls on the snow. Christmas here, too, but it does not mean much; not much in the way of parties and presents. Joe Sky will get drunk. Alex Bodidash will buy his children red mittens and a new sled. Alex is a Carlisle man[4] and tries to keep his home

---

[4] a man who went to the Carlisle School in Pennsylvania, the first reservation school, established by the government in 1879

up to white standards. White standards. Funny that my people should be ever falling farther behind. The more they try to imitate whites, the more tragic the result. Yet they want us to be imitation white men. About all we imitate well are their vices.

The village is not a sight to instill pride, yet I am not ashamed; one can never be ashamed of his own people when he knows they have dreams as beautiful as white snow on a tall pine.

Father and my brother and sister are seated around the table as I walk in. Father stares at me for a moment; then I am in his arms, crying on his shoulder. I give them the presents I have brought, and my throat tightens as I watch my sister save carefully bits of red string from the packages. I hide my feelings by wrestling with my brother when he strikes my shoulder in token of affection. Father looks at me, and I know he has many questions, but he seems to know why I have come. He tells me to go on alone to the lodge, and he will follow.

I walk along the trail to the lodge, watching the northern lights forming in the heavens. White waving ribbons that seem to pulsate with the rhythm of the drums. Clean snow creaks beneath my feet, and a soft wind sighs through the trees, singing to me. Everything seems to say, "Be happy! You are home now—you are free. You are among friends—we are your friends; we, the trees, and the snow, and the lights." I follow the trail to the lodge. My feet are light, my heart seems to sing to the music, and I hold my head high. Across white snow fields blue winds are dancing.

Before the lodge door I stop, afraid. I wonder if my people will remember me. I wonder— "Am I Indian, or am I white?" I stand before the door a long time. I hear the ice groan on the lake, and remember the story of the old woman who is under the ice, trying to get out, so she can punish some runaway lovers. I think to myself, "If I am white, I will not believe that story; if I am Indian, I will know that there is an old woman under the ice." I listen for a while, and I know that there is an old woman under the ice. I look again at the lights and go in.

Inside the lodge there are many Indians. Some sit on benches around the walls; others dance in the center of the floor around a drum. Nobody seems to notice me. It seems as though I were among a people I have never seen before. Heavy women with long black hair. Women with children on their knees—small children that watch with intent black eyes the movements of the dancers, whose small faces are solemn and serene. The faces of the old people are serene, too, and their eyes are merry and bright. I look at the old men. Straight, dressed in dark trousers and beaded velvet vests, wearing soft moccasins. Dark, lined faces intent on the music. I wonder if I am at all like them. They dance on, lifting their feet to the rhythm of the drums, swaying lightly, looking upward. I look at their eyes and am startled at the rapt attention to the rhythm of the music.

The dance stops. The men walk back to the walls and talk in low tones or with their hands. There is little conversation, yet everyone seems to be sharing some secret. A woman looks at a small boy wandering away, and he comes back to her.

Strange, I think, and then remember. These people are not sharing words—they are sharing a mood. Everyone is happy. I am so used to white people that it seems strange so many people could be together without someone talking. These Indians are happy because they are together, and because the night is beautiful outside, and the music is beautiful. I try hard to forget school and white people, and be one of these—my people. I try to forget everything but the night, and it is a part of me; that I am one with my people and we are all a part of something universal. I watch eyes and see now that the old people are speaking to me. They nod slightly, imperceptibly,[5] and their eyes laugh into mine. I look around the room. All the eyes are friendly; they all laugh. No one questions my being here. The drums begin to beat again, and I catch the invitation in the eyes of the old men. My feet begin to lift to the rhythm, and I look out beyond the walls into the night and see the lights. I am happy. It is beautiful. I am home.

---

[5] extremely slightly, gradually, or subtly

REVIEWING AND INTERPRETING

Record your answers to these questions in your personal literature notebook. Follow the directions for each part.

REVIEWING Try to complete each of these sentences without looking back at the selection.

Recalling Facts **1.** The author's home is in
   a. Colorado.
   b. Wisconsin.
   c. Minnesota.
   d. New Mexico.

Understanding Main Ideas **2.** Whitecloud wants to go home because he
   a. feels free there and at peace with himself.
   b. wants to please his father and family.
   c. looks forward to traveling home by train.
   d. is bored with college life.

Identifying Sequence **3.** Whitecloud suddenly becomes afraid of what his father and others will think about his return
   a. before he meets the man headed for Albuquerque.
   b. when he buys presents for his family.
   c. after he enters the lodge.
   d. when he is just twenty miles from home.

Finding Supporting Details **4.** As an example of Whitecloud's feeling of inferiority in the white world, he mentions
   a. that his professor says Native Americans have not adjusted to white society.
   b. reports of intelligence tests that say his race is behind.
   c. that his classmates will say "he has gone back to the blanket."
   d. that hobos think there should be a better distribution of wealth.

Getting Meaning from Context

5. "I look at their eyes and am startled at the rapt attention to the rhythm of the music." The word *rapt* means
a. foolish.
b. absorbed.
c. uninterested.
d. concerned.

INTERPRETING

To complete these items, you may look back at the selection if you'd like.

Making Inferences

6. One of Whitecloud's main purposes in writing this essay is to show
a. that hobos were really ordinary men.
b. how easy it was to ride cattle and coal-tender trains.
c. how difficult it was to go home.
d. how much he longed for the peace he found at home.

Generalizing

7. Whitecloud's relationship with his family can best be described as
a. distant.
b. angry.
c. affectionate.
d. uncomfortable.

Drawing Conclusions

8. When Whitecloud says, "These civilized white men want us to be like them—always dissatisfied, getting a hill and wanting a mountain," he means that
a. in the white world progress is built on always wanting and buying more.
b. Native Americans want to be a part of the white world and economy.
c. Native Americans want to live in the mountains.
d. all people are concerned with getting ahead in life.

Recognizing Fact and
Opinion

9. Which of the following is a statement of opinion?
   a. A pine fighting for existence on a windy knoll is much more beautiful!
   b. But home is beyond the mountains, and I am here.
   c. I find a fellow headed for Albuquerque, and talk road-talk with him.
   d. On the boardwalk there are some Indian women in colored sashes selling bits of pottery.

Identifying Cause and
Effect

10. Whitecloud must keep an eye out for Denver Bob, a railroad bull, because he
   a. stops the train and tells hobos and bums to leave.
   b. runs the east-bound railroad.
   c. throws people who have not paid from the train.
   d. will have those who ride the train illegally, put into jail.

Now check your answers with your teacher. Study the items you answered incorrectly. What skills are they checking? Talk to your teacher about ways to work on those skills.

Style, Use of Language, and Comparison

"Blue Winds Dancing" is a personal essay. An *essay* is a brief work of nonfiction that expresses a person's opinions or views about a particular subject. The purpose of an essay may be to analyze, to inform, to entertain, or to persuade. The author of a personal essay re-creates a personal experience, allowing you to live that same experience through his or her eyes. By reading personal essays, you have the chance to experience insights, thoughts, or feelings that may be outside of your own everyday experience.

The reader's interest in a personal essay often has at least as much to do with the author as it does with the subject of the essay. The author's style and how well the author presents his or her opinions or views about the essay's subject are important factors in engaging the reader's interest. In some personal essays the writer may make use of a comparison to help achieve his or her purpose in writing the essay.

In the lessons that follow we will examine several aspects of an author's style and use of language, as well as the use of comparison, in telling his or her story.

1. **Author's Style**   Each writer's style is unique, but all writers structure their writing and use language in ways that help them to express their thoughts and feelings. The style of each writer differs depending on how each chooses to express those thoughts and feelings.

2. **Use of Figurative Language**   Writers use words and phrases in unusual ways to create strong, vivid images. One of the most effective ways a writer has to make you picture something clearly in your mind is to compare it with something else—something the writer thinks is familiar to you. Such comparisons, when they compare two things that are in most ways unlike, are called *figures of speech,* or figurative language.

3. **Use of Comparison**   Writers sometimes use comparison or contrast as a way to help get their main points across. A *comparison* focuses on the similarities between two things or ideas, whereas a *contrast* focuses on their differences. The term *comparison* is generally used to cover both techniques.

LESSON 1 AUTHOR'S STYLE

In literature, *style* refers to the way a writer expresses himself or herself in writing. The writer's choice of *sentence structure* and choice of words are two elements of a writer's style.

Sentence Structure   The pattern the writer uses to connect words is called *sentence structure*. The most common sentence structure is the simple declarative sentence with a subject-verb-object pattern. This is a simple declarative sentence from "Blue Winds Dancing": "Chipmunks make tiny footprints on the limbs."

If Whitecloud used the same sentence pattern throughout the essay, it would become monotonous and would produce a piece of writing that was uninteresting and probably boring. Good writers vary their sentence patterns by mixing compound and complex sentences with simple sentences and by interspersing questions and exclamations with their statements. They also vary the length of their sentences—some long and some short. Notice in the following passage how Whitecloud mixes short declarative sentences with longer compound sentences in this passage:

> I look around the room. All the eyes are friendly; they all laugh. No one questions my being here. The drums begin to beat again, and I catch the invitation in the eyes of the old men. My feet begin to feel the rhythmn, and I look out beyond the walls into the night and see the lights. I am happy. It is beautiful. I am home.

Another element of style writers use to express their feelings or to emphasize their ideas is parallelism. *Parallelism* is the repetition of forms, phrases, or clauses that are similar in structure. For example: *If I make my bed and [if I] clean my room and [if I] take out the trash, may I go out?* Such repetitions add continuity within a paragraph and highlight connections between ideas.

Look at Whitecloud's use of parallelism in the following passage. It not only helps you understand how weary and desperate he is to get home, but you also feel his weariness and desperation.

> I am tired. I want to walk again among the ghost-birches. I want to see the leaves turn in autumn, the smoke rise from the lodgehouses, and to feel the blue winds. I want to hear the drums; I want to hear the drums and feel the blue whispering winds.

Another technique that Whitecloud uses effectively is *alliteration*—the repetition of consonant sounds, especially at the beginning of words. For example: *The sun set slowly*. People often think of alliteration as a device used mostly by poets, yet you probably use alliteration every day. "Bread and butter" and "rock and roll" are just two examples. Alliteration helps create a particular atmosphere and adds a musical quality. Notice this example of alliteration in the previous excerpt: *whispering winds*. The repetition of the *w* sound calls your attention to Whitecloud's description of the wind and produces a soft, lyrical sound that is peaceful and restful. What example of alliteration can you in the following passage?

> Morning and the desert. Noon and the Salton Sea, lying more lifeless than a mirage under a somber sun in a pale sky. Skeleton mountains rearing on the skyline, thrusting out of the desert floor, all rock and shadow and edges.

Did you notice the repetition of the consonant *s* at the beginning of several words in that passage?

Imagery   Another important aspect of a writer's style is imagery. *Imagery* is the use of words or phrases that appeal to one or more of the senses of sight, sound, taste, smell, and touch. It is language that helps a reader to visualize a scene or to summon up a sound, a taste, a smell, or a feeling. When people describe experiences, they often begin by telling you what they see. You do absorb many impressions through your sight, but you also absorb impressions and images through your other senses. Read the following passage that describes Whitecloud's home state of Wisconsin.

> In my Wisconsin, the leaves change before the snows come. In the air there is the smell of wild rice and venison cooking; and when the winds come whispering through the forests, they carry the smell of rotting leaves. In the evenings, the loon calls, lonely . . .

In the above passage, Whitecloud uses several strong images. Note how he appeals to the sense of smell and perhaps taste with the following images: "In the air there is a smell of wild rice and venison cooking; . . . they carry the smell of rotting leaves." Then he appeals to the sense of sound with these images: "the winds come whispering through the forests. . . . In the evenings, the loon calls, lonely . . ." Notice how Whitecloud's use of sensory details makes his description vivid. Which of your senses does Whitecloud appeal to in this passage?

> There is one from which comes black coal smoke that rises lazily and drifts out over the tops of the trees.

EXERCISE ⟨1⟩

Read these paragraphs from the essay. Use what you have learned in this lesson to answer the questions that follow them.

> That land which is my home! Beautiful, calm—where there is no hurry to get anywhere, no driving to keep up in a race that knows no ending and no goal. No classes where men talk and talk, and then stop now and then to hear their own words come back to them from the students. No

constant peering into the maelstrom of one's mind; no worries about grades and honors; no hysterical preparing for life until that life is half over; no anxiety about one's place in the thing they call Society.

I hear again the ring of axes in deep woods, the crunch of snow beneath my feet. I feel again the smooth velvet of ghost-birch bark. I hear the rhythm of the drums.

1. What example of parallelism does Whitecloud use? What do you think he is emphasizing through his use of parallelism in that paragraph?

2. Whitecloud uses imagery in the second paragraph to appeal to the senses of sound and touch. What specific words does he use to help you "hear" and "feel" what he is describing?

Now check your answers with your teacher. Review this lesson if you don't understand why an answer was incorrect.

 WRITING ON YOUR OWN

In this exercise you will use what you have learned in this lesson to begin to develop a description of your experience. Follow these steps:

• Review the graphic organizer you filled in for Writing: Describing a Personal Experience. Choose one of those experiences to develop.
• Use the details from your graphic organizer to write two or three paragraphs describing your experience. Before you begin, think about the structure and length of your sentences. Try to mix simple, declarative sentences with compound sentences. Vary their lengths—some short, some long. Try to use words and phrases in your descriptions that will paint a vivid image for the reader by appealing to two or more of the senses: sight, sound, taste, smell, and touch. Finally, include an example of parallelism or alliteration in your paragraphs—

but only if its use would fit naturally into your description. Don't force it.

- When you have finished writing your paragraphs, reread them. Is there any other information you could add that would help a reader "share" your experience better?

LESSON 2 — USE OF FIGURATIVE LANGUAGE

The use of figurative language also contributes to the writer's distinctive style. *Figurative language* refers to words or phrases used in unusual ways to create strong, vivid images, to focus attention on certain ideas, or to compare things that are basically dissimilar. When words or phrases are used figuratively, they have meanings other than their usual, or literal, meanings. If someone said, "The stars were diamonds in the night sky," you would know that the speaker did not mean that the stars were literally diamonds; he or she would mean that the stars resembled diamonds in the way they sparkled in the night sky. The speaker would be using a figure of speech to describe the stars. *Figures of speech* are words or phrases used in ways other than their literal meanings to create vivid images—for example, by comparing unlike things.

People often think that figurative language belongs in the domain of fiction writers and poets, yet good nonfiction writers often use figures of speech to convey precise images and enliven their descriptions. The most common figures of speech are similes, metaphors, and personification.

Simile   A *simile* is a direct comparison between two basically dissimilar things that have some quality in common. A simile uses the words *like, as,* or *than,* or a verb such as *appears* or *seems,* to make the comparison. If a writer said, "The old farmer's hands were like sandpaper," he or she would mean that the farmer's hands were coarse, or rough, as is sandpaper. Although the two things being compared—the old farmer's hands and sandpaper— are dissimilar in most ways, they are similar in that they are both rough.

Whitecloud describes the giant cacti along the highway as "giant cacti that look like petrified hitchhikers along the highways." You don't normally think of cacti and hitchhikers as being alike at all, yet your mind can easily see giant cacti with their "arms" raised into the sky just as hitchhikers raise their arms while hitchiking.

Metaphor   A *metaphor* is an implied comparison, comparing two basically dissimilar things without using a word of comparison such as *like* or *as*. A metaphor suggests that one thing *is* another. For example, if you traveled to a foreign country and didn't speak the language, you might describe yourself by saying, "I'm a fish out of water." This does not mean that you are calling yourself a fish. Rather, you are suggesting that you feel as out of place as a fish is when it is out of the water.

Instead of using a simile to describe the cacti as Whitecloud did in the example cited above—"giant cacti that look like petrified hitchhikers along the highway"—he could have written the description as a metaphor instead: "giant cacti were petrified hitchhikers along the highway." In the simile the cacti were *like* hitchikers; in the metaphor the cacti would *be* hitchikers.

Personification   Another effective figure of speech that Whitecloud uses is *personification*—a form of figurative language in which an animal, an object, or an idea is given human characteristics. Read the following excerpts from the essay. How many examples of personification can you find?

> Across the valley there are heavy mountains holding up the night sky, and beyond the mountains there is home. Home, and peace, and the beat of drums, and blue winds dancing over snow fields. The Indian lodge will fill with my people, and our gods will come and sit among them. I should be there then. I should be at home.

You know that mountains do not really hold up the sky and that wind does not really dance. Whitecloud has personified the mountains and the wind, however, to make his description more vivid and to let you know that nature is a real, living part of his life.

EXERCISE

Read this sentence from the essay. Use what you have learned in this lesson to answer the questions that follow it.

"Noon and the Salton Sea, lying more lifeless than a mirage under a somber sun."

1. What kind of figure of speech has Whitecloud used in that sentence?

2. What two unlike things does he compare? In what way does Whitecloud mean the two things are alike?

Now check your answers with your teacher. Review this lesson if you don't understand why an answer was incorrect.

 WRITING ON YOUR OWN

In this exercise you will use what you have learned in this lesson to add figurative language to your description. Follow these steps:

• Reread the paragraphs you wrote for Writing on Your Own 1. Look carefully at how you have described your experience. Where in your paragraphs would the use of figurative language help to make the images you created more vivid?

• Now add a simile or metaphor to the description. Is it possible to add personification? Think of how Whitecloud uses figurative language to describe his images: pine trees wearing shawls of snow, trains wailing into the night, blue winds dancing over snow fields.

• When you have finished rewriting your paragraphs, you may want to have a classmate read your description to see whether the images you created provide the reader with a clear, interesting picture of your experience.

LESSON 3 — USE OF COMPARISON

Thomas S. Whitecloud was a Chippewa who, like most Native Americans, experienced great difficulty trying to live in a society that is predominately white and whose culture, or way of living, is dramatically different from the cultures of native peoples. Whitecloud found himself torn between two worlds—the white world, which he disliked but in which his future would lie, and the Indian world, which he loved but in which he feared he no longer fit.

To show you how he feels about the worlds he lives in, Whitecloud compares the two. Remember, the term *comparison* generally refers to both *comparison*, which focuses on similarities between two things or ideas, and *contrast*, which focuses on their differences. In Whitecloud's comparison he focuses on the differences between the two worlds.

In the following passage from the essay, note Whitecloud's use of comparison to show what he feels are dramatic differences between the white world of the city and the Indian world of his home.

> The railroad on which I stand comes from a city sprawled by a lake—a city with a million people who walk around without seeing one another; a city sucking the life from all the country around; a city with stores and police and intellectuals and criminals and movies and apartment houses; a city with its politics and libraries and zoos.
>
> I walk along the trail to the lodge, watching the northern lights forming in the heavens. White waving ribbons that seem to pulsate with the rhythmn of the drums. Clean snow creaks beneath my feet, and a soft wind sighs through the trees, singing to me. Everything seems to say, "Be happy! You are home now—you are free. You are among friends. . .

Through his effective use of comparison, Whitecloud helps you to understand his strong feelings for his Indian heritage.

EXERCISE 3

Read this passage from the essay. Use what you have learned in this lesson to answer the questions that follow it.

> . . . Being civilized means trying to do everything you don't want to, never doing anything you want to. It means dancing to the strings of custom and tradition; it means living in houses and never knowing or caring who is next door. These civilized white men want us to be like them—always dissatisfied, getting a hill and wanting a mountain.

1. Whitecloud suggests several differences between being "civilized" (white) and being Indian. What are three of those differences?

2. What does Whitecloud mean by "white men are always dissatisfied—getting a hill and wanting a mountain?"

Now check your answers with your teacher. Review this lesson if you don't understand why an answer was incorrect.

 WRITING ON YOUR OWN 3

In this exercise you will use what you have learned in this lesson to add comparison to your description. Follow these steps:

- Reread the paragraphs you wrote for Writing on Your Own 2. The description of your personal experience should include varied sentence structure, strong images, and figurative language.
- Now you will write a paragraph or two comparing your personal experience with another, one. For example, if you first wrote about your first day in high school, you could compare that experience with your first day in kindergarten or middle school. This related experience may have similarities to or differences from the subject of your description. You may choose to include both similarities and differences, or to emphasize only the similarities or the differences.

DISCUSSION GUIDES

1. A *motif* is a recurrent theme in a piece of writing. In "Blue Winds Dancing," a recurrent theme is "going home." Together with a small group skim Whitecloud's essay and find each reference to home. What does going home mean to Whitecloud? Why does he prefer home to the environment at college in California? Once your group has discussed these questions, share your opinions with the rest of the class.

2. You learned in Building Background that Whitecloud's father was a graduate of Yale Law School, yet he decided not to practice in white America and returned to the reservation instead. When young Whitecloud is 20 miles from home, he suddenly feels afraid. He says, "I sit by a fire and think about myself and all the other young Indians. We just don't seem to fit in anywhere—certainly not among the whites, and not among the older people." With a partner discuss what the older Whitecloud might say to his son. Do you think he would understand how his son feels? What advice do you think he might give to his son? Develop a short dialogue between father and son. Then present your dialogue to the rest of the class.

3. Whitecloud's essay is well known, not only for its theme but also for its lyrical language. For example, geese don't simply fly south; they wedge southward. In Redlands, California, the weather isn't just temperate; winter never comes down from the mountains. Whitecloud's use of words and images are mostly related to nature. In a small group discuss what you think he means by the title "Blue Winds Dancing." Also discuss what he means when on his trip home after leaving school in California, he says, "They will say he has gone back to the blanket." Share your opinions with the class.

WRITE A DESCRIPTION OF A PERSONAL EXPERIENCE

In this unit you have seen how Whitecloud's unique style of writing and his effective use of figurative language and comparison combine to create a powerful presentation of his thoughts and feelings about his personal experience in going home. Now you will complete your description of a personal experience.

Follow these steps to complete your description. If you have questions about the writing process, refer to Using the Writing Process (page 250).

- Gather and review the following pieces of writing you did in this unit: 1) the graphic organizer from Writing: Describing a Personal Experience; 2) paragraphs describing your experience from Writing on Your Own 1; 3) paragraphs you rewrote to include figurative language from Writing on Your Own 2; 4) paragraphs comparing your experience with another, related personal experience from Writing on Your Own 3.
- Complete the description of your personal experience by combining the paragraphs you wrote for Writing on Your Own 2 with the paragraphs you wrote for Writing on Your Own 3. You may simply add your comparison paragraphs after your description paragraphs, or you may interweave your comparison with the descriptive paragraphs as Whitecloud does in his essay.
- Exchange finished work with a classmate. After reading, critique each other's work and make suggestions for improvements. If changes seem warranted, revise your description accordingly.
- Proofread your final draft for errors in spelling, grammar, punctuation, and capitalization. Make a final copy and save it in your writing portfolio.

UNIT 2

Selecting and Organizing Facts

Mount Rainier: Washington's Tranquil Threat

◆

by Jon Krakauer

INTRODUCTION

BUILDING BACKGROUND

Mount Rainier, a volcano that has erupted in the past, rises majestically behind Tacoma, Washington. Geologists are concerned that another eruption will have devastating effects on cities like Tacoma.

At an elevation of 14,410 feet, majestic Mount Rainier in the state of Washington towers above the other peaks in the Cascade Range. It is sculpted by ice and surrounded by 41 glaciers. In 1792 English explorer George Vancouver sighted the summit and named it after Peter Rainier, a fellow explorer. The mountain, a popular tourist and recreation area, is sometimes referred to by its Indian name, Mount Tacoma.

Writer and avid climber Jon Krakauer probably considers Mount Rainier an old friend, having spent many hours the past 30 years climbing over its surface. In his feature article in the July 1996 issue of *Smithsonian* magazine, Krakauer takes an in-depth, scientific look at Rainier—a volcano that experts say could become a dangerous enemy. He explains what is brewing inside the volcano and why even the smallest "burp" by it could unleash a deadly flow of debris.

In researching the article, Krakauer relied on the expertise of geologists and other scientists, but also used his own observations and impressions. The article provides numerous facts and predictions to consider about Mount Rainier.

ABOUT THE AUTHOR

Jon Krakauer has lived most of his life in the Northwest. At age eight, his father introduced him to volcanoes, and he has been climbing mountains ever since. His passion for scaling the world's highest mountains culminated in May 1996 when he climbed Mount Everest, the highest of them all. He wrote an article about his climb for *Outside* magazine and a book about the expedition titled *Into Thin Air.* "I had this invitation to climb with the best, and to go to this amazing place with these beautiful, huge fins of granite sticking out of the ice that had never been climbed before. It was a once-in-a-lifetime opportunity, and I took it." The expedition, however, ended in tragedy. Nine members of the team died on the descent when a storm closed in on them. Krakauer has vowed never to return to Mount Everest.

Before becoming a writer, Krakauer worked as a commercial fisherman and a carpenter. His first published article detailed his three ascents of unclimbed peaks in Alaska. The experience led him to pursue a career of freelance writing. He most enjoys writing about the outdoors and says his outdoors pieces are his best work. Besides being published in *Rolling Stone, National Geographic, Smithsonian,* and *Outside* magazines, Krakauer has written several books, including *Into Thin Air, Into the Wild,* and *Eiger Dreams.* He currently lives in Seattle, Washington with his wife.

ABOUT THE LESSONS

The lessons that follow "Mount Rainier: Washington's Tranquil Threat" focus on how writers of informational articles select the facts to include in an article and how they organize those facts in a way that not only informs and makes a point about their subject but also interests the reader.

In his article the author presents the past, the present, and the possible future of the volcano, supporting his main points with various facts and information about Mount Rainier and other volcanoes. You will learn what influenced the author to select the facts that he did and why he chose to organize and present those facts to the reader in the way that he did.

WRITING: DEVELOPING A MAGAZINE ARTICLE

At the end of this unit you will write a magazine article. You will use what you learn in this unit about selecting and organizing facts. The suggestions below will help you get started:

- Think about an interesting topic for your article. You may want to write about a serious issue affecting your school or age group such as the role (or value) of varsity sports in school life. Or perhaps your town has experienced some kind of natural disaster, such as a tornado, hurricane, blizzard, fire, or flood. What was the impact on your town? How did your town cope with the emergency?

- Write down a topic that interests you and that you think will interest others. Write a sentence or two next to the topic explaining why you think others might be interested in that topic.

- Consider these questions: Do I have firsthand knowledge about the topic? Are there any people with information or opinions about my topic whom I can interview? Are there any written materials or other sources that I can research?

- Gather and write down as many facts and other information about your topic that you can. You may include background information and personal knowledge and observations.

AS YOU READ

Think about these questions as you read the article. They will help you see how the author organizes his article about Mount Rainier.

- How does John Krakauer immediately attract your attention and interest?

- What poses the greatest threat to the people who live near Mount Rainier?

- What is the theme, or central idea, of the article?

- Think about the information Krakauer provides in the beginning, the middle, and the end of the article. Why do you think he organized the material in this way?

Mount Rainier:
Washington's Tranquil Threat

by Jon Krakauer

The experts believe Mount Rainier will give plenty of notice before it erupts again—the problem is that it can kill in other ways

Fourteen thousand four hundred and ten feet above sea level, I have to pause for breath between each plodding step as I arrive at the crest of Mount Rainier, the highest point in the Cascade Range. I've climbed this huge volcano many times over the past 30 years—for fun, for exercise, for escape from the urban grind. On this occasion, however, the impetus[1] is morbid curiosity.

Recent geological reports have suggested that Rainier poses a serious threat to thousands of people who live in the shadow of the mountain—as I do—even if it does not erupt. My hope is that this ascent will shed a little light on the matter. It took two exhausting days to reach the top. Now, a caustic wind is screaming across the summit crater, flash-freezing the skin on my face and turning my mittened hands into blocks of ice.

Before my eyes is a chunk of country that stretches from Canada to central Oregon, some 200 miles away. Scanning the craggy spine of the Cascades, one can't help noticing that this

---

[1] a driving force

corner of the planet is lousy with volcanoes: from my lofty vantage I count no fewer than nine of them. The most riveting— and most notorious—is Mount St. Helens, whose truncated[2] cone squats immediately to the southwest. At the moment, its yawning crater is belching a plume of steam high into the troposphere,[3] a gentle admonition that St. Helens—along with some two dozen other Cascade peaks—is very much an active volcano.

On Sunday, May 18, 1980, shortly before 9 in the morning, I happened to look up from a salmon net I was mending outside Tacoma, Washington, and saw what appeared to be a massive cumulonimbus cloud boiling toward the heavens, where a moment earlier there had been nothing but blue sky. Unbeknownst to me, avalanches had carried millions of tons of rock and ice off the top of Mount St. Helens, in essence suddenly removing the cap that had enabled the mountain to contain the molten rock and the superheated steam within. The resulting explosion obliterated what the avalanches had left of the upper 1,300 feet of the volcano and sent it hurtling into the sky.

The blast devastated plant and animal life for 150 square miles. The cloud of ash that caught my eye soared to a height of more than 60,000 feet, turning day to night across much of Washington, and scattered 540 million tons of volcanic debris across the Western United States. Fifty-seven people were killed, a remarkably small number considering the violence of the eruption. The death toll was so low due to evacuation measures, and because the mountain's rugged environs were sparsely populated and largely undeveloped.

Fifteen years later, as I mull the scenery from atop Mount Rainier, the merest glance between my boots suggests that the consequences could be much more dire when it's this peak's turn to blow. Hard to the northwest sprawl Tacoma, Seattle, and their myriad suburbs. I can plainly make out the Space Needle, skyscrapers, and 747s landing at Sea-Tac Airport.

---

[2] flattened, having part of the cone cut off

[3] the lowest part of the earth's atmosphere

Given that Rainier has erupted numerous times in the past (most recently, just 150 years ago), the proximity[4] of so much humanity is troubling. Geologists warn that there is no way of knowing when the mountain will blow again—it could go off in 10 years or not for 10,000—but blow it will, eventually.

Hunkered on the crest of Rainier, watching freighters and ferryboats ply[5] the dazzling waters of Puget Sound, it's easy to imagine that the volcano is ready to erupt at any moment. The rim of the summit crater is riddled with fumaroles[6] actively venting hot gases from the bowels of the earth, filling my nostrils with their sulfurous stink. Even though the air temperature is well below freezing and most of the rest of the mountain wears a carapace[7] of glacial ice hundreds of feet thick, the rocky ground beneath me is utterly bare of snow and disturbingly warm to the touch. Scientists have recorded surface temperatures on the crater rim as high as 176 degrees F. The heat I feel through my insulated trousers makes it impossible to forget that somewhere not too far below lies a reservoir of fidgety, red-hot magma,[8] itching to elbow its way to daylight.

Sixty miles north of Rainier, in a cluttered, windowless room on the University of Washington campus, banks of humming machines keep close tabs on the mountain's every seismological twitch, lest an eruption take the region by surprise. Antennas on the roof of the building gather signals from some 30 remote-sensing devices on or near various Cascade volcanoes: telephones and microwaves carry signals from 120 more. Twelve devices monitor Rainier. Tremors large and small show up as squiggly lines on an array of rotating drum graphs in the center of the room.

"Actually," confesses Steve Malone—a cheerful, bearded geophysicist attired in shorts and sandals, who oversees the seis-

---

[4] nearness

[5] make regular trips

[6] a hole in a volcanic region from which hot gases and vapor escape

[7] a protective shell

[8] molten rock within the earth

mology lab— "the drums provide some useful data, but they are mostly for the benefit of news media. They give TV crews something to point their cameras at whenever there's an earthquake. Here at the lab, we glance at the drums now and then, but mostly we rely on a fairly sophisticated computer system." Should any remote sensor record a seismic[9] event of a magnitude greater than 2.4, the computers are programmed to trigger a beeper that Malone wears on his belt. Additionally, if the event is stronger than 2.9, the system will automatically send out a flurry of faxes and e-mail communiqués to scientists and emergency-management agencies throughout the region.

The big St. Helens blast in 1980 was preceded by a series of minor earthquakes prompted by movement of magma up the throat of the volcano; similar tremors would almost certainly give geologists plenty of notice before Mount Rainier next erupts. "With this system in place," Malone concurs, "the available seismic data should give us warning of an impending eruption weeks or even months in advance."

Truth be told, Malone doesn't think Rainier is a very likely candidate for an explosive, St. Helens-like eruption, in any case. Extrapolating[10] from past eruptions, he and most other volcanologists believe that when Rainier blows its lid, it is apt to do so in a much less histrionic fashion, producing relatively modest explosions or extrusions of lava rather than a cataclysmic detonation.

Malone cautions, nevertheless, that it would be a grave mistake to conclude thereby that the mountain presents no great threat: "In fact, Rainier is perhaps far more dangerous than St. Helens. The frightening thing about Rainier is the hazard posed by catastrophic debris flows—a hazard most people aren't even aware of." Known to geologists as lahars (an Indonesian term), such flows are flash floods of semiliquid mud, rock, and ice that surge down from the heights with terrifying speed and destructive power.

---

[9] of, having to do with, or caused by an earthquake

[10] inferring that which is not known from that which is known

"Lahars have occurred throughout Rainier's history," warns Malone, "and they can happen more or less spontaneously, in the complete absence of an eruptive event, with practically no warning at all. Horribly, we remember what happened to Armero, and worry that something similar might happen around here."

Armero was a prosperous farming community nestled in the Andes in Colombia, not far from Bogotá. On the evening of November 13, 1985, residents of the town felt the earth tremble and heard a series of rumbling explosions emanating from a 17,453-foot volcano called Nevado del Ruiz, 30 miles away. According to a local woman named Marina Franco de Huez, an ominous cloud rose from the mountain's crater, raining ash down on Armero, "but we were told it wasn't anything serious."

Although the volcano was erupting, at first there seemed to be little reason for concern. Indeed, newspaper reports later described the event as a "relatively small eruption, a volcanic burp" that melted only about 5 percent of the ice and snow covering the uppermost reaches of the peak. The "burp" was sufficiently powerful, however, to collapse a steep buttress below the summit crater, initiating an avalanche of rock, snow, and ice—a classic lahar—that swept down the slopes of Nevado del Ruiz from an elevation of 15,000 feet.

Liquefying and gathering momentum[11] as it rocketed down a river drainage toward the valley bottom, the lahar wiped out a natural dam, sending a colossal mud slide downvalley. As one resident of Armero remembered the ensuing cataclysm,[12] "I heard a sound like a huge locomotive going at full steam, and then I felt water swirling around my neck."

Within moments, the town was inundated with a slurry resembling wet concrete, burying the community beneath 30 feet of gray-brown muck. The next morning, where their homes had once stood, survivors gazed upon a stark, lunar-like plain

---

[11] strength or force gained by motion

[12] an upheaval that causes destruction; a catastrophe such as a flood or earthquake

covering 600 acres and littered with smashed cars, corpses, and uprooted trees. An estimated 23,000 people lost their lives, and more than 60,000 were left homeless. It was the worst natural disaster in Colombia's history.

Kevin Scott, a senior geologist at the U.S. Geological Survey's Cascades Volcano Observatory in Vancouver, Washington, warns that there are a number of disquieting parallels between Nevado del Ruiz and Mount Rainier. As he tells me this, he is standing in a field beside a new housing development in Orting, a rapidly growing town in the lowlands near Puget Sound. "The Mountain" (as Rainier is known locally), gleaming in the summer sun, looms to the southeast less than 30 miles away.

Living on top of an old lahar

A solitary block of lava as big as a Volkswagen Beetle rests incongruously[13] on a manicured sward[14] behind a recently constructed house. "You know how that boulder got here?" Scott asks. "It was carried down from Rainier by a lahar. This development, like most of the rest of Orting, was built on 20 feet of debris deposited by the Electron Mudflow, a lahar that came down the Puyallup River Valley about 500 years ago." The geologic record indicates that at least 60 major lahars have roared down from Rainier over the past 10,000 years; a few of them ran all the way to Puget Sound, more than 50 miles from the mountain.

Scott points out that Armero, like Orting, was built on debris from an old lahar: "Armero had already been destroyed at least once, in 1845, before the most recent disaster—by a mudflow that killed hundreds of people. Yet the town was rebuilt in the same place. We can be fairly certain that sooner or later another lahar is going to plow through Orting too—we just don't know when.

"Judging from the frequency of mudflows on Rainier in the past, we are reasonably confident that the recurrence interval

---

[13] out of harmony; not compatible

[14] a portion of ground covered with grass

for major lahars is between 500 and 1,000 years. That sounds like an awfully long time, long enough that we don't really need to worry. Statistically, however, it's been calculated that a house built on the floodplain of a lahar is many times more likely to be destroyed by a lahar than by fire. Almost nobody would consider owning a home without fire insurance and smoke alarms, yet people think nothing of living in the path of mudflows without safeguards. Most folks simply don't take the risk of lahars seriously."

Geologists take lahars very seriously, which is why Mount Rainier makes them so nervous. More than 100,000 people live in homes built on debris washed down by lahars. Two hundred thousand Puget Sound residents go to work each day at businesses lying in the path of documented mudflows. A report published in 1994 by the National Research Council warns, "This metropolitan area is the high-technology industrial center of the Pacific Northwest and one of the commercial aircraft manufacturing centers of the United States. . . . A major volcanic eruption or debris flow could kill thousands of residents and cripple the economy."

Lahars are a hazard of virtually all volcanoes, but Rainier has some unique geologic traits that make it especially dangerous. Thanks to its great height and the sodden Northwest climate, Rainier wears a stupendously robust mantle of ice. Twenty-six named glaciers drape Rainier's broad flanks, a reservoir of snow and ice approximately equal to that of all the other Cascade volcanoes combined. The melting of just a tiny fraction of this frozen water during a volcanic event could unleash lahars of biblical proportions.

"Compared to any other volcano in the Cascades," Scott declares, "Rainier is in a class by itself in terms of risk to human life and property."

"Rainier is covered with 36 square miles of perennial snow and ice," muses Carolyn Driedger, a hydrologist with the Cascades Volcano Observatory who has carefully measured the size and thickness of the mountain's glaciers. During the eruption of Mount St. Helens, she says, three-quarters of that volcano's glacial ice melted over a very short time, creating gargantuan mudflows that ran all the way to the Columbia River, filling its channels with enough debris to disrupt international shipping for three months. "And remember that St. Helens," Driedger points out, "only had about 4 percent as much year-round ice and snow as Rainier has. That's pretty sobering to think about."

Stewing in its own juice

Rainier's prodigious[15] mantle of ice contributes to the potential danger in a less obvious, more insidious way, as well. The peak's subterranean heat is continuously melting its glaciers from below, feeding water into a complex system of geothermal aquifers.[16] Constantly circulating through the mountain, this abundance of hot liquid combines with sulfur-bearing gases to produce acids that are eroding Rainier from the inside out, undermining its structural integrity. "The entire edifice of the mountain is stewing in its own hot chemical juices," explains Scott, "and as a consequence it's becoming increasingly rotten and unstable."

Geologists, who call this phenomenon hydrothermal alteration, have only recently begun to appreciate its impact on Mount Rainier. "We don't have a very complete picture of what's going on up there yet," says Don Swanson, a geologist with the U.S. Geological Survey and a contributor to the 1994 National Research Council report. "But the hydrothermal alteration of all that rock is alarming to contemplate. I firmly believe that learning the extent of the alteration is among the most important things to find out about Rainier."

Most of what we know thus far comes from the efforts of Tom Sisson and David Zimbelman, geologists who have spent many months on the mountain, painstakingly studying and mapping it. "It's extremely hard work," Zimbelman admits. Because altered rock is inherently unstable, he and Sisson had

---

[15] treacherous; awaiting a chance to entrap

[16] any geological formation containing water

to climb some of Rainier's more dangerous slopes to conduct their research.

The research has shed considerable light on the degree to which strong acids percolating through Rainier's innards are transforming solid rock into soft, crumbly clay, a process that is readily apparent on the rim of the summit crater. The thin air up here reeks of rotten eggs: the telltale scent of hydrogen sulfide gas, which condenses and mixes with water to form sulfuric acid, the primary agent of alteration on Rainier. Around the steaming summit fumaroles, clumps of reddish brown mud cling to the spikes of climbers' crampons. This spongy stuff is hydrothermally altered rock.

Zimbelman and Sisson have discovered bands of weak, highly altered rock that locally penetrate the mountain. It is the nature of clay to absorb water, and expand when it does so. As zones of newly altered rock on Rainier swell with moisture, dry out, and re-expand, the clay acts as a sort of natural crowbar, prying apart the more solid rock around it, further weakening the edifice.

As soon as part of Rainier grows sufficiently rickety, a catastrophic lahar is bound to result. "What would it take to trigger a significant mudflow?" asks Zimbelman. "Certainly an earthquake could do the job. But so could a much lesser event like a minor steam explosion. You have all this gravitationally unstable rock becoming weaker and weaker; eventually it's going to reach a point where it won't take much of a jolt to break off a big piece of mountain and send it tumbling toward Puget Sound. In fact, you could have a major sector collapse without any triggering mechanism at all. That's what's so scary: something huge could come down simply under its own weight, with no advance warning."

When Rainier is viewed from southern Puget Sound, it looks like a large part of the summit cone is missing, as though removed by some Brobdingnagian[17] ice-cream scoop. The cliffs that form the walls of the hollow are mottled with yellowish

---

[17] huge in size; gigantic; tremendous

orange splotches: zones of rotten, clay-rich altered rock that hold clues to what happened here. The scooped-out area is called the Sunset Amphitheater, and its existence hints at what can happen when a really big piece of the mountain lets go. The hollow is where the Electron Mudflow started.

Around the corner from the Sunset Amphitheater, on the north face of the mountain, scars from an even bigger cataclysm are visible with the naked eye from downtown Seattle. They were left behind by the Osceola Mudflow, the largest known lahar ever spawned by Mount Rainier. It came thundering down about 5,000 years ago, when something—perhaps an earthquake or a buildup of steam within the volcano, perhaps nothing more than the tug of gravity on hydrothermally weakened rock— caused the upper 2,000 feet of the peak to cleave off and slide away. A dusting of airborne ash sprinkled over the region at the time of the mudflow indicates that it was accompanied by a modest volcanic eruption, but many geologists have come to believe that the landslide may have triggered the eruption, rather than vice versa.

The Osceola Mudflow began as an avalanche of mind-boggling size, carrying 60 times as much rubble as the lahar that wiped out Armero in 1985. Much of the flow consisted of clay saturated with geothermal fluids, an avalanche of semiliquid muck that roared downslope at a speed in excess of 100 miles per hour.

As it reached the base of the mountain and churned down the valleys of the White, Green, and Puyallup rivers, the lahar slowed to between 30 and 50 miles per hour, but it nevertheless scoured the earth of everything in its path. Thanks to its high clay content, the Osceola Mudflow was what geologists call a cohesive lahar: a thick, gooey mass viscous[18] enough to suspend house-size boulders and 200-foot trees within its flow. Indeed, it swallowed up entire forests and carried them down onto the plains below.

Cohesive lahars tend to travel farther and pack a greater punch than more dilute, clay-poor, noncohesive lahars, and the

---

[18] sticky

Osceola Mudflow was no exception. It ran all the way to Puget Sound, whose shores lay considerably east of where they do now. The lahar blanketed at least 200 square miles with a layer of concrete-like muck that averaged 25 feet deep, burying the sites of present-day Orting, Enumclaw, Auburn, Puyallup, Kent, Sumner, and some of the Tacoma waterfront.

If a similar lahar came down Rainier tomorrow, it would take about one to two hours to reach the densely populated lowlands. According to Kevin Scott, residents of Orting would see "a wall of trees, rocks, and mud rolling down the canyon of the Carbon River at perhaps 30 miles per hour. The sound would be deafening and the earth would tremble. In Armero, survivors reported hearing a loud roar and feeling the ground shake when the lahar was still five kilometers away, but they didn't know what was happening—they thought it was an earthquake—they didn't run to high ground."

Hoping to avoid such deadly confusion, in February of last year the Orting Fire Department hand-delivered copies of an emergency evacuation plan to each of the town's roughly 3,000 residents. The plan explains that if a debris flow is expected, sirens will sound throughout Orting, indicating that people should immediately leave town via evacuation routes described on an attached map. In conjunction with the plan, the local schools regularly practice lahar evacuation drills.

"The last time the schools held a drill," says Orting Fire Chief Scott Fielding, "all the kids were out of the city and bused to high ground in 15 minutes. I'm more concerned about our adult citizens. We've told them, 'When you hear the sirens, get in your car and leave! Immediately!' But adults are more likely to doubt the seriousness of the situation, to question it, to fool around. Realistically, I doubt we'd get more than 50 or 60 percent of the people to actually evacuate."

Fielding acknowledges that for the evacuation plan to work at all, moreover, the town will have to have some advance warning that the mud is bearing down. "And at present," he laments, "no early-detection system is in place. If someone up toward the mountain doesn't happen to see the debris flow and phone the fire department, it's going to be bad news for the people downstream. Personally, I live on a hill above town, so I sleep well at night. But I worry about my friends who live on the valley floor."

Scientists and government officials have discussed establishing a network of electronic sensing devices in each of the threatened drainages to sound a warning when a lahar is on the way. Such a system, however, would probably be far from foolproof. "The technology for implementing something like that would be pretty straightforward," says Steve Malone. "The problem will be maintaining it in the long term, and getting people to take it seriously when the alarm goes off after decades or even centuries without anything happening."

What, then, can we who live in the shadow of the mountain do to protect our lives and property the next time a tsunami[19] of mud comes rumbling down from the heights? Civil engineers have suggested constructing massive containment dams in each of the half-dozen river drainages that snake down from Rainier to Puget Sound. Such structures could be designed to catch most of the sediment released by a lahar.

Although containment dams would probably stop a lahar, says Patrick Pringle, a geologist with the Washington State Department of Natural Resources, "the cost of building and maintaining them would be substantial, and I don't think the public is willing to commit those kinds of funds in this economic climate. It's hard to galvanize[20] people to do anything until after a disaster has already happened. Mudflows occur so infrequently that people would rather just take their chances. They'd rather spend their tax money on a new baseball stadium. Such dams would also pose environmental problems."

In the absence of containment dams and a reliable early-warning program, an obvious way to reduce the risk would be to enact zoning laws that would prevent people from building homes or businesses in the path of documented mudflows. "But

---

[19] a series of giant waves

[20] startle into action

most of the land we're talking about is prime real estate," laments Don Swanson. "It's probably unrealistic to think that very much of it will be placed off-limits."

Given fiscal and political realities, Swanson, Scott, Pringle, and other experts believe the best course of action for the time being is to learn as much as possible about the hazards posed by the mountain and aggressively share that knowledge with the public. Toward that end, the International Association of Volcanology and Chemistry of the Earth's Interior has designated Rainier, along with 14 other mountains worldwide, a "Decade Volcano": an unusually dangerous volcano earmarked for intensive study.

"We're trying to come up with hard statistical data," says Pringle, "actual numbers people can use to get a handle on the risk. We want to give people enough knowledge to make rational decisions concerning their options. The challenge is to get the public's attention without alarming anybody unnecessarily."

"It's extremely hard to quantify these kinds of risks," Swanson concedes. "How do you put large but infrequent hazards into any sort of meaningful statistical context? A catastrophic mudflow is not likely to happen on Rainier in our lifetime. But it will happen somewhere down the road, in one or more generations—and when it does, a lot of people will lose everything."

REVIEWING AND INTERPRETING

Record your answers to these questions in your personal literature notebook. Follow the directions for each part.

REVIEWING

Try to complete each of these sentences without looking back at the selection.

Recalling Facts

1. Krakauer climbed Mount Rainier in
   a. four days.
   b. three days.
   c. one week.
   d. two days.

Understanding Main Ideas

2. Even if it doesn't erupt, Mount Rainier poses a threat because
   a. its glaciers continue to shift and move down the mountain.
   b. there are no emergency plans in place.
   c. lahars could destroy everything near the base of the mountain.
   d. there could be an earthquake.

Identifying Sequence

3. The lahar that destroyed Armero, Colombia, for the second time happened
   a. a few years after Mount St. Helens erupted.
   b. decades before Mount St. Helens erupted.
   c. after Krakauer climbed Mount Rainier.
   d. before scientists knew about lahars.

Finding Supporting Details

4. You know that officials in Orting, the town at the base of the Mount Rainier, take the threat of lahars seriously because they have
   a. asked people in the most dangerous areas to move.
   b. set up an advance emergency warning system.
   c. already experienced the devastation of a lahar.
   d. made plans to relocate the entire town.

Getting Meaning
from Context

5. "Now a caustic wind is screaming across the summit crater, flash-freezing the skin on my face. . . ." In this context *caustic* means
   a. gentle.
   b. warm.
   c. swirling.
   d. biting.

INTERPRETING

To complete these sentences, you may look back at the selection if you'd like.

Making Inferences

6. From the interview with Kevin Scott, you can infer that he
   a. feels the emergency warning system will protect Orting.
   b. feels that a lahar won't do much damage to Orting.
   c. thinks it is foolish to build a new housing development in Orting.
   d. estimates that a lahar won't occur for thousands of years.

Generalizing

7. Most of the adult population in Orting
   a. evacuate the town during the drill.
   b. want a more sophisticated warning system.
   c. are planning to move to a higher location.
   d. don't take the threat of a lahar seriously.

Recognizing Fact and
Opinion

8. Each of the following statements based on the article is fact except
   a. Most of Orting was built on a lahar that came down the mountain 500 years ago.
   b. People would rather spend money on a new baseball stadium that on containment dams.
   c. In 1985 Armero, Colombia, was destroyed by a lahar.
   d. Scientists cannot tell exactly when another lahar will occur on the mountain.

Identifying Cause and Effect

9. It is difficult to convince people that lahars pose a serious threat because
a. people don't believe the scientists.
b. lahars are so infrequent.
c. people are not aware of the real dangers.
d. if a lahar occurs, it may miss the town completely.

Drawing Conclusions

10. Jon Krakauer's main purpose in writing this article is to
a. make people aware of the danger posed by Mount Rainier.
b. show how few people are concerned about the dangers.
c. show the advances in scientific equipment in the last 20 years.
d. demonstrate the effectiveness and importance of warning systems.

Now check your answers with your teacher. Study the items you answered incorrectly. What skills are they checking? Talk with your teacher about ways to work on those skills.

Selecting and Organizing Facts

All nonfiction writers make use of one or more of the four basic kinds of writing: description, narration, exposition, and argumentation. *Description* is the kind of writing that helps you picture a person, a place, or an event. *Narration* is the kind that presents the events and actions of a story. *Exposition*, sometimes called expository writing, explains a subject by presenting information and analysis, and *argumentation* is the kind of writing that uses reasons, arguments, and logic to make a point.

"Mount Rainier: Washington's Tranquil Threat" is an example of expository writing. Its purpose is to give the reader information about the subject of the article. The author is objective; that is, he or she presents facts rather than opinions. The writer tries to give the reader an unbiased, or balanced, treatment of the topic, allowing the reader to draw his or her own conclusions. In other articles, the writer may not only present facts but may also include his or her own viewpoint and interpretation of the facts.

Nonfiction articles are generally found in magazines and newspapers, and the topics vary. They can be about science, history, cooking, sports, people, or any number of subjects. Whatever the topic may be, every writer wants his or her article to be accurate, meaningful, interesting, and well organized.

There are several considerations to think about when writing an exposition for a magazine. In the lessons that follow, we will examine these:

1. **Selection of Facts**   When writing a magazine article, the writer must select the facts to include in the article carefully. The writer's selection of the facts is influenced by the article's audience, or readers, and the central idea that the writer wants to impart to the readers.

2. **Organization of the Article**   After selecting the relevant facts for the article, the writer must think about how to organize them. The writer wants the introduction, the opening paragraph or paragraphs of an article, to capture the atten-

tion and interest of the readers. In the main body, or middle, of the article, the writer develops his or her central idea. In the close, or end, of the article, the writer may summarize what was said in the article, draw conclusions, or suggest some possible future development or action. In any case, the writer hopes the reader enjoys reading the article and understands its message.

3. **Main Idea and Supporting Details**   Within the article the writer needs to organize information into main ideas and supporting details. Facts, like directions, need to be presented in a logical, connected way.

LESSON 1 SELECTION OF FACTS

Feature articles, such as "Mount Rainier: Washington's Tranquil Threat," often require many hours of research. In their research, writers usually compile more facts than they can possibly use. Then they map out their plan for writing the article and select which facts and ideas to include and which to omit. Two important considerations play a part in this decision: the author's purpose in writing the article and the audience, or readers, who will most likely read the article.

Krakauer makes his purpose known in the second paragraph of the article:

> Recent geological reports have suggested that Rainier poses a serious threat to thousands of people who live in the shadow of the mountain—as I do—even if it does not erupt. My hope is that this ascent will shed a little light on the matter.

Krakauer's purpose is not only to inform his readers about the possible threat posed by Mount Rainier, but also to support his belief and the findings of the recent geological reports that Mount Rainier does indeed pose a serious threat to the thousands of people who live near it. With his purpose in mind, the author carefully selected facts that would help him achieve his purpose—facts such as the following from the article:

> Given that Rainier has erupted numerous times in the past (most recently, just 150 years ago), the proximity of so much humanity is troubling. Geologists warn that there is no way of knowing when the mountain will blow again—it could go off in 10 years or not for 10,000—but blow it will eventually.

In reviewing the collected facts for the article, Krakauer noticed that one main, or central, idea emerged—it is the lahars, not an eruption, that pose a deadly threat to the residents living near Mount Rainier. This idea is the theme of the article. A *theme* is the underlying message, or central idea, in a piece of writing. The theme may be directly stated by the author, or it may only be implied, as it is in this article. In selecting facts to include, Krakauer chose ones that developed and supported his theme. For example, he chose to include the following information obtained from an interview with a geophysicist:

> Truth be told, Malone doesn't think Rainier is a very likely candidate for an explosive, Mount St. Helen's-like eruption. . . .
> Malone cautions, nevertheless, that it would be a grave mistake to conclude thereby that that the mountain presents no great threat: "In fact, Rainier is perhaps far more danger-ous than Mt. St. Helens. The frightening thing about about Rainier is the hazard posed by catastrophic debris flows—a hazard most people aren't even aware of." Known to geolo-gists as lahars (an Indonesian term), such flows are flash floods of semiliquid, mud, rock, and ice that surge down from the heights with terrifying speed and destructive power.

Before writing the article Krakauer considered his audience. He knows that the *Smithsonian* is a scholarly magazine published by the Smithsonian Institution in Washington, D. C. The magazine contains articles on all aspects of the sciences as well as history and the arts. Its readers are generally well educated and interested in informational articles that include technical terms and information.

Because he knew his audience, Krakauer included scientific data and scientific terms such as "hydrothermal alteration." He anticipated that his readers would find a detailed explanation of the alteration phenomenon interesting. He also knew that he had to consult with experts who could provide him with historical background, accurate facts and statistics, and credible opinions. For this, he chose geophysicists, geologists, and a hydrologist. The only nonscientist quoted was a local fire chief. Had Krakauer written the article for a magazine devoted to opinions, such as *The Atlantic Monthly*, he would have included his own opinions and offered his own conclusions about the scientists' predictions. Had he written the article for *People*, a magazine intended for a more general audience, he would have avoided using a lot of technical information and perhaps would have focused on the concerns of the residents of Seattle and Tacoma.

EXERCISE ⟨1⟩

Read this passage from the article. Use what you have learned in this lesson to answer the questions that follow it.

A solitary block of lava as big as a Volkswagen Beetle rests incongruously on a manicured sward behind a recently constructed house. "You know how that boulder got here?" Scott asks. "It was carried down from Rainier by a lahar."

1. How do the facts contained in this paragraph help support and develop the author's theme?

2. Which words in the passage indicate that Krakauer recognizes his audience is well educated?

Now check your answers with your teacher. Review this lesson if you don't understand why an answer was incorrect.

WRITING ON YOUR OWN

In this exercise you will use what you have learned in this lesson to begin to develop your magazine article. Follow these steps:

- Before you write be sure to keep your audience in mind as you choose the facts to include.
- Review carefully the facts and other information about your topic that you gathered for Writing: Developing a Magazine Article.
- After reviewing them, decide what underlying message, or central idea, seems to emerge. This idea is your theme. Write down the theme in the form of a sentence.
- With your theme in mind, select only those facts and other pieces of information that develop and support your theme. Write each of these in sentence form.

LESSON 2   ORGANIZATION OF THE ARTICLE

After selecting all the facts and deciding on the theme for an article, the writer has to decide how to organize the facts and develop the theme. Which facts and ideas should come in the introduction of the article? Which should come in the body? Which should the writer use to close the article?

Introduction   How to begin? Every writer who stares at a blank computer screen or at a clean, white sheet of paper in a type-writer is faced with this question. The writer knows that he or she must demonstrate in the opening paragraphs that the article will be worth the reader's time and effort.

The opening paragraph of an article is called the *lead*. The lead should capture the reader's immediate attention and inter-est. Some writer's begin a lead with a question, a catchy phrase, or an anecdote (a brief story about an interesting incident or event). An effective lead is one that amuses, excites, or startles the reader, or appeals to his or her emotions. In Krakauer's lead, he tries to excite his readers by having them join him at the crest of Mount Rainier, 14,410 feet above sea level, and by refering to his "morbid curiosity."

After the second paragraph readers have an idea of where the article is headed—Rainier poses a threat to people who live in its shadow. Krakauer then lays the foundation for his theme by creating a little mystery. He describes the hot gases venting from the volcano and how the ground beneath his feet is "disturbingly warm." He hasn't revealed yet what geologists believe is the hidden threat of Mount Rainier. He wants the audience to continue reading to find out.

Body   The body, or middle part, of the article develops the theme. It presents specific facts and examples that are directly related to the theme. While you are reading, you may not even be aware that the facts and examples the writer is giving are developing the theme. Note how the following passages from the body of the article all relate to the article's theme:

> Geologists take lahars very seriously, which is why Mount Rainier makes them so nervous. More than 100,000 people live in homes built on debris washed down by lahars.

> Lahars are a hazard of virtually all volcanoes, but Rainier has some unique geologic traits that make it especially dangerous.

> As soon as part of Rainier grows sufficiently rickety, a catastophic lahar is bound to result.

Krakauer further develops his theme when he discusses historic events: the lahar that destroyed the town of Armero in Columbia and the lahars that flowed from Mount Rainier hundreds of thousands of years ago. His inclusion of the geologist's explanation of the phenomenon known as hydrothermal alteration, a process that is causing Rainier to erode from the inside out, adds to his development of the theme.

Close   When a writer has said everything that he or she has to say about the subject of the article, it's not enough simply to stop writing. It's important to give the reader a satisfying conclusion.

There are several ways to close an article. The writer may summarize the main points, draw conclusions, or suggest some possible future developments or action. In closing his article, Krakauer asks, "What, then, can we who live in the shadow of the mountain do to protect our lives and property the next time a tsunami of mud comes rumbling down from the heights?" He then provides a summary of the experts' answers to that question.

EXERCISE ◇2◇

Read the following passage from the article. Use what you have learned in this lesson to answer the questions.

> "Lahars have occurred throughout Rainier's history," warns Malone, "and they can happen more or less sponta-neously, in the complete absence of an eruptive event, with practically no warning at all. Horribly, we remember what happened to Armero, and worry that something similar might happen around here."

1. How does the author further develop the theme of the article in this passage?

2. How can you infer what happened in Armero? Does the author effectively set up and make a connection to the events that follow?

Now check your answers with your teacher. Review this lesson if you don't understand why an answer was incorrect.

 WRITING ON YOUR OWN ◇2◇

In this exercise you will use what you learned in this lesson to help you organize your facts and write a lead paragaph for your article. Follow these steps:

- Review the sentences you wrote for Writing on Your Own 1. Decide which facts and ideas in those sentences should come in the introduction, which should come in the body, and which should come in the close of your article.

- In paragraph form, write and group the sentences that go into the introduction first, followed by those that go into the body, and finishing with those that go into the close.

- Now think about how you want to begin your article. What can you say to attract your readers' attention and interest? Will you use a question, a catchy phrase, or an anecdote? You may want to try several approaches before deciding which one works best for your article. Write your lead paragraph.

- When you have finished writing the draft of your lead, reread it. Is it an "eye-catcher." Revise your lead until you are satisfied that it will "hook" your reader's attention. Then place it at the beginning of the introduction as your opening paragraph.

LESSON ③   MAIN IDEA AND SUPPORTING DETAILS

Within the main parts of the article—the introduction, the body, and the close—the writer needs to organize the information into main ideas and supporting details. At this stage the writer reviews all the information he or she has gathered and decides what main ideas are contained in that information. They are the important points about the topic the author is writing about. The writer then makes a judgment about which main ideas to include and which to leave out, which to emphasize and which just to mention briefly. The more important ideas, of course, will have more supporting details.

The body of Krakauer's article includes several main ideas, such as that lahars can happen without warning; there are a number of disquieting parallels between Nevada del Ruiz and Rainier, and Rainier has some unique geological traits that make it especially dangerous. Krakauer introduces each new idea with a topic sentence or a quotation.

Topic Sentence   A *topic sentence* states the main idea of a paragraph. Although it often appears at the beginning of the paragraph, it can appear anywhere in the paragraph. If a topic sentence appears at the beginning of the paragraph, one or more supporting details follow it. If the topic sentence appears elsewhere, it summarizes the preceding details. Read the following passage from the article and see whether you can identify the topic sentence.

> Within moments, the town was inundated with a slurry resembling wet concrete, burying the community beneath 30 feet of gray-brown muck. The next morning, where their homes had once stood, survivors gazed upon a stark, lunar-like plain covering 600 acres and littered with smashed cars, corpses, and uprooted trees. An estimated 23,000 people lost their lives, and more than 60,000 were left homeless. It was the worst natural disaster in Colombia's history.

Did you choose the last sentence in the paragraph as the topic sentence? It clearly sums up the preceding details about the mudflow that destroyed Armero, Colombia. By placing the topic sentence at the end, the author adds drama to the paragraph.

Order of Ideas   Once a writer selects the main ideas and supporting details, he or she then must decide in what order to present the ideas. Some writers use a formal outline; others just make a few notes. If a writer does not begin with a plan, the outcome will be a hodgepodge of random thoughts.

Usually the subject matter dictates the most logical sequence for organization. The six most common methods of ordering ideas are chronological order, spatial order, order of importance, developmental order, general-to-specific order, and specific-to-general order.

Chronological order is the arrangement of events in the order in which they occurred. Biographies and how-to articles are ideal for chronological organization.

Spatial order is the order in which objects are arranged in space. It is often used to describe a scene, telling what is in the foreground and what is in the background, or what is at the left and what is at the right.

Order of importance is an ordering of topics and events based on the significance the writer places on each.

Developmental order is an ordering of facts that highlights the natural relationship of one fact to another.

General-to-specific order organizes information by starting with a general discussion of the main points and then proceeding to specific examples, facts, or other evidence.

Specific-to-general order organizes the information by starting with specific examples, facts, or other evidence and then proceeding to a general discussion of the main points.

Although most articles are written in developmental order, some include other methods as well. Krakauer uses mainly developmental order in his article but also uses paragraphs written in general-to-specific and spatial order. For example, he begins his article by explaining that he climbed Mount Rainier looking for answers. When he saw steam rising from Mount St. Helens, it reminded him of where he was when the volcano erupted. This led him to think about Rainier erupting because he could see and smell plumes of hot gases and feel the volcano's warmth. As you can see, Krakauer then uses developmental order to discuss lahars, to give examples of lahars, and to speculate what would happen if a lahar came down Rainier.

In the following passage from Krakauer's article, see if you can identify the method of organization.

Fifteen years later, as I mull the scenery from atop Mount Rainier, the merest glance between my boots suggests that the consequences could be much more dire when it's this peak's

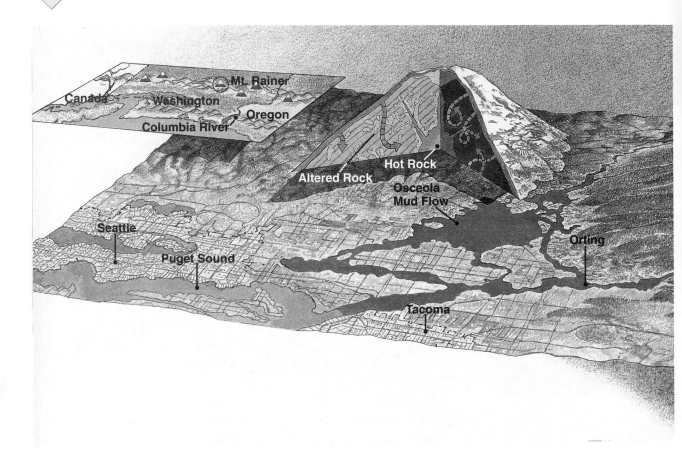

Mount Rainer (in cutaway, above) has 25 times as much ice as Mount St. Helens did. Ice can cause catastrophic debris slides known as lahars. The cutaway shows how infiltrating water is heated; it meets glacier bottoms and, with hydrogen sulfide added, turns rock to clay.

turn to blow. Hard to the northwest sprawl Tacoma, Seattle, and their myriad suburbs. I can plainly make out the Space Needle, skyscrapers, and 747s landing at Sea-Tac Airport.

Krakauer first places the reader atop Mount Rainier; then he describes from his vantage point what he sees below to the northwest: Tacoma and Seattle, points of interest, and planes landing at the airport. This is an example of spatial order. His description places the reader atop Mount Rainier, where one can visualize the view.

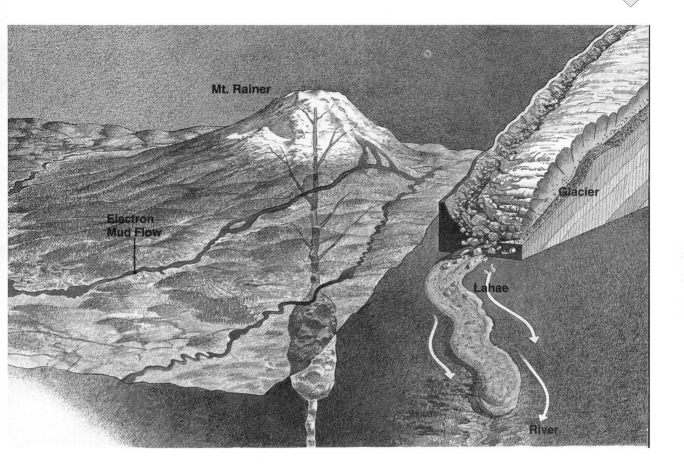

Graphic Aids   When a complex, difficult-to-understand fact or idea is presented in an article—for example, the description of the hydrothermal-alteration phenomenon—sometimes even a detailed, thorough explanation by the writer may not be enough for the reader to understand it. In such cases, the use of a graphic aid can greatly help the reader's understanding. A graphic aid can be an illustration, a photograph, a chart, or a diagram. It usually appears on the same page as, or facing the page, where the topic is discussed. This allows the reader to refer easily to the graphic aid for clarification.

Notice how the illustration above from the article, helps simplify the concept of hydrothermal alteration. The illustration helps show how the hot rock within the mountain is melting its glaciers from below. This continuous melting causes water to flow into the mountain, where it is further heated, and to circulate. The hot liquid combines with sulfur-bearing gases to produce acids that are eroding and altering the rock of Rainier from the inside out. Note that the arrows show the circulation of the hot liquid and gases throughout the mountain. The graphic also shows the path of the Osceola Mudflow, demonstrating just how far it traveled.

EXERCISE ⟨3⟩

Read this passage from the article. Use what you have learned in this lesson to answer the questions that follow it.

> Rainier's prodigious mantle of ice contributes to the potential danger in a less obvious, more insidious way, as well. The peak's subterranean heat is continuously melting its glaciers from below, feeding water into the complex system of geothermal aquifers. Constantly circulating through the mountain, this abundance of hot liquid combines with sulfur-bearing gases to produce acids that are eroding Rainier from the inside out, undermining its structural integrity. "The entire edifice of the mountain is stewing in its own hot chemical juices," explains Scott, "and as a consequence it's becoming increasingly rotten and unstable."

1. What is the topic sentence in this paragraph?

2. What details support the main idea of the paragraph?

Now check your answers with your teacher. Review this lesson if you don't understand why an answer was incorrect.

 WRITING ON YOUR OWN ⟨3⟩

In this exercise you will use what you have learned in this lesson to organize your main ideas and supporting details. Follow these steps:

- Reread what you wrote for Writing on Your Own 2. You should have a lead and one or more paragraphs for each part of your article: the introduction, the body, and the close.
- Now you will organize each of your paragraphs so that it has a topic sentence stating the main idea and one or more details that support that main idea. To help you, first copy the graphic organizer shown below onto a sheet of paper.

Main Idea

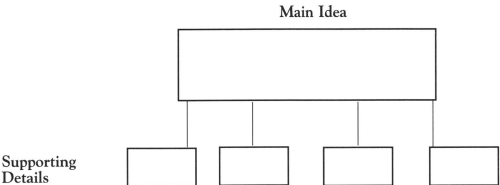

Supporting Details

- For each paragraph, write a topic sentence that states the main idea in the main idea box at the top of the organizer. Then write each of the details that support that main idea in one of the boxes below it. You will need an organizer for each paragraph.
- When you have finished, number the paragraphs in the order in which you wish to present them in your article. Is the order you chose logical? Will you be able to make a smooth transition from one main idea to the next?

DISCUSSION GUIDES

1. Many people live in or near locations where natural disasters have occurred and will probably occur again sometime in the future. People live on the flood plains of major rivers, on fault lines, on hillsides prone to mudslides, on the shores of oceans where hurricanes have hit, and in locations that have frequent tornado activity. When a disaster does occur, many people rebuild their homes on the same site. With the class discuss why you think many people choose to live in dangerous areas rather than move.

2. In a small group discuss any questions you may have about volcanoes that you feel the author did not cover or did not explain well enough. Have someone in your group list the questions. Next to each question, write down how you would find an answer. Share your list of questions and where the answers might be found with the rest of your class.

3. With a partner choose a volcano that has had a major eruption—Mount St. Helens, Mount Vesuvius, Mount Pelee, Nevado del Ruiz, Mauna Loa, Krakatoa, or Mount Etna, for example. Do some research on the one you choose and put together a brief report telling where the volcano is located, when it last erupted, and what damage it caused. Then present your report to the class.

WRITE A MAGAZINE ARTICLE

In this unit you have seen the steps that writers follow when writing a magazine article. Now you will write your own magazine article.

Follow these steps to complete your article. If you have questions about the writing process, refer to Using the Writing Process (page 250).

- Gather and review all the writing execises you did for this unit: 1) the name of your topic and sentences explaining why others might be interested in it, and a list of facts and other information about your topic; 2) your theme and facts, and other pieces of information that develop and support your theme, written in sentence form; 3) paragraphs organized into an introduction, body, and close, and a lead paragraph; 4) paragraphs with a main idea and supporting details numbered in the order of presentation.
- Write a first draft of your magazine article. As you write, keep your audience in mind. Are you using any technical or scientific terms? If so, will your readers understand them? Can you add information that would explain these terms? Consider using a graphic aid to help explain any difficult ideas you're presenting.
- When you have finished your first draft, reread it, keeping these questions in mind: Does your lead paragraph catch your readers' attention? Are the paragraphs arranged in a logical order? Does each paragraph flow easily into the next? Does each of your main ideas have sufficient details to support it? Revise your article accordingly.
- Think about the theme that runs throughout your article. Write a title for your article. Remember, you want to catch your readers' attention right away. An interesting title will help.
- Exchange articles with a partner. Read and comment on each other's work. Make suggestions for improving each other's article. Revise your article accordingly.
- Proofread your article for errors in spelling, grammar, punctuation, and capitalization. Make a final copy and share it with your class.

Remember Who You Are

◆

by Cathy Guisewite

INTRODUCTION

BUILDING BACKGROUND

Readers can easily identify with Cathy Guisewite's ironic view of the responsibilities and concerns of women in today's society. Cathy was first introduced over 20 years ago and is still popular today.

Being asked to be the keynote speaker at a university graduation ceremony is quite an honor. Graduation committees usually debate for months before selecting a speaker. They look for someone who not only has achieved success but also could be an inspiration to others. In April 1994 cartoonist Cathy Guisewite stepped before a microphone and delivered the commencement address at the University of Michigan. Just imagine how the character in her nationally known *Cathy* comic strip would have felt at that moment. Would her speech be informative, insightful, well-organized, entertaining, creative, funny, and appealing to a very large audience? "Yikes!"

College graduation ceremonies are called "commencements" because they mark the end of a school experience and the beginning of a promising future. It is an exciting time for the graduating class and perhaps an uncertain one too. Students are leaving the security of college life and going out on their own, often moving to new locations. Most commencement speakers offer advice on how to meet the challenges of the future and accept the disappointments. They often use personal experiences to emphasize their main ideas. In her speech, "Remember

Who You Are," Guisewite lists four survival tips that she
believes will help students fulfill their dreams and cope with
"the little stuff" that lies ahead. As you read the speech, you will
learn how Guisewite applies those tips to her own life.

**ABOUT THE
AUTHOR**

Cathy Guisewite is one of only a few successful female cartoon-
ists. Both she and her comic strip character *Cathy* are well-
known role models for the young, single career woman.

    Born in 1950 in Ohio, Guisewite grew up in Midland,
Michigan. She received a Bachelor of Arts degree in English
from the University of Michigan in 1972. Four years after graduating, she was a vice president at an advertising agency but was
unhappy in her work. In letters home to her parents, she
included funny, stick-figure drawings of herself looking overweight, overworked, and unhappy. Guisewite's mother thought
the sketches had potential for being a comic strip. She "constantly nagged" her daughter to submit her drawings to
Universal Press Syndicate, which distributes strips to newspapers. Guisewite decided to follow her mother's advice. To
Cathy's surprise, she immediately received a contract to create
the cartoon strip *Cathy.*

    Cathy has gained a wide audience since it first appeared in
1976. In 1987 Guisewite won an Emmy, an award for excellence
in television, for an animated television special for adults called
"Cathy."

**ABOUT THE
LESSONS**

The lessons that follow "Remember Who We Are" focus on
two related elements: structure and style. Both elements are
important in creating a well-written and well-presented speech.

    In this unit you will see how Cathy Guisewite's excellent
commencement speech was structured, or organized, by her, and
how her unique style, or way, of writing and speaking made her
speech a memorable one

WRITING: DEVELOPING A SPEECH

At the end of this unit, you will write an informal speech about some meaningful experience that you've had in your life. The suggestions below will help you get started:

- Think about an experience you've had that is particularly meaningful to you—one that you think would make an interesting topic for a speech.
- Write it down in the form of a topic—for example, your first driving experience.
- Under the topic write down as many details that you can recall about the experience. Write each of these details in sentence form. Are there any humorous details you could include?
- Review these sentences. Then use them to write two or three paragraphs describing the experience. Be sure your sentences and paragraphs follow a logical order.

AS YOU READ

Think about these questions as you read the selection. They will help you focus on the structure and style of Guisewite's speech.

- How does Guisewite get the audience's immediate attention and interest?
- How does she organize her speech?
- What are the four survival tips that she gives to the graduates?
- How does the author make her speech conversational?

Remember Who You Are

by Cathy Guisewite

University of Michigan
Ann Arbor, Michigan
April 30, 1994

The fact that the University of Michigan would have a commencement speaker who has publicly admitted to hiding in the
ladies' room with a box of doughnuts as a way of coping with
business pressure means a lot to me. The committee was also
willing to overlook the fact that I balance my checkbook by
switching banks and starting all over every six months . . . that I
sometimes call in sick because I can't get my hair straight . . .
and that I end each day in my brilliant career with a tiny, secret
prayer that my desk will burn down in the night.

   This is a school that understands that success is not something we achieve once and get to keep, but something we have
to each re-earn in our own way every day.

   This is a school that understands that every hope, every
dream, and every single speck of your fabulous education still
has to be filtered through you. The human element . . . that
your ability to cope daily with the little stuff is going to have as
much to do with how your future works as the four years you just
spent getting your degree.

The world expects so much of you. You will be expected to be a dynamic businessperson; financial wizard; nurturing home-maker; enlightened, involved parent; environmental activist; physical fitness expert; a sexy and alluring yet responsible part-ner; champion of human rights; independent thinker; commu-nity activist; and if you're a woman, a size 5, all at once.

Today, when the message is that anyone can do anything, it is going to be very hard not to feel that everyone else is doing something, and that you personally are standing still in the same old ruts.

It is already hard not to get the impression that everyone else is coping better, isn't it? Everyone seems more efficient, more organized, more confident.

Everyone else not only knew how to get to North Campus but knew there was one. Everyone else knew it was a mistake to sign up for the 8:00 A.M. art history lecture, where the first thing they do is turn out all the lights and start talking about dream visions.

Everyone has a better direction, a better love life, a better day planner, and a better therapist . . . not to mention a clue what they are going to do tomorrow. It is hard not to be depressed by the very examples that are supposed to inspire you.

And just in case normal human insecurity does not nail you when you get out in the world, you will be bombarded by images which, even when you know better than to believe them, will do their little number on your brains.

Look at how women are bombarded in 1994. Look at the commercials. Look at how they picture men and women. The men are still doing one thing in the commercials. The women are doing six things at once.

The man in the commercial is mowing the lawn. One job. The woman is giving herself a beauty treatment for her hands while she does the dishes. The man is grilling a steak. One job. The woman is simultaneously cleaning the oven, disinfecting the floor, popping a five-course meal in the microwave, and fax-ing the office while explaining the magic of feminine hygiene products to her daughter.

If you think that does not translate into real-life expectations, head for Detroit during rush hour some morning and look around you on the freeway. The men are driving to work. One job. The women are driving to work, steering the car with their knees, applying eyeliner with one hand, rehemming their power suits with the other hand, singing songs to the children they are dropping off at day care, while listening to French language tapes and doing isometric butt exercises.

We like to believe that women are equals in the workplace, but to even look acceptable for her first interview, a woman will spend more on her haircut, more on her makeup, more on her underwear, more on her shoes, and more on her outfit, which will take a hundred times more time to get together, since the pieces are in twelve different departments and women's stores do not do alterations, and five minutes after the Visa bill arrives the woman will have to start all over again because it all just went out of style.

It is a microcosm[1] of the extra expectations that come with being a woman, and the extra sense of isolation that many women will feel when they try to do everything and cannot.

Compounding the loneliness for many women has been the fact that if we expressed any vulnerability in the process of trying to live up to fifty images at once, we were shaming our gender by being stereotypically weak.

Men are bombarded with their own set of impossible images. They have been honed and handed down by a zillion generations of protectors and providers and have smacked head-on into a world which is simultaneously screaming for and rejecting the kinder, gentler kind of guy.

A lot of my work as a cartoonist revolves around coping with the pressures that result from the images, trying to close the gap between who we are supposed to be, versus who we want to be, versus who we actually were at 7:30 this morning.

I have searched for answers. I have prayed for inspiration. I have begged for miracles. I have scoured the mall. I humbly offer the four clues I have so far.

---

[1] a little world

1. Give up the quest for perfection and shoot for five good minutes in a row. When I came to the University of Michigan as a freshman, I was five pounds overweight and desperate to lose the weight immediately so I would be liked by each of my 34,000 classmates. My first crash diet resulted in a gain of four more pounds, and then I was really desperate. I quit eating completely for three days.

I slipped into a Diet Coke-induced delusionary stupor[2] during my first all-nighter and gained another seven pounds when I accidentally ordered and ate pizza for the entire Mosher-Jordon Dorm.

I vowed to not only lose the weight instantly but to look my demons directly in the eye, so I got a job at Drakes, where I gained another twenty-nine pounds, for a grand total of forty-five pounds by the end of my senior year, which I figure means my college education cost my parents a thousand dollars a pound.

In retrospect, it all could have gone so differently if I had just refrained from eating for five minutes in a row. The only thing I have ever succeeded at instantly was failing.

Every one of you knows someone who did better than you at something in college because they approached it with a slow, steady, dignified attack, rather than going for the screaming, end-of-semester, bluebook miracle.

A lot of what you just experienced at the University of Michigan is unfortunately exactly how it works on the outside. Just like in college, you will be able to luck out now and then and get an A without trying, but if you bank on that as your system, you will flunk life in general. Just like in college, you will be tempted to take on too much at once and will have diminished results in all the categories. Just like in college, you will eventually have to do your laundry and call your parents to beg for money. And mostly, just like in college, you will be graded not for how dramatic your plans are but for what you actually sit down and do, slowly, deliberately, for five minutes in a row. If you can succeed for five minutes in a row, you can do anything.

[2] a dazed condition

2. Remember what you love. I know that a lot of your parents are here, and that this day means as much to them as it does to you. Graduation is the sort of rich, precious, intensely emotional day that has always brought out the very worst in my family. In the eight hours I spent with them on Graduation Day, we managed to have a miniature recap of every psychodrama we had had since I arrived here as a freshman.

It took us two and one-half hours to buy a cup of coffee in the cafeteria line in the Union the morning of my graduation. My father wanted to take a picture of Mom and me in line. My mother said no, that my dad should be in the picture, and that she would take it. My father said my mother always cuts off everyone's head, and that he should take all the pictures.

Neither one of them could get the flash to work, so I said I would take the picture. At this point there were twenty people backed up in line behind us, and all twenty were pleading to take our picture as a group and be done with it.

Mom did not want to inconvenience anyone, so she said she would take everyone else's picture and started simultaneously snapping shots and looking for a pencil so she could write down their names and addresses to send them copies.

Dad felt guilty that Mom was decapitating an entire group of strangers with her photography and offered to buy doughnuts for everyone in line. Mom worried that there were now thirty-five people getting crumbs on the floor and went into the kitchen to get a broom so she could help sweep.

I stood in the middle and just started shrieking, "This is who I am! This is the gene pool! This is why I never get anything done!"

By the end of Graduation Day, it was as though we had assembled our own little psychological parent-child yearbook. When I flip through the pages of that yearbook now, I see the tangle of love and impatience and dependence and defiance that makes up the most important relationship of my life. When I look at my family, I know who I am.

But it is more than just family. The experience of going to the University of Michigan bonds people in a bizarre way that I can only describe by saying that even though I did not graduate with a big circle of friends in my class, almost all the people who have become my best friends since college went to school here and graduated at different times.

I did not even know them when I was here, and every single one of them has helped keep me more connected to what I believe in than anyone else I have met. Every single one of them came here today to be at your graduation with me. One of my friends who not only came to your graduation but brought his whole family is Larry Kasdan, who wrote *The Big Chill* and told the whole world about the depth of friendship and connection that happens on this campus.

Every year you are out of school you will have more names in your phone book and fewer actual friends. A lot of the ones that really count will be people who mapped out their dreams on the diag just like you. When I look at my friends from the University of Michigan, I believe in who I am.

But it is not just friends and family. You might not even realize it today, but each one of you has had one pivotal experience here that will eventually define what you do with the rest of your life. I am talking about the kind of experience that felt so right, was so exhilarating, tapped into your essence in such a way that you will look back on it and say, "That was the moment my calling was revealed to me."

My pivotal experience at the University of Michigan was the book *Ulysses*. The two-million-page, twenty-pound masterpiece *Ulysses*, which I took one entire, semester-long class on. I never read the book. I never made it through the "Cliff Notes." I went into Angel Hall for my written essay final on *Ulysses* knowing only that it had something to do with a guy in Ireland. I left Angel Hall an hour and fifteen minutes later with an A in the class and the knowledge that I had a gift for creative writing.

The exhilaration of creating ten poignant insightful pages out of nothing but complete hysteria is what convinced me I should write for a living; and that reconvinces me every time I remember it. When I look at my *Ulysses* bluebook twenty-two years later, I trust who I am.

Look at what you love on graduation day. Take the classes, the friends, and the family that have inspired the most in you. Save them in your permanent memory and make a backup disk. When you remember what you love, you will remember who you are. If you remember who you are, you can do anything.

3. *If you want something to change, do something different.* When I look back and think about the things I could have done and should have done and wish I had said and wanted to try and thought of changing, time and time again I see the only brick walls that were ever really in my way were the ones I lovingly built myself, brick by brick, and then proceeded to smash my head against. I just could not get out of my own way.

Stuck with myself, I have had no choice but to do some deep, introspective[3] thinking, and like so many bright, intelligent Americans, to really search my own soul until I found a way to blame someone else.

I blame the products I buy for funding the TV channels I subscribe to for desensitizing me to violence. I blame the company I paid a fortune to for my car for mucking up my air. I blame the fashion industry I spend thousands on for degrading women, leaving me with the sickening feeling that I am financing my own destruction, which, of course, I blame on the politicians whose salaries I pay, which I lump into a pool with all the other miscellaneous unpleasantries of life and blame on my parents.

If people responded honestly to everything that was simultaneously going wrong in their own lives and in the world on any given day, we would all just run around screaming all the time.

On a personal level, it is hard to make changes because of the fear that if we change, something might be different. In the world at large, it is hard to make changes because of the fear that no matter what we do, nothing will be different. And in both cases, we are hit with the bonus fear that even if things are different, they will be worse.

I graduated with a class committed to open love, open thinking, open doors, open everything. Twenty-two years later a

---

[3] looking inward

whole generation of flower children are spending four thousand dollars each on burglar alarms for our cars and homes so that no one will take our things.

My graduating class rejected the depersonalized greed of corporate structure. We believed in people. Our goal was to understand people, to relate to people, nothing would ever come before the people. Twenty-two years later the people of my class are getting cash out of a machine, dinner out of a clown's mouth, and it is not even possible to get a human being on the phone at the phone company. In Los Angeles, my only chance of having a meaningful encounter with a person is if I smash into one with my car.

My graduating class demanded information. We wanted to know why our revolution was backfiring. We got 150 cable channels. One third are eyewitness crime shows. One third are entertainment crime shows. One third are news commentary shows, showing in graphic detail how all the crime shows are warping our minds and creating the next generation of little villains.

I have fantasized that I could really change and have an impact if I could just move to a different city, take on a new identity and start fresh, where everyone, including me, did not already know what sort of person I was. Every single person in the audience who is not graduating today is jealous of the fact that most of you who are graduating get to do just that.

We all appreciate that it will not be that easy. You have grown up in a strange time where people seem more bonded by the bad stuff than the good, where in a lot of communities the main common link between neighbors is that everyone knows someone who has AIDS, everyone knows someone who has been mugged, everyone knows someone in rehab,[4] and everyone has been touched by a life that ended way too soon.

If you want something to change, you personally have to do something different. You have to take a stand when it is not convenient. Say something in a relationship when it hurts to

---

[4] short for *rehabilitation*—a program to restore one's health

do it. Work harder than you are used to working. Try something nobody else has tried. Defy your own group. Rebel against yourself. Knock down your walls and get out of your own way. If you are brave enough to do something different, you can do anything.

4. *Let yourself regraduate every four years.* In one of my mother's really annoying moments of being right about something, Mom told me that life deserves an overhaul every four years. She said four years is exactly enough time in any situation to know what is working, what is not, what is worth saving, and what or who you ought to dump. As with most of her advice, I staged my own personal rebellion and hung onto everything I ever owned, clung to relationships way past when it was appropriate, and not only settled into ruts, but dug them so deep they became like little subterranean villages stuffed with cable TV and bad habits.

In another really annoying moment of being right about something, my mother quit mentioning the four-year-overhaul thing completely a few years ago, which forced me to rebel again and bring it up myself and, even though I was twenty years overdue, to stage my own overhaul.

When I took a really good hard look at things, I saw that I was great at my career, horrible at personal relationships, and that I had fifteen minutes left in which to meet someone, fall in love, get married, get pregnant, and have a child, if I ever wanted to be a parent. I used the full fifteen minutes I had left on my biological clock to call my mother and scream at her for not being pushy enough. I then started the process that eventually resulted in my adopting a beautiful baby girl named Ivy.

Adopting Ivy was without question the hardest and loneliest thing I have ever done. I had to change every single fantasy about how I thought I would have a child, who I thought I would have a child with, how I thought a family should work, not to mention change every single minute of how I was used to living.

Twenty years after getting down on my hands and knees and begging my University of Michigan Spanish professor to pass me out of the language requirement that I would never use, I have had to sign up for a Spanish Berlitz course so I could keep up with what my two-year-old is learning on *Sesame Street*. Like many psychotic, exhausted mothers, I can only say that if I had it to do all over again, I only wish I would have done it a little bit sooner.

Let yourself regraduate every four years. Celebrate what you have done. Admit what you are not doing. Think about what is important to you and make some changes. If you give yourself a chance to move on, you can do anything.

For all the women and men of the class of 1994, the only thing greater than the frustration of attempting to do it all will be the seduction of wanting to try.

Both personally and professionally, I believe very strongly in visualizing goals way beyond what seems humanly possible. I got this from my parents, who are great dreamers themselves and always insisted my sisters and I could do anything, way past the point of all logic.

When my mother first suggested I submit some scribbles to a comic-strip syndicate, I pointed out that I knew nothing about comic-strip syndicates or comic strips. Mom said, "So what? You will learn."

When I submitted my scribbles to a comic-strip syndicate and I pointed out to Mom that I did not know how to draw, she said, "So what? You will learn."

When the syndicate sent me a contract to do a comic strip for them, I asked Mom how she thought I could possibly think of something worth printing 365 days a year for the next forty years. Mom took me by the hand, sat me down at a table, and together we ate a Sara Lee cheesecake.

All parents believe their children can do the impossible. They thought it the minute we were born, and no matter how hard we have tried to prove them wrong, they all think it about us now. And the really annoying thing is, they are probably all right again.

You are no different from the graduate sitting next to you who might solve the world's energy problems. You are no different from the one behind you who might bring about the most important changes yet in human rights. You are no different from the one in front of you who might inspire all of our children with his or her brilliant teaching.

Each of us wages a private battle each day between the grand fantasies we have for ourselves and what actually happens. Between the graceful, meaningful way others seem to use their time, versus the chaos of our own.

We all have to learn to not give up if we are not perfect tomorrow and to somehow stay optimistic that we will be perfect the day after tomorrow.

As graduates, you have to set standards for how you work, how you treat others, how you let yourself be treated. You have to simultaneously celebrate yourself and rebel against yourself. You have to defy your group, knock down your walls, and get out of your own way. You have to separate yourself from the 10,000 things that are expected of you and concentrate on something one day at a time. I suggest these four clues to start:

1. *Give up the quest for perfection and shoot for five good minutes in a row.*
2. *Remember what you love.*
3. *If you want something to change, do something different.*
4. *Let yourself regraduate every four years.*

And when you are demoralized, with no hope in your heart and a pint of Häagen-Dazs[5] in your stomach, crawl over to the box of junk you never quite got organized, pull out your diploma, and remember the best clue of all:

If you made it through this place, you can do anything.

---

[5] a popular brand of ice cream

REVIEWING AND INTERPRETING
Record your answers to these questions in your personal literature notebook. Follow the directions for each part.

REVIEWING

Try to complete each of these sentences without looking back at the selection.

Recalling Facts

1. Cathy Guisewite
   a. graduated from the University of Michigan in 1994.
   b. gained forty-five pounds while she was a freshman in college.
   c. got an A on her college Spanish final exam.
   d. discovered her gift for creative writing in college.

Understanding Main Ideas

2. The author thinks modern women have a difficult time because
   a. the culture says they must be thin in order to be beautiful.
   b. men do not give them the help and support they need.
   c. they are expected to fill too many roles simultaneously.
   d. they are educated to think like men.

Identifying Sequence

3. Cathy Guisewite adopted a child
   a. soon after graduating from college.
   b. when she became a successful cartoonist.
   c. after her marriage ended.
   d. less than two years before she delivered this speech.

Finding Supporting Details

4. As an example of the confusion felt by university freshmen, Guisewite mentions
   a. her experiences on graduation day with her parents.
   b. taking an exam on *Ulysses* without ever reading the book.
   c. not knowing the university had a North Campus.
   d. taking a Berlitz course in Spanish.

Getting Meaning
from Context

5. "In retrospect, it all could have gone so differently if I had just refrained from eating for five minutes in a row." The word *retrospect* means
   a. believing.
   b. forgetting.
   c. looking backward.
   d. looking forward.

INTERPRETING

To complete these items, you may look back at the selection if you'd like.

Making Inferences

6. Which statement best expresses Cathy Guisewite's attitude toward her mother's advice?
   a. She wishes she had paid more attention to it.
   b. She feels her mother had interfered too much.
   c. She feels her mother didn't understand her.
   d. She wishes she hadn't followed it.

Generalizing

7. Guisewite's attitude toward her parents is
   a. distant.
   b. unforgiving.
   c. affectionate.
   d. uncomfortable.

Recognizing Fact and
Opinion

8. Which of the following is *not* a statement of opinion?
   a. "If you can succeed for five minutes in a row, you can do anything."
   b. "All parents believe their children can do the impossible."
   c. "Each one of you has had one pivotal experience here that will eventually define what you do with the rest of your life."
   d. "It took us two and one-half hours to buy a cup of coffee in the cafeteria line. . . ."

Identifying Cause and Effect

9. Guisewite submitted her cartoons to a comic-strip syndicate because
   a. she wanted to make a career change.
   b. friends told her she was very funny.
   c. her mother kept urging her to.
   d. she was proud of her drawing ability.

Drawing Conclusions

10. Which statement most accurately expresses the message Guisewite wants to give her audience?
   a. "If people responded honestly to everything that was simultaneously going wrong in their own lives and in the world on any given day, we would all just run around screaming all the time."
   b. "Every year you are out of school you will have more names in your phone book and fewer actual friends."
   c. "We all have to learn to not give up if we are not perfect tomorrow and to somehow stay optimistic that we will be perfect the day after tomorrow."
   d. "If you want something to change, you personally have to do something different."

Now check your answers with your teacher. Study the items you answered incorrectly. What skills were they checking? Talk to your teacher about ways to work on those skills.

Structure and Style

What makes a truly great speech? Is it the speaker's message, the way it is delivered, the length, or some humorous stories? Some people can give a superb impromptu speech. If suddenly asked to talk about an issue, they can present their ideas in a clear, concise manner without having a prepared text. When delivering an important speech, however, most people take the time to write and rewrite, carefully defining their main points, or ideas.

You learned in Unit 1 that style refers to the way writers express themselves in their writing and speaking. It involves *how* something is said in addition to *what* is said. It is what makes a writer sound unique. It is the kinds of words a writer chooses, as well as the kinds of images he or she creates. A writer's style is also expressed by the structure he or she uses. *Structure* is the writer's arrangement or overall plan for a work. Structure refers to the way words, sentences, and paragraphs are organized to create a complete work. In Unit 1 you learned about different ways writers structure sentences. In this unit you will learn how the author structured a complete work—a speech.

Presentation, or speaking style, is another important element of a speech. How the written words on a page come to life depends on the inflection in the speaker's voice or the facial expressions and gestures used. If a speaker merely reads a funny anecdote, the story probably will fall flat. For humor to be effective, the writer must feel comfortable using it.

There are many elements that combine to make an interesting, well-written speech. In this unit we will talk about some of those elements:

1. **Structure of the Speech**   A speech needs structure. It should be focused on one or two main ideas and have an introduction, body, and close.

2. **Elements of Style**   When writing a speech, an author makes choices about tone and diction—two elements of style.

3. **Humor and Style**   Humor, another element of style, can be an effective tool in a speech. An author's personality is often revealed through his or her use of humor.

LESSON 1   STRUCTURE OF THE SPEECH

In preparing her speech, Cathy Guisewite had to decide not only what she was going to say, but also how she was going to structure, or organize, her speech. Before deciding on the structure of her speech, Guisewite first had to consider who her audience was and decide what the purpose of the speech would be. She knew her audience was a group of young and eager men and women who were about to graduate from college and go out into the "real" world. Her purpose was to show them through her own experiences that success is not easily achieved but must be earned and then reearned every day. Finally, she had to decide on a theme for her speech. You learned in Unit 2 that a theme is the underlying message that the writer wants to convey. Perhaps the best way to examine the structure of Guisewite's speech is to examine its three main parts: the introduction, the body, and the close.

Introduction   In the opening paragraph, Guisewite immediately captures the audience's interest and at the same time puts them at ease. She begins by poking fun at herself. She readily admits to having flaws, anxieties, and insecurities. Her candor lets her audience know that she is far from being perfect, but it doesn't matter because here she is—giving the commencement address at a prestigious university. Her introduction has enabled her to make a direct connection between herself and the young graduates who are her audience.

In the next few paragraphs, her underlying message, or theme, begins to become apparent: The graduates must find ways to cope with life and unrealistic expectations. She alludes to this theme when she says:

. . . your ability to cope daily with the little stuff is going to have as much to do with how your future works as the four years you just spent getting your degree.

She shows she understands that many of these young graduates, perhaps most, have some degree of self-doubt and that she shares their insecurities:

It is already hard not to get the impression that everyone else is coping better, isn't it? Everyone seems more efficient, more organized, more confident. . . . Everyone has a better direction, a better love life, a better day planner, and a better therapist. . . .

Having secured the audience's attention and interest, and having established her theme in the introduction, Guisewite's speech moves into the body, or main part, of the speech.

Body In the body of the speech, the writer develops the theme fully. Although this is the most important part of the speech, effective speechwriters try to limit themselves to just a few important points, and they try to avoid getting bogged down with too many supporting details. Sometimes the writer will repeat or restate his or her main points one or more times. The audience may need to be reminded of what has already been said in order to be able to link these ideas with the new ones they are now hearing.

In developing her theme, Guisewite identifies four main points to help the graduates cope with life after school and with unrealistic expectations. After making each of her points, she summarizes what she said earlier:

1. **"Give up the quest for perfection and shoot for five good minutes in a row."**

. . . you will be graded not for how dramatic your plans are but for what you actually sit down and do, slowly, deliberately, for five minutes in a row. If you can succeed for five minutes, you can do anything.

2. "Remember what you love."

Look at what you love on graduation day. Take the classes, the friends, and the family that have inspired the most in you. Save them in your permanent memory and make a backup disk. When you remember what you love, you will remember who you are. If you remember who you are, you can do anything.

3. "If you want something to change, do something different."

Try something nobody else has tried. Defy your own group. Rebel against yourself. Knock down your walls and get out of your own way. If you are brave enough to do something different, you can do anything.

4. "Let yourself regraduate every four years."

Celebrate what you have done. Admit what you are not doing. Think about what is important to you and make some changes. If you give yourself a chance to move on, you can do anything.

Close You learned in Unit 2 that there are several effective ways to close an article. A speech may be closed in similar ways. The speaker's closing remarks may repeat the main points, give a summation of the writer's opinion or point of view concerning issues addressed in the speech, or even be a call for some kind of action.

Guisewite closes her speech by repeating the four main points she makes in the body of the speech and then ends with this final remark: "If you made it through this place, you can do anything." It is an uplifting, thought-provoking ending.

EXERCISE ◁1▷

Read the following passage from the speech. Use what you have learned in this lesson to answer the questions.

A lot of my work as a cartoonist revolves around coping with the pressures that result from the images, trying to close the gap between who we are supposed to be, versus who we want to be, versus who we actually were at 7:30 this morning.

I have searched for answers. I have prayed for inspiration. I have begged for miracles. I have scoured the mall. I humbly offer the four clues I have so far.

1. Does this passage demonstrate how the author has structured her speech? Explain your answer.

2. What images is the author referring to? How does this passage link the introduction and body of the speech?

Now check your answers with your teacher. Review this lesson if you don't understand why an answer was incorrect.

WRITING ON YOUR OWN

In this exercise you will use what you learned in this lesson to begin developing a structure for your speech. Follow these steps:

- Copy the graphic organizer on the facing page.
- Reread the paragraphs you wrote earlier in this unit. Decide what you think is the underlying message in those paragraphs. That is the theme of your speech. Write the theme in your organizer.
- To introduce your speech, think of ways to grab the audience's attention and interest. Then in the introduction part of the organizer, write a short paragraph to open your speech.
- Following the opening paragraph, and still in the in the introduction part, write a paragraph that clearly expresses the theme of your speech. It is here that you want to give your audience an idea of what your speech is about.

Speech Title

Theme

Introduction

Body

Close

LESSON 2 ⟩ ELEMENTS OF STYLE

In writing "Remember Who You Are," Guisewite had to decide on the the proper tone of her message. *Tone* is the speaker's or writer's attitude toward his or her subject or audience. Did she want to sound enthusiastic or reserved, funny or serious, scholarly or informal? The attitude of some speakers and writers toward their subject or audience is serious, and it is reflected in their work. Others are less serious, perhaps even humorous, in their tone. In which category would you place Cathy Guisewite?

You probably noticed that because her message to the graduates is a serious one, Guisewite's tone moves back and forth between lightheartedness and seriousness. By making fun of herself in her opening remarks in the first paragraph, she clearly reveals that the basic tone of her speech will be lighthearted. She reinforces this tone throughout her speech by painting humorous images of herself when she describes her efforts at coping with life.

Diction works naturally with tone. *Diction* refers to a speaker's or writer's choice and arrangement of words. Good diction is clear. The writer's or speaker's words are chosen to say exactly what he or she means. For example, Guisewite tells the graduates that the world expects a great deal of them; each is expected to be a " dynamic businessperson; financial wizard; nurturing homemaker; enlightened, involved parent; environmental activist; physical fitness expert." She deliberately chose such words as "dynamic," "wizard," "enlightened," to emphasize the point that the graduates are expected to be more than just average or good at what they do in life—they are expected to be superior.

To affect how a speech "sounds" to the reader or listener, a writer may use a series of words having the same ending to give emphasis or affect the pace of the reading, or may insert pauses or use run-on sentences to exaggerate a point or build suspense. Diction also involves the enunciation of words. A speech should be delivered with clear pronunciation, ensuring that listeners will be able to understand it easily.

EXERCISE

Read this passage from the speech. Use what you have learned in this lesson to answer the questions that follow it.

> If you think that does not translate into real-life expectations, head for Detroit during rush hour some morning and look around you on the freeway. The men are driving to work. One job. The women are driving to work, steering the car with their knees, applying eyeliner with one hand, rehemming their power suits with the other hand, singing songs to the children they are dropping off at day care, while listening to French language tapes and doing isometric butt exercises.

1. What is the author's attitude toward the working woman versus the working man?

2. Read this passage aloud. What happens as you read? How does the repetition of words ending in "ing" affect the pace of your reading of the passage?

Now check your answers with your teacher. Review this lesson if you don't understand why an answer was incorrect.

 ## WRITING ON YOUR OWN

In this exercise you will use what you have learned in this lesson to help you write the body part of your speech. Follow these steps:

- Reread the paragraphs you wrote earlier in this unit for Writing: Developing a Speech. You will be rewriting them, where necessary, to describe the experience in your life that is the subject of your speech.
- Before rewriting these paragraphs, consider what tone, or attitude, you want to express toward your subject or audience.
- Write the revised paragraphs in the body part of your organizer. Do the paragraphs develop and support the theme of your speech?

LESSON ③ HUMOR AND STYLE

Have you ever heard a funny story and then repeated it to a friend, only to have your friend not laugh? Did you try to redeem yourself by saying, "I guess you had to be there"? Maybe the problem wasn't with the story but with the storyteller. Professional comedians, such as Bill Cosby and Lucille Ball, or writers, such as Mark Twain and James Thurber, have a great natural talent and unique style for humor. If given the same story to tell, each would take a different approach or attitude to make you laugh. By studying the basic techniques of humor, you too can develop a humorous style.

Humor is an effective element in a speech. It can warm up an audience, relieve tension, or provide a welcome pause after a serious point. When thinking of using a humorous story, however, a writer needs to look at his or her own natural strengths. Do you make your friends laugh with little jokes or deadpan humor? Are you more amusing when telling a story about something that happened to you? Whatever form works best in normal conversation will work best for you in a speech. That is what style is all about.

You no doubt noticed Cathy Guisewite's wit, her self-mocking but good-natured humor. Her style reveals much about her personality. The cartoonist's real-life stories are very similar to those in her comic strip, *Cathy*. Guisewite is not afraid to show humility and talk about those embarrassing, awkward moments that most people would just as soon forget. Her humorous style comes from knowing how to laugh at herself.

> Mom did not want to inconvenience anyone, so she said she would take everyone else's picture and started simultaneously snapping shots and looking for a pencil so she could write down their names and addresses to send them copies.
>
> Dad felt guilty that Mom was decapitating an entire group of strangers with her photography and offered to buy doughnuts for everyone in line. Mom worried that there were now thirty-five people getting crumbs on the floor and went into the kitchen to get a broom so she could help sweep.
>
> I stood in the middle and just started shrieking, "This is who I am! This is the gene pool! This is why I never get anything done!"

This scene is painted so well that you can imagine yourself being a part of it. You can almost see Guisewite's face turning red when her mother goes to find a broom so she can sweep. "Dad" and "Mom" could be your parents!

Besides self-mocking humor and humorous visual images, Guisewite also uses *exaggeration*, an intentional overstatement of facts or events so that their meanings are intensified. Exaggeration is not meant to deceive you but to create humorous results. Look back at the description of the woman driving to work near the beginning of Guisewite's speech. Notice how Guisewite exaggerates how many things the woman is doing besides driving the car, to create an image of a modern-day superwoman.

EXERCISE ⟨3⟩

Read the following passage and answer the questions about it, using what you have learned in this lesson.

> I graduated with a class committed to open love, open thinking, open doors, open everything. Twenty-two years later a whole generation of flower children are spending four thousand dollars each on burglar alarms for our cars and homes so that no one will take our things.
>
> My graduating class rejected the depersonalized greed of corporate structure. We believed in people. Our goal was to understand people, to relate to people. . . . Twenty-two years later the people of my class are getting cash out of a machine, dinner out of a clown's mouth, and it is not even possible to get a human being on the phone at the phone company. In Los Angeles, my only chance of having a meaningful encounter with a person is if I smash into one with my car.

1. How does Guisewite use exaggeration to make the passage more humorous?

2. How does the author reveal her personality in the passage? Does she seem pleased or disappointed with her graduating class?

Now check your answers with your teacher. Review this lesson if you don't understand why an answer was incorrect.

 ## WRITING ON YOUR OWN ⟨3⟩

In this exercise you will use what you have learned in this lesson to add a humorous moment or story to your speech. Follow these steps:

• Reread the paragraphs you wrote for Writing on Your Own 1 and Writing on Your Own 2. Is there a place in those paragraphs where humor would be appropriate?

- Try to insert an element of humor somewhere in your paragraphs. It could be an anecdote or a longer humorous story that is relevant to the experience you are describing.
- To add another element of humor, try to use exaggeration.
- After rewriting you paragraphs, read them. Does the humor seem natural to your writing style? You may wish to read your paragraphs aloud to a classmate to see whether he or she finds the humor amusing.

DISCUSSION GUIDES

1. In a group of three, have each member choose one section of Guisewite's speech to read aloud to the others. As one student reads, take notes about the delivery. Do you think the speaker is using the right tone? emphasizing the right words? pausing in the right places? After the first reading, discuss your observations and recommendations. Then practice reading the sections of the speech again, using the other students' suggestions if justified. Once your group is comfortable with the readings, present them to the class.

2. In a small group discuss current television commercials and compare how men and women are portrayed in them. Do the commercials reflect the comparisons that Guisewite makes? From your own experience, do you think Guisewite and the television commercials are accurate in the way they portray the differences between men and women? Share your observations with the rest of the class.

3. Imagine that you have been asked to give advice to an eighth-grade class on what to expect in high school. In a small group discuss what those students should know about high school. Make a list of tips you would give the students about how to succeed in their freshman year.

WRITE A SPEECH

In this unit you have seen how Cathy Guisewite structured her speech and how her unique style helped make her speech a memorable one. Now you will write a 2–5 minute informal speech about some meaningful experience that you've had in your life.

Follow these steps to complete your speech. If you have questions about the writing process, refer to Using the Writing Process (page 250).

- Gather and review all of the writing exercises you did for this unit: 1) a topic for your speech and two or three paragraphs describing the personal experience that will be the subject of your speech, from Writing: Developing a Speech; 2) your graphic organizer, in which you wrote the theme and introduction of your speech; 3) your completed graphic organizer, in which you wrote the body of your speech; 4) the revised paragraphs you wrote for the body of your speech—to include some elements of humor, including exaggeration.
- Reread the introduction and body of your speech. Think about how you will close your speech. Will you repeat the main points, or ideas? Will you give a summation of your opinion or point of view concerning the experience you described?
- In the close section of your organizer, write some ideas in the form of notes about how to end your speech. From these notes write the close of the speech.
- Write a title for your speech. The title may be different from the name you gave to your topic at the beginning of the unit. For example, the topic may have been your first driving experience, but the final title could be "Disaster on Wheels."
- Read your completed speech to a classmate, a friend, or a family remember. Ask your "audience" to comment on your speech and to suggest any ways that you might improve it. If any suggested changes seem warranted, revise your speech accordingly.
- Proofread your speech for errors in spelling, grammar, punctuation, and capitalization. Make a final copy and save it in your writing portfolio.

Author's Purpose

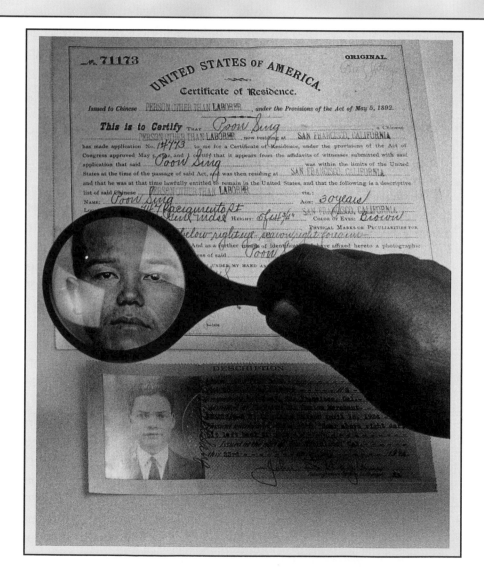

Sojourners Who Came to Stay

❖

by Donald Dale Jackson

INTRODUCTION

BUILDING BACKGROUND

Throughout its history the United States has had a contradictory attitude toward immigrants to this country. On the one hand, America is proud to be a "nation of immigrants"—a "melting pot" of all races and creeds. Every person in this country—unless of Native American ancestry—can trace his or her heritage back to some other part of the world. On the other hand, the United States has not treated newly arrived immigrant groups well. At various times Irish, Italian, Eastern European, and Southeast Asian immigrants have all experienced prejudice and unfair treatment.

As you will read in "Sojourners Who Came to Stay," Chinese immigrants were treated as second-class citizens during the end of the 1800s and the beginning of the 1900s. They were discriminated against when they sought jobs, housing, and education. In 1882 Congress even passed a law known as the Chinese Exclusion Act, the first law in U.S. history to bar people from one specific country from entering the country. The Exclusion Act was not repealed until 1943. Despite the legal barriers and the social and economic hardships they faced, the Chinese continued to come to this country seeking their fortunes. They

Pictured are an 1892 Certificate of Residence for Poon Sing and another document describing Chun Pick Sang (below). Each of these men came to the United States as a "merchant" despite the hated Exclusion Act.

arrived in the United States hoping to save enough from their labors to return to their homeland in a few years with enough valuable U.S. dollars to build a comfortable life for themselves and their families. Actually, few Chinese did return to China, although many continued for most of their lives to think of themselves as temporary visitors, or sojourners, rather than permanent residents of the United States.

ABOUT THE AUTHOR

Donald Dale Jackson is the author of nearly a dozen books as well as numerous articles for national magazines. His wide-ranging interests have led him to write books about such diverse subjects as the California Gold Rush, international cave exploration, the deserts of the American Southwest, American trial judges, unusual animals of Australia, polar exploration, and the American Civil War.

Jackson was born in San Francisco in 1935. He graduated from Stanford University in 1957 and received a master's degree from the Columbia School of Journalism in 1958. After two years of military service in the Counter Intelligence Corps, he began his writing career as a reporter for United Press International. In 1963 he became a reporter for *Life* magazine, to which he contributed major articles on a wide variety of people and subjects. Recently he has been a regular contributor to *Smithsonian* magazine.

ABOUT THE LESSONS

The lessons that follow "Sojourners Who Came to Stay" focus on the author's purpose and his methods of organization. You will learn how an author's purpose affects his or her organization, the facts and opinions he or she presents, and the techniques he or she uses to present them.

As with most magazine articles, the primary purpose of "Sojourners Who Came to Stay" is to provide its readers with information. Donald Dale Jackson gives you information about conditions facing Chinese immigrants to this country during the late 19th and early 20th centuries, particularly those who settled in California and the western part of the country. You will see how Jackson organized the article in a way that he felt best accomplished his purpose.

WRITING: DEVELOPING AN INFORMATIONAL ARTICLE

At the end of this unit, you will write an informational article that reports on a personal interest, skill, or activity. The following suggestions will help you get started:

- Make a list of some of your favorite activities and interests. Write down any hobbies or talents you have. Also list such things as your favorite sport, music, books, food, or games.
- Share and discuss your list with a small group of classmates. You may be surprised to discover that there is an interest or activity in your life that has given you knowledge or experience that is not shared by your classmates. Perhaps you have played and studied baseball, basketball, soccer, or hockey for as long as you can remember. Maybe you have been playing interactive computer games for a very long time and now engage in on-line games with people scattered all over the country. You may have talent as a musician or an artist.
- Choose one interest or activity from your list to write about. The purpose for writing your article will be to give your readers information about your special interest or activity.
- Write a paragraph briefly describing the interest or activity you have chosen to write about.
- On a separate sheet of paper, jot down notes about the reasons you particularly like this activity. Make notes also about reasons you think others might enjoy the same activity.
- Think about what information others might like to have about your topic. As you think of questions a reader might ask,

write them down. If you do not know the answer to any question, can you think of how to find it? Is there a person you can interview? Are there written materials you can research?

Think about these questions as you read the article. They will help you see how Jackson organizes his article to accomplish his purpose.

- How does Jackson organize and present his material to keep your interest?
- What new facts and details do you learn about Chinese immigrants to the United States?
- Why did Chinese immigrants face prejudice, and how did they react?

Sojourners Who Came to Stay

by Donald Dale Jackson

With brilliance and a stoic willingness to persevere, Chinese-Americans remember, their people climbed the "Gold Mountain."

As the railroad pushed through the Sierra Nevada in 1865, the men from China toiled from sunrise to sunset, six days a week. Their pay started at $26 per month and could reach $36. They worked in crews of 12 to 20, each crew with a cook who also furnished hot water for sponge baths.

When the crews reached a perpendicular promontory[1] called Cape Horn, they had to gouge a roadbed out of a sheer granite cliff more than a thousand feet above the American River. Chinese workmen lowered down the rock face in wicker baskets had to drill holes for explosives, light the fuses, and then make as swift an exit as they could before the powder blew.

Roberta Yee, a real estate broker in Palo Alto, California, remembers hearing about the rail workers from her elders: "You know that expression 'a Chinaman's chance'?" she asks. "I always heard that it started with those men that went down the cliff in baskets."

Slight and quiet, the Chinese workers didn't look like railroad builders. The Central Pacific hadn't wanted to hire them at

---

[1] a high ridge of land or rock

all in the race for the historic coast-to-coast linkup in Utah. In fact, officials took on these pigtailed immigrants only because they couldn't recruit enough whites to do the job. At least a thousand perished in building the roadbed, some after taking that Chinaman's chance, some in avalanches, some from blistering heat or disease or simply overwork. But they worked so hard and so well that hundreds more were hired. In 1869 a group of Chinese and Irish workers laid a record ten miles of track in just under 12 hours, though the Chinese and their sacrifice were barely mentioned in the flossy[2] speeches that year when the historic meeting of the rails was celebrated.

Things had been different a generation before the railroad building, when many Chinese began arriving in California. In 1849 and 1850, when the discovery of gold ignited a worldwide rush to the tawny Sierra foothills, a Chinaman's chance seemed as good as anyone else's. "The Celestials," one newspaper declared, in reference to immigrants from the "Celestial Kingdom," as China called itself, "are good citizens, deserving of the respect of all." When California joined the Union in 1850, blue-coated Chinese had a prominent place in the admission-day parade through downtown San Francisco. They tossed firecrackers and pinwheels as they marched, and a speaker at the ceremony afterward spoke admiringly of the ethnic mix that gold had lured to California. "We . . . meet here today as brothers," he proclaimed. "Henceforth we have one country, one hope, one destiny."

They called their new home Gum Sahn—Gold Mountain. Then and later the great majority of Chinese immigrants came from a single province, Kwangtung, in southern China. Many grew up in the city of Canton. In the 1850s they began sailing under the "credit-ticket" system, with a broker advancing passage money to be repaid out of future earnings. Their goal was to make a stake and return to China and their families. They saw themselves as sojourners,[3] and the sojourner mentality persisted even when the years stretched into decades and the decades into

---

[2] (slang) flashy

[3] someone who stays in a place briefly, a visitor

lifetimes. China was home. They went home to marry and to father children and then returned here. They sent money home regularly and created little self-contained islands of China— Chinatowns—mostly in large cities.

Writer Connie Young Yu, 49, of Los Altos Hills, California, visited China seven years ago to see where her immigrant ancestors started from: "If you saw the villages they came from, you'd know why they left. They didn't come for freedom but for survival. My great-grandfather worked on the Central Pacific railroad. He learned a little English, and they made him foreman. Those men never complained. It was like one generation simply sacrificed itself."

"If you have a daughter," a Cantonese folk song warned, "don't marry her to a Gold Mountain man. Out of ten years, he will not be in bed for one." In 1852 the number of Chinese arrivals in California exceeded 20,000. Toting their belongings in bags suspended from bamboo poles across their shoulders, the newcomers were organized into companies by Chinese associations. At the goldfields they provided their own rice and dried fish, and their own diversions, mainly gambling and opium. They specialized in digging in placer sites[4] that white miners had abandoned as played-out.

Thomas Chinn, 81, a scholarly man who used to own a typesetting business in San Francisco, is the grandson of a forty-niner. Like many older Chinese-Americans, he has tried to trace his family's roots in Gum Sahn: "My maternal grandfather got to San Francisco in September 1849. He went back to China to marry and left his wife there. He mined tailings[5] and worked on the railroad. I don't know where he died. I've checked records all over the state. They aren't much help because they often got the names wrong. I don't think I'll ever know."

By the 1870s the easygoing cordiality that greeted the first Chinese in America had been replaced by an ugly resentment that often boiled into violence. Racism and economic fear led

---

[4] a place where gold is mined by sifting sand

[5] dirt and rocks left behind after a mine is excavated

many Westerners to believe that the Chinese, who were willing to work cheap, were stealing their jobs. A "Workingmen's Party" arose, demanding that "the Chinese Must Go" and intimidating firms that hired them. An English-Chinese phrase book from that time shows a little of what the Chinese were up against. Its sampling of frequently helpful phrases includes "He took it from me by violence," "He cheated me out of my wages," and "They were lying in ambush."

In 1871 a mob enraged by the shooting of a white man killed 19 Chinese in Los Angeles. In California's Central Valley, where the Chinese found work on reclamation projects and as tenant farmers, they were hounded out of one town after another, a time they remember as "the driving out." A particularly bloody outburst came in 1885 in Rock Springs, Wyoming. There, coal miners infuriated by the refusal of Chinese coworkers to join in a strike attacked their camp, burning 79 houses and killing 28 men.

Legal persecution took the form of taxes and statutes aimed at their livelihood, their customs, and even their looks. Chinese families had to pay special taxes. Their children were barred from local public schools. A San Francisco ordinance, vetoed by the mayor at the last moment, would have required that the queues[6] of Chinese jail inmates be cut off. Other harassments included laws making it illegal to carry baskets suspended from poles while walking on sidewalks, as Chinese laundryman did, or to rent rooms with less than 500 cubic feet of space per person, as most Chinese had to do. The courts even prohibited Chinese from giving testimony in cases that involved whites.

By 1880 Chinese immigrants represented only .002 percent of the population, yet the "Chinese Question"—which boiled down to finding ways to keep them out—had become a major national issue. Two years later Congress passed the Chinese Exclusion Act, the first immigration law in America's history designed to bar a specific nationality. The law suspended the immigration of Chinese laborers for ten years, though it did permit the entry of teachers, students, merchants, and travelers—a

---

[6] a pigtail

loophole the Chinese would learn to exploit. Subsequent legislation extended the ban on laborers indefinitely. In 1913 California added another twist of the knife by prohibiting Chinese, as "aliens ineligible for citizenship," from owning land.

The Chinese responded to prejudice and persecution in two ways. First, they created an insulated society-within-a-society that needed little from the dominant culture. Second, they displayed a stoic willingness to persevere, and to take without complaint or resistance whatever America dished out.

"I was in downtown Portland once with my parents a long time ago," Thomas Chinn recalls. "We went to first one restaurant and then two others and they wouldn't serve us or even sell us bread. My father spat on the sidewalk, and a policeman came over and told him to clean it up. He took out his handkerchief and wiped the spittle off the sidewalk."

The Chinese were neither the first nor the last immigrants in America to tote their culture in their baggage. What set them apart—and this is true of other, more recent Asian immigrants to the United States as well—was the extent of their mutual support systems. They established their own schools taught in their own language, read their own newspapers, and attended their own operas. Wherever possible they made a living working with, and selling to, one another. Groups of merchants organized de facto[7] banks by putting money into a pool from which anybody in the group could borrow. They banded together in associations based on their home districts in China.

"Our self-sufficiency was a specific response to persecution," Connie Young Yu explains. "The district and family associations were employment agencies, welcome wagons, labor contractors, and rooming houses. They also arranged the shipment of bones back to China." (Quite separate from such associations were the protective societies, called "tongs"—from the Cantonese t'ong, or "hall"—which ultimately degenerated into feuding, criminal gangs.)

The face Chinese immigrants showed to strangers was impassive or agreeable, never angry. They swallowed their anger.

---

[7] something that happens in reality, or in fact, but not through proper channels

Chinese parents taught their children to *bai hoi*—stand aside—to avoid conflict. "We kept our place, stayed where we belonged," Roberta Yee remembers. "You knew where you weren't wanted. To this day I know that." Controlling anger preserved dignity and asserted a deeper strength, but is an approach that young Chinese condemn in retrospect.

"A white friend once told me, 'You people are used to suffering,'" says Philip Choy, 64, a San Francisco architect who has written about Chinese-Americans. "We *were* passive for so long; we didn't make waves. This generation accuses us for that, but they don't realize that the threat was always there. Always."

The years between the 1880s and the 1930s were a test of their tenacity[8] and ingenuity. The Chinese were not yet fully American, either in their own eyes or in the view of the U.S. Government or of Americans generally. Most were still clustered in Chinatowns and rural areas in the West, with small contingents in the South and East. They worked on Arkansas farms and on railroads in Mississippi (where, one story has it, the town of Canton took its name from Canton, China), and—as strikebreakers—in the Sampson's shoe factory in North Adams, Massachusetts. Chinese immigrants were still predominantly male: only 5 percent of the roughly 90,000 here in 1900 were women.

The Chinese found a small crack in the Exclusion Act, the provision that permitted merchants to immigrate, and mined it as assiduously as they had once washed gold at secondhand claims. Chinatown businesses took on "paper partners" who could then claim merchant status; stores were established for the purpose. The main result was to let wives come in, and so, gradually, increasing numbers of Chinese women began to arrive. Chinatowns now flourished in a number of large cities, but whites visited them rarely. Anyone who did so was usually treated to a hoked-up tour of opium dens and dim alleys haunted by slave girls (both of which did indeed exist). Restaurants courted American palates with chop suey and chow mein, both, like fortune cookies, first concocted on these shores.

───────

[8] stubbornness; persistence

Historically, the greatest boon to Chinese immigration was the 1906 San Francisco earthquake, which destroyed the city's birth records. Thereafter, thousands of Chinese could (and did) claim, with no evidence to refute them, that they had been born in the United States and thus were U.S. citizens. Almost more important, all their children, even those born in China, were then entitled to citizenship too.

Life was still cramped and mean in the 12-block Chinese enclave in San Francisco—known as Dai Fou (Big City); Sacramento was Yee Fou (Second City). Single men slept 10 and 12 to a room; several families shared a kitchen and bathroom. They couldn't get housing elsewhere because whites would not sell or rent to them; even venturing outside Chinatown meant risking harassment or worse. In cities there were two kinds of work, doing laundry or serving in restaurants. As late as 1920 nearly one-third of all Chinese in the labor force toiled in laundries. "When I was a kid in Chinatown, we were afraid to cross the border at Pacific Street," Thomas Chinn remembers. "I started to do it once with some friends, and a bunch of Italian kids got out their knives, so we ran back. When my wife and I found a house we wanted to buy in 1930—it was out of Chinatown—a policeman visited us and advised me not to do it. He said some friends of his might make it tough on us if we moved there."

For Chinese sharecroppers and seasonal laborers the daily grind was equally gritty. They grew fruit and vegetables on Sacramento River delta land protected by levees they had helped build. In 1915 a group of Chinese in the delta founded an all-Chinese village they named Lockeport, later shortened to Locke, for the family that owned the land. With its blocklong main street of ramshackle buildings in the shadow of the levee, its Chinese school and stores and casinos, and its brothels (the only enterprises in town owned by whites), Locke became a mecca and a sanctuary.

Roberta Yee: "I grew up in Locke during the 1930s. When someone won the lottery at the casino, the kids would run to find the winner, hoping he'd give us something. I remember the bok-bok man used to bang a stick on a wooden box on the hour at night to say that all was well. My father had been a landowner in China, but in the delta he sprayed trees and picked fruit. He didn't feel persecuted. His investment was us kids; that's what it was all about."

Even that late, most Chinese in America still saw themselves as sojourners. On rare occasions one would let his mask drop to reveal the bitterness behind it. "When I young fellow I felt that I American," a merchant named Pany Lowe told a researcher in 1924. "Now I got more sense. I know I never be American, always Chinaman. I no care now anymore. . . . I think very few American people really know anything about Chinese." When a group of young Chinese-Americans were polled in 1935 on whether their future lay in America or China, three-fourths said China.

For a people who embraced the Confucian ideal that one's first loyalty was to the family, the rupture in family relations that accompanied immigration to America was the cruelest blow. Couples were sometimes separated for as long as 50 years. Though intermarriage with whites later became common, the sojourners wanted Chinese-born wives—"They like family more, better mothers, not spend so much," one man explained. When Chinese families finally began to flourish here, they stuck to their old values—father received unconditional respect and obedience, everyone worked together. A whole family would run a Chinese store. The payoff came in a good education and better life for the next generation.

"My father's father came in 1881," says Connie Young Yu. "He hit a keno number the first month he was here and sent two $10 gold pieces back home. His parents thought he was already rich. When he went back to get married, he brought raisins and lemon-scented soap—they loved that—and cotton cloth and cigars." It was a onetime piece of luck—everything else came hard.

"The family was like a cause," she adds. "It was the key to strength. My parents taught me their way of getting along here: always behave like your actions reflect on all Chinese. Education was everything. My father always said that they can burn your house or even Chinatown, but they can never take away your education."

Immigrants whose citizenship status was questionable were held at the grim, prisonlike immigration detention station on Angel Island in San Francisco Bay. They were locked in barracks where bunks were stacked three high, women and the younger children in one large room, men in another. New arrivals were separated from relatives and friends so they couldn't discuss their testimony before immigration officers.

Most of the Chinese were boys from 15 to 21 who entered the United States illegally as "paper sons," using the loophole in the law that gave Chinese-born children of U.S. citizens the right to citizenship. The ploy began when a Chinese man already here claimed citizenship as American-born (someone calculated that if every such claim were true, each Chinese mother in San Francisco before 1906 would have had to bear 800 children). The "paper father" reported that he had sons in China. The boy's real family bought documents that included his ticket to America, a birth certificate stating that he was his paper father's son, and instructions on how to deal with the grilling by Angel Island's immigration officials. The boy adopted the name of his bogus father and tried to memorize hundreds of facts about the man's family and native village.

Confined for weeks, sometimes months, while awaiting interviews that would decide their future, some men etched their feelings in poems on the wooden barracks walls. "Nights are long and the pillow cold," one lamented. "Why not just return home and learn to plow the fields?" Another promised vengeance once he was released: "I will certainly behead the Barbarians and spare not a single blade of grass."

At the crucial interrogation, the immigrant faced one or two inspectors, with an interpreter and a stenographer also present. The questioning sometimes went on for two or three days, with questioners pressing for minute details about the home village and the father's house—how many steps the temple had, the location of the pond, how many rooms in the house. The answers given by father and son were then carefully compared. The boys sometimes studied crib notes smuggled to them via the Chinese kitchen staff.

"I was 5 when I came through Angel Island with my mother

in 1930," Roberta Yee recalls. "They herded us to meals in a chow line, and we ate with silverware instead of chopsticks. My father and brothers visited us every day and brought Bartlett pears from the delta. You could see the ferry pier from the room where we met. But it's the pears I remember best."

In the mid-1930s one of the inspectors at Angel Island was a young man named Zalph B. Jackson—my father. "Those kids never showed any expression," he told me. "We were trying to catch them lying with our questions. If there were, say, a half-dozen discrepancies[9] we'd reject them." It was his recollection that most applicants survived the gauntlet of questions. Ronald Takaki, author of *Strangers from a Different Shore*, a recent book on Asians in America, estimates that only 10 percent of the Chinese who passed through Angel Island were deported.

The disgrace for those who were, especially the women, could be unbearable. Paul Chow, 61, a retired highway engineer and head of a foundation created to restore the Angel Island site as a monument like Ellis Island, has interviewed former detainees who remember suicides. "The women faced humiliation if they returned to China," he says.

Chow, a round-faced, sunny-tempered man, remembers that Angel Island was a taboo subject when he was growing up. "Whenever my mother would mention it, she'd say, 'Angel Island, shhh.' I thought it was all one word— 'Angelislandshhh.' They didn't talk about it because of the shame. I found out later that my father bribed an immigration officer with $500 to get his card in 1922. That's why we kept quiet about it." The Angel Island station closed after a fire in 1940.

World War II brought the long-delayed turning point for America's Chinese. China was our ally against Japan, and Generalissimo Chiang Kai-shek was a world-famous leader. Chinese in the United States—the population had dwindled to 78,000—eagerly embraced the cause. Nearly a fourth of the Chinese adult males in the country either enlisted or were drafted (though many Chinese recruits were routinely sent to

---

[9] disagreement or inconsistency between claims or statements

cook school). As civilians, Chinese workers were for the first time welcomed in higher-paying industrial jobs.

In 1943 Congress took up a bill to repeal the Exclusion Act. President Franklin D. Roosevelt supported it in a message to Congress. Exclusion, he said, was a "historic mistake." In December he signed the bill into law. The immigration quota specified by the act was hardly generous—permitting just 105 Chinese to enter each year. Applicants for U.S. citizenship, moreover, had to prove that they had entered the country legally. But the glad news was that the stigma[10] was at long last gone and the door was open, if only a crack.

Becoming Americans, a dream deferred for a century, remained a slow adjustment for many. Even though he was born here, Philip Choy remembers that his own uncertainty persisted into the 1940s. "Even then a lot of us still thought we'd get our education here and then go home to China," he says. Choy became Americanized almost by default: "The war came, China was in turmoil, I got married—all of a sudden my roots were here."

Stereotyping had not evaporated, of course. In 1949, when the chief Chinese delegate to the United Nations rang the bell of the wrong room at a New York hotel, the woman who opened the door handed him her laundry without a word. Prejudice also remained. Some Chinese-Americans chose to work in fields like engineering, where their careers would depend more on skill than on social contact across ethnic lines.

But for a heartening number, the passage to Americanization became natural and inevitable. "I have a photograph of my father wearing his San Jose High sweater and standing by his Model T," Connie Young Yu says. "I think that was the turning point. This is an American kid. He went to Stanford and graduated in engineering, but wound up as the co-owner—how Chinese can you get?—of a soy sauce factory."

Thomas Chinn: "I remember my father saying, 'This is our home. Our descendants will be born here.' My mother had bound feet like so many Chinese girls. But after she married she

---

[10] a mark of disgrace

removed the bindings. That was a symbolic act, a commitment to the West. The pendulum swung for us after World War II. We could get jobs and buy a house outside Chinatown. My mother finally became a citizen at 89. This is my country. If you threw me back into China now, I'd be a stranger."

An end to hysteria and legal persecution

The final, culminating breakthrough came with the historic immigration act of 1965, which once and for all abolished the old quota system. Under this law, after July 1, 1968, China and every other nation was allowed 20,000 immigrants a year (families of a legal immigrant, however, don't count toward the quota). In 1982 the quota was extended to apply separately to Taiwan and the People's Republic. A tremendous influx of Chinese families, and other Asians, followed, creating what is now the fastest-growing ethnic minority in America. Yet the Chinese population, never larger than 1 percent of the U.S. total during all the years of hysteria and persecution, was projected at just over a million, or .42 percent, in 1985.

Chinese fanned out through the culture and excelled in ways their oppressed forerunners could scarcely have imagined. In 1970 fifty-six percent of working Chinese held white-collar jobs, a figure well above the national average. Their education and family-income levels far exceeded national norms, and so, proportionally, does Chinese representation at demanding, high-prestige colleges.

Paul Chow and I stood outside the deserted barracks on Angel Island in a brisk winter wind. He looked past the marble monument that memorializes the immigrants detained there and focused on the choppy blue-gray bay beyond. He spoke intently. "Every group has its story," he said. "This is ours. These were our heroes. They taught us how to survive; they sacrificed and suffered so my family and I could live a better life. I'm not saying this is a perfect country, but it's better than where they came from—despite discrimination, despite Angel Island, despite everything."

REVIEWING AND INTERPRETING

Record your answers to these questions in your personal literature notebook. Follow the directions for each part.

REVIEWING Try to complete each of these sentences without looking back at the selection.

Recalling Facts

1. Most Chinese immigrants came to the United States
   a. with their wives and children.
   b. planning to work on the railroad.
   c. to escape political repression.
   d. planning to return to China.

Understanding Main Ideas

2. Most of the hardships Chinese immigrants endured during this time were caused by
   a. their inability to speak English.
   b. their disdain for Western ways.
   c. whites' mistrust and prejudice.
   d. staying in their own communities.

Identifying Sequence

3. Conditions for Chinese-Americans began to improve
   a. after they helped build the transcontinental railroad.
   b. during and after World War II.
   c. after the Exclusion Act was passed.
   d. after the second generation was born.

Finding Supporting Details

4. As an example of the legal barriers the Chinese faced, Jackson writes
   a. "By 1880 Chinese immigrants represented only .002 percent of the population . . ."
   b. "A 'Workingman's Party' arose, demanding that 'the Chinese Must Go . . . .'"
   c. "The face Chinese immigrants showed to strangers was impassive or agreeable, never angry."
   d. "In 1913 California added another twist of the knife by prohibiting Chinese, as 'aliens ineligible for citizenship,' from owning land."

Getting Meaning from Context

5. "The Chinese found a small crack in the Exclusion Act, the provision that permitted merchants to immigrate, and mined it as assiduously as they had once washed gold at second-hand claims." In this context *assiduously* means
a. quietly.
b. constantly.
c. cautiously.
d. secretly.

INTERPRETING

To complete these items, you may look back at the selection if you'd like.

Generalizing

6. The Chinese-Americans whom Jackson interviewed all seem to agree that
a. they would have returned to China rather than deal with the hardships their parents and grandparents faced.
b. first-generation immigrants made great sacrifices to ensure a better future for their children.
c. the government owes them something for the unfair treatment of their families.
d. they no longer are treated differently because they are Chinese.

Recognizing Fact and Opinion

7. Which of the following statements expresses an opinion?
a. "Then and later the great majority of Chinese immigrants came from a single province, Kwangtung, in southern China."
b. "In 1871 a mob, enraged by the shooting of a white man, killed 19 Chinese in Los Angeles."
c. ". . . I think very few American people really know anything about the Chinese."
d. "Most of the Chinese were boys from 15 to 21 who entered the United States illegally as 'paper sons,' using the loophole in the law that gave Chinese-born children of U.S. citizens the right to citizenship."

Making Inferences

8. From Jackson's description of the lives and working conditions of Chinese railroad builders, you can infer that
   a. the railroad owners thought Chinese lives had little value.
   b. the railroad could have been built without Chinese help.
   c. the writer thinks the Chinese workers were braver than Irish workers.
   d. many Chinese gave up their railroad jobs and returned to China.

Identifying Cause and Effect

9. Chinese immigrants built their own separate, self-sufficient communities because
   a. they mistrusted white people.
   b. they were safer there from persecution.
   c. it was easier for their district and family associations to control them.
   d. this allowed them to continue to practice their own religion.

Drawing Conclusions

10. Which of the following statements is a reasonable conclusion to draw from this article?
   a. Many modern Chinese-Americans feel their families made a mistake immigrating to this country.
   b. Chinese-Americans now hold an unreasonably large proportion of white collar jobs.
   c. There is no longer any prejudice against Chinese-Americans in the United States.
   d. Chinese-Americans are proud and grateful for the sacrifices made by their parents and grandparents.

Now check your answers with your teacher. Study the items you answered incorrectly. What skills are they checking? Talk to your teacher about ways to work on those skills.

Author's Purpose

Author's Purpose is the writer's reason for creating a particular work. The purpose may be to inform, to instruct, to entertain, to express an opinion, or to persuade readers to do or believe something. An author may have more than one purpose for writing, but usually one is the most important.

In "Sojourners Who Came to Stay," Donald Dale Jackson's primary purpose is to inform—to give information. He wants to tell about the difficult living and working conditions Chinese immigrants faced in the United States. He also wants to explain the sources of the white prejudice and discrimination that caused these conditions and to explain how and why the Chinese endured and overcame the hardships they faced.

Much of the information Jackson gives is unpleasant. To keep the reader interested in reading such grim material, Jackson must keep his writing interesting and enjoyable. He does this through his style—his tone, sentence structure, diction, and imagery. He keeps our interest through the way he presents his material: one interesting fact or detail leads naturally to the next. He also keeps your interest by including the personal memories and experiences of several Chinese-Americans.

You are probably accustomed to thinking of history as a complete record of all the facts about what happened in the past. You should realize, however, that written history is filtered through the interests and the purposes of the writer. For example, the information in the one or two chapters on the American Revolution in your history textbook will not be as thorough as an entire book about the same subject. Your textbook writer's purpose is to teach you the most important facts about the war and to give you a simple analysis of its causes and effects. On the other hand, a professional historian who is writing an entire book about the war would provide an enormous number of facts and offer a complex analysis. A history article is different from both a textbook and a professional history book. An article will usually focus on a much smaller subject than the entire American Revolution, and it will offer more detailed information and a deeper analysis than your history textbook.

Many elements combine to make a well-written, informative history article. Understanding an author's purpose is important because that purpose influences not only *what* the writer says but *how* he or she says it. In the lessons that follow, you will look at three ways a writer reveals his or her purpose.

1. **Purpose and Chronological Order**   An author's purpose affects the order in which he or she presents information. The writer's purpose also determines the emphasis the writer gives to each piece of information.

2. **Purpose and General-to-Specific Order**   A writer usually uses more than one type of organization to support the central idea of an article. Often a writer starts with a general discussion of the main points and then proceeds to specific examples, facts, or other evidence—details that support the writer's main points.

3. **Purpose and Exposition**   Expository writing explains the *whys* about a subject. The methods of explanation a writer chooses are determined by his or her purpose. Donald Dale Jackson, whose purpose is to describe and explain a series of historical conditions and events uses two methods of explanation—cause-and-effect analysis and historical analysis.

LESSON 1   PURPOSE AND CHRONOLOGICAL ORDER

When a writer plans an article for a magazine, his or her first task—after settling on the general topic—is to determine what the focus of the article will be. In writing about Chinese immigrants to the United States, Jackson could have given you details about the lives of several individual immigrants. He could have chosen to give you all the reasons that so many Chinese came to the United States in the late 1800s and early

1900s. Instead, he focuses on the deplorable living and working conditions and the deep prejudice Chinese immigrants faced upon their arrival. He describes the "sojourner mentality" many Chinese adopted in order to survive—a belief that they were only visitors and would someday return to China.

In doing his research, Jackson became impressed by the courage with which Chinese faced conditions in their new homeland and with their ingenuity in gaining entry to the United States despite immigration laws designed to keep them out. In interviewing the descendants of Chinese immigrants, Jackson also learned that the close-knit communities and mutual support system that first-generation immigrants established had paid off in citizenship, financial success, and social acceptance for their children and grandchildren. This idea (that the Chinese survived and became successful because of their close-knit communities and mutual support system) became the *thesis*—the chief point—of his article. Jackson's *thesis statement*—a one-sentence statement asserting the writer's chief point is "What set the Chinese apart from other immigrants was the extent of their mutual support."

Jackson develops his thesis in two ways: he gives information about the Chinese and their situation, and he *explains* the relationship between the pieces of information he gives. The information he gives answers the questions *who, what, where, when,* and *how.* His explanations tell you *why* these things happened. In his article Jackson frequently moves back and forth between giving information and offering explanations—often within the same paragraph. Look at the diagram on the next page, which shows the relationship between the information and explanations in Jackson's article.

As you learned in Unit 2 the six most common methods of organization used by writers are chronological order, spatial order, order of importance, developmental order, general-to-specific order, and specific-to-general order. As you were reading "Sojourners Who Came to Stay," you should have noticed that Jackson's overall method of organization is chronological—the order in which events happen in time. The beginning of his article talks about the arrival of immigrants during the

Subject:

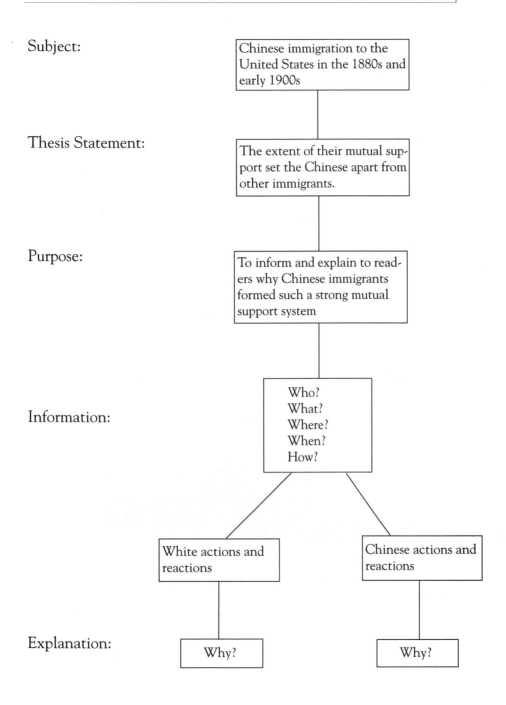

Thesis Statement:

Purpose:

Information:

Explanation:

California Gold Rush of 1849. The article then covers the history of Chinese immigrants over the years, ending with a discussion of the 1985 population census information about modern Chinese-Americans. Look at the time line on page 121. It uses chronological order to show important events in the history of the Chinese immigrants in America. You will answer some questions about the information missing from the time line in the next exercise.

EXERCISE

Copy the time line onto a sheet of paper. Then use what you have learned in this lesson to answer the questions.

1. What important events happened in 1871, 1906, 1913, 1915, and 1943? You may look back at the selection. Use your answers to fill in the missing information on your copy of the time line.

2. What two events on the time line support Jackson's thesis statement?

Now check your answers with your teacher. Review this lesson if you don't understand why an answer was incorrect.

WRITING ON YOUR OWN

In this exercise you will use what you have learned in this lesson to write a thesis statement and a description using chronological order. Follow these steps:

• Review the paragraph you wrote describing your special interest or activity. Write a thesis statement—a one-sentence statement that asserts, or states, the chief point of your article.
• Look at the time line in the lesson. On a sheet of paper,

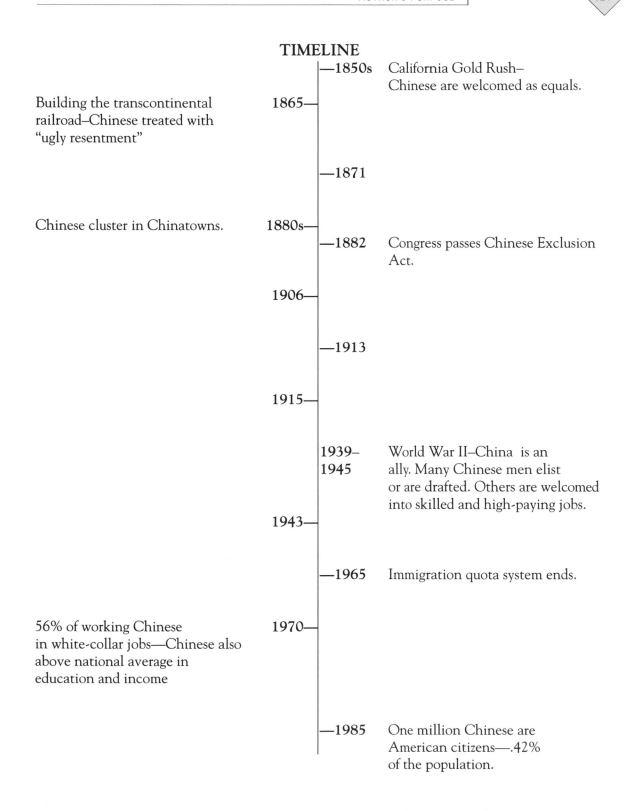

TIMELINE

—1850s   California Gold Rush–
          Chinese are welcomed as equals.

Building the transcontinental   1865—
railroad–Chinese treated with
"ugly resentment"

—1871

Chinese cluster in Chinatowns.   1880s—

—1882   Congress passes Chinese Exclusion
         Act.

1906—

—1913

1915—

1939–   World War II–China is an
1945   ally. Many Chinese men elist
         or are drafted. Others are welcomed
         into skilled and high-paying jobs.

1943—

—1965   Immigration quota system ends.

56% of working Chinese   1970—
in white-collar jobs—Chinese also
above national average in
education and income

—1985   One million Chinese are
         American citizens—.42%
         of the population.

create a similar time line that shows the time and the sequence in which you gained your experience or knowledge about the special interest or activity.

• Using your time line, write a description of how you gained your knowledge or experience in this activity or interest. Try to use a variety of words or phrases in your description to give your readers cues about chronological order. For example, if you were writing about becoming a skilled interactive game player, you might begin by writing, "When I was eight, I got my first small computer. I didn't go on-line until 1997, though." At a later point in your description, you might write, "It wasn't until the summer between middle school and high school that I became seriously involved in role-playing games."

LESSON 2 PURPOSE AND GENERAL-TO-SPECIFIC ORDER

A time line outlines the who, what, where, when, and how information about Chinese immigrants. This is the chronological order of Jackson's article. But an article based only on dates and events is neither very informative nor very entertaining. Jackson supports his thesis and maintains the reader's interest by filling out the chronological order with the specific, detailed information he has gathered through his research and interviews. These details about conditions and events in the lives of Chinese immigrants are what keep the reader interested in the article. To present these details, Jackson uses the general-to-specific order, which organizes information by starting with a general discussion of the main points and then proceeds to specific examples, facts, or other evidence.

In the passage below notice how Jackson picks a point in his chronological order and then uses general-to-specific order to support his thesis that the Chinese survived because of their close-knit communities and mutual support.

For Chinese sharecroppers and seasonal laborers, the daily grind was equally gritty. They grew fruit and vegetables on Sacramento River delta land protected by levees they had helped build. In 1915 a group of Chinese in the delta founded an all-Chinese village they named Lockeport, later shortened to Locke, for the family that owned the land. With its block-long main street of ramshackle buildings in the shadow of the levee, its Chinese school and stores and casinos, and its brothels (the only enterprises in town owned by whites), Locke became a mecca and a sanctuary.

Roberta Yee: "I grew up in Locke during the 1930s. When someone won the lottery at the casino, the kids would run to find the winner, hoping he'd give us something. I remember the *bok-bok* man used to bang a stick on a wooden box on the hour at night to say that all was well. My father had been a landowner in China, but in the delta he sprayed trees and picked fruit. He didn't feel persecuted. His investment was us kids; that's what it was all about."

In the article, Jackson identifies this particular point in the chronological order of his story by saying: "In 1915 a group of Chinese in the delta founded an all-Chinese village they named Lockeport . . . ." He moves from that general statement to add specific facts and examples to bring the town to life. He gives details about the village's physical appearance—the ramshackle buildings; the "shadow of the levee" serving as a constant reminder that the river might break through at any moment; the striking contrast between schools and stores on the one hand and the casinos and brothels on the other. Then Jackson uses Roberta Yee's own poignant memories of her childhood in the village to add further colorful details about life in the village. Through rich and varied details such as these—and the personal point of view provided by someone who actually lived in the village—Jackson creates a clear picture of Lockeport and what it was like to live there.

EXERCISE ◇2◇

Read this passage from the article. Use what you have learned in this lesson to answer the questions that follow it.

> They called their new home Gum Sahn—Gold Mountain. Then and later the great majority of Chinese immigrants came from a single province, Kwangtung, in southern China. Many grew up in the city of Canton. In the 1850s they began sailing under the "credit-ticket" system, with a broker advancing passage money to be repaid out of future earnings. Their goal was to make a stake and return to China and their families. They saw themselves as sojourners, and the sojourner mentality persisted even when the years stretched into decades and the decades into lifetimes. China was home. They went home to marry and to father children and then returned here. They sent money home regularly and created little self-contained islands of China— Chinatowns—mostly in large cities.

1. How is this passage an example of Jackson's use of general-to-specific order?

2. What specific details in the passage support Jackson's description of the sojourner mentality? What details show how unrealistic this attitude was?

Now check your answers with your teacher. Review this lesson if you don't undertand why an answer was incorrect.

 WRITING ON YOUR OWN

In this exercise you will use what you have learned in this lesson to add supporting details to your informational article. Follow these steps:

- Reread the chronological description you wrote for Writing on Your Own 1.
- Look at each event, experience, or step in the learning process you have described. Ask yourself what facts or details you can add to each point so that your readers will clearly understand what happened at each step along the way. In "Sojourners Who Came to Stay," Donald Dale Jackson organized his information using general-to-specific order. You may wish to do the same, or you may wish to use specific-to-general order. If you were writing about your involvement with basketball, for example, you might choose to describe how your interest began when you first joined an elementary school or town-sponsored youth basketball program. You might begin by talking generally about how many years you played in youth leagues and later in junior-high-school and high-school programs, then give details about several important or memorable games or plays you were involved in. Or you might choose to describe how you gradually acquired one or more specific skills (such as dribbling, passing, shooting, or rebounding) and then generalize about how your interests began to center on playing one particular position. After these considerations, revise your description accordingly.
- Remember that you are writing about a topic that you know much more about than your readers. Review what you have written and add definitions for any words or specialized language that may not be familiar to your readers. Also remember that what may seem like basic or obvious information to you may be completely unfamiliar to your readers. Check to see whether you have left out any important details.

LESSON ③ PURPOSE AND EXPOSITION

You learned in Unit 2 that nonfiction writing is divided into four basic types: description, narration, exposition, and argumentation. There are six questions most informational articles should answer: who, what, where, when, how, and why? The first five questions are usually answered through description (writing that helps readers picture a person, place, or event) and narration (writing that gives the events and actions in a story). To answer the sixth question (why?) the writer must use *exposition*—writing that explains a subject by presenting information and analysis.

In "Sojourners Who Came to Stay" Jackson's purpose was to answer several questions: Why was prejudice so widespread and deep against Chinese immigrants? Why did prejudice and discrimination increase over time? Why did prejudice diminish over time?

To answer these questions and to show how the events and situations are related to one another, Jackson uses two methods of explanation—*cause-and-effect analysis* and *historical analysis*.

Cause-and-Effect Analysis   When you are asked to examine any idea, event, or action, you want to know its *causes* (what brought it into existence) and its *effects* (what consequences it has produced or will produce). Two events are related as cause and effect if one brings about, or causes, the other. The event that occurs first is the cause; the one that follows is the effect. *I leave my computer turned on all day because it takes so long to restart.* The cause-and-effect relationship in this example is signaled by the word *because*. It explains why you leave your computer on all day.

Expository writers use cause and effect to explain why things happen. Writers often signal cause-and-effect relationships with words and phrases such as *because, next, therefore, since, so that,* and *in order that.* In writing and in life, however, few relationships are that simple. Effects often have several causes, and one cause frequently leads to several effects: *I bought a new car because my old one died. My car payments and insurance went up because the car was new. I can no longer afford to eat out so frequently as I used to because my car payments and the cost of my insurance went up.* Look at the chain of results caused by the purchase of a new car.

In his article Jackson shows the linked causes and effects that influenced the lives of three generations of Chinese-Americans. The diagram on the next page shows how relations between the

Chinese did not plan to establish permanent roots here—sojourner mentality.

Whites mistrusted Chinese and treated them with prejudice.

Chinese retreated into their own isolated communities—Chinatowns.

Whites' mistrust of Chinese increased, and discrimination continued.

Chinese mistrust of whites increased, and they withdrew further into dependence on their own families and communitities.

Whites continued to see Chinese as "different" and "foreign."

Chinese and whites remained locked into a closed cycle until some part of the chain of causes and effects was broken.

This cause-and-effect analysis explains the negative effects of the long period of Chinese separateness within American culture. Jackson also shows that the same chain of events had a positive face as well. Because the Chinese were forced to remain together, they developed strong ties of mutual support within their families and community—everyone worked together. The first generation sacrificed and, as Jackson writes, "The payoff came in good education and better life for the next generation."

Historical Analysis   Another method of explanation Jackson uses to answer the question why is historical analysis. *Historical analysis* puts an idea, an event, or an action into historical perspective. It shows how the lives of individuals or small groups were shaped by large political, social, or economic forces or events. The event that began the immigration of large numbers of Chinese to the United States was the California Gold Rush of 1849. In the scramble to get rich quick, all men were equal; but when the gold ran out, work was scarce for many of the new arrivals. To survive, large numbers of Chinese had to take risky, low-paying jobs building the railroad. Historically, it was this change in economic conditions that changed the country's attitude toward the Chinese. They went from being regarded as "good citizens, deserving of the respect of all" to seeming to be an indistinguishable mass of laborers who could be worked to death.

Jackson also uses historical analysis to explain how the tragedy of the San Francisco earthquake of 1906 had a beneficial side-effect for many Chinese who wished to become citizens. The earthquake destroyed the city's birth records. As a result, thousands of Chinese, with no evidence to refute their assertions, could claim they were born in the United States.

EXERCISE ⟨3⟩

Read the following passage from the article. Use what you have learned in this lesson to answer the questions that follow it.

World War II brought the long-delayed turning point for America's Chinese. China was our ally against Japan, and Generalissimo Chiang Kai-shek was a world-famous leader. Chinese in the United States—the population had dwindled to 78,000—eagerly embraced the cause. Nearly a fourth of the Chinese adult males in the country either enlisted or were drafted (though many Chinese recruits were routinely sent to cook school). As civilians, Chinese workers were for the first time welcomed in higher-paying industrial jobs.

In 1943 Congress took up a bill to repeal the Exclusion Act. President Franklin D. Roosevelt supported it in a message to Congress. Exclusion, he said, was a "historic mistake." In December he signed the bill into law.

1. What cause-and-effect relationships does the author explain in this passage?

2. How is the use of historical analysis demonstrated in the passage?

Now check your answers with your teacher. Review this lesson if you don't understand why an answer was incorrect.

 WRITING ON YOUR OWN

In this exercise you will use what you learned in this lesson to explain to your readers some process or activity related to your topic. Follow these steps:

- Review the thesis statement you wrote for Writing on Your Own 1 and the paragraphs you wrote for Writing on Your Own 1 and 2.
- Now you are going to explain your topic from a "how" or "why" standpoint. Is there a particular method, activity, or process involved in the interest or activity you are writing about that needs to be explained or analyzed in order for readers to understand it?

- Write a paragraph or two of explanation for your article, using cause-and-effect anaysis or historical analysis. For example, if your interest or hobby is tropical fish, you might use cause-and-effect analysis to explain how different species of fish have different care and feeding requirements and why these requirements must be met exactly. If you were writing about your basketball experiences, you might include a brief history of the game.
- Reread what you have written. If there is still some part of your explanation that seems hard to follow, consider adding a graphic aid or illustration that will support or expand on what you have written.

DISCUSSION GUIDES

1. The author of this article reports that Chinese immigrant parents taught their children to *bai hoi* (stand aside) to avoid conflict. Do you think this is a good policy for an individual or group that is being mistreated or treated unfairly? What do you think would have been the result if the Chinese had organized and demanded fair treatment and equal rights? With a small group discuss these issues and come to a group decision. Then share the group's decision with the rest of the class.

2. What do you know about the treatment of other national groups when they immigrated to this country? In a large-group discussion, compare and contrast those experiences with what happened to Chinese immigrants. Do you think they were treated better or worse than other groups? Why? Share what you know with other members of your class. Discuss the reasons that, in your view, new immigrant groups are often treated poorly. What factors do you think make the transition to full acceptance quick or slow?

3. The author of this article and the people he interviewed all seem to agree that the present above-average status of Chinese-Americans in jobs, income, and education is a result of the sacrifices and suffering of the immigrant grandparents and parents. As a class, discuss the evidence in the article that supports that view.

WRITE AN INFORMATIONAL ARTICLE

In this unit you have learned how an author's purpose affects the organization and exposition of an informational article. Now you will write an informational article about one of your favorite activities or interests—and how and why you became invoved in it.

Follow these steps to complete your article. If you have questions about the writing process, refer to Using the Writing Process (page 250).

- Gather and review the following pieces of writing you did for this unit: 1) the paragraph, notes, and questions from Writing: Developing an Informational Article; 2) the thesis statement, the time line, and the descriptive paragraph, from Writing on Your Own 1; 3) the revised descriptive paragraph from Writing on Your Own 2; 4) the paragraph(s) of explanation from Writing on Your Own 3.
- Plan and write an introduction for your article. You may wish to begin with a thesis statement and several sentences previewing what your article will cover. Or you may decide to open with a lead that includes an anecdote or incident to capture your audience's attention. For example, if you were writing about your cooking hobby, you might begin with a dramatic story of how you successfully created and served a very fancy dessert, or you might begin with a comic incident that occured when everything went wrong in the kitchen. If you begin with an anecdote or incident, use a paragraph containing your thesis statement as a transition from the anecdote to the main body of your article.
- Use the paragraphs you have developed for Writing on Your Own 1, 2, and 3 as the basis for the body of your article.
- After you complete the draft for the body of your article, review your list of questions that a reader might ask about your topic. Does your article answer all the questions? If not, try to add further information or details that will answer these questions.

- Write a close for your article. You may decide to end by restating your thesis and summarizing why you enjoy this activity. Or you may decide to close, as Donald Dale Jackson does in his article, with another anecdote.
- Invite a classmate to read your article. When your classmate is finished, ask whether he or she has any questions about your topic that were not answered in the article. Ask whether he or she can suggest any ways you might improve your article. Revise your article as needed.
- Proofread your article for errors in spelling, grammar, punctuation, and capitalization. Make a final copy and save it for your writing portfolio. You may wish to share your article with the class before filing it in your portfolio.

UNIT 5

Biography: Sources and Interpretations

QUEEN OF THE WEST VS. MORNING STAR

Mark Twain:
The Early Years

❖

from *The Importance of Mark Twain* by Skip Press

INTRODUCTION

BUILDING
BACKGROUND

"Mark Twain: The Early Years," the selection you will read in this unit, consists of the first two chapters from *The Importance of Mark Twain*, a biography written by Skip Press. The excerpt covers the early years of Twain's life up until age 26.

Mark Twain was the pen name of Samuel Langhorne Clemens. He was born in 1835 in Florida, Missouri, and died on April 21, 1910. He is considered one of America's greatest writers and humorists. Ernest Hemingway, another renowned American writer, called *The Adventures of Huckleberry Finn* the greatest American novel ever written. Many of the characters and incidents Twain describes in his books and lectures were based on the experiences of his own adventurous childhood and early manhood.

When young Twain was four, his family moved to Hannibal, Missouri, on the banks of the Mississippi River. The Mississippi River and the town of Hannibal inspired some of Twain's greatest works. After his father's death, 12-year old Sam had to leave school and work as an apprentice to a printer in Hannibal. Setting type for newspaper articles and stories sparked his interest in reading, and reading eventually led him to writing. At 18, the young man left Hannibal and for a few years supported himself as a printer in cities from the frontier to the East Coast. For

Before the Civil War started in 1861, the Mississippi River was a major north-south trade and travel route. From 1859 until the War broke out, Mark Twain worked as a pilot on steamboats like those pictured here.

several exciting years, beginning in 1857, he realized a boyhood dream by working as a steamboat pilot on the Mississippi. When he later became a reporter for the *Virginia City* (Nevada) *Territorial Enterprise* in 1863, Clemens adopted the now-famous name Mark Twain. The words *mark twain* are a river-boating term meaning "two fathoms deep" (12 feet)—safe water for a riverboat. Young Clemens traveled to Hawaii and Europe as a reporter, and his humorous accounts of those trips so delighted newspaper readers and lecture audiences that he soon became famous. He won international attention after *The Innocents Abroad*, a record of his experiences in the Mediterranean region and the Holy Land, was published.

Twain's fame as an author rests mainly on his work between 1872 and 1889, the happiest and most productive period of his life. Among his best-known books written during that period are *The Adventures of Tom Sawyer*, *The Prince and the Pauper*, and *The Adventures of Huckleberry Finn*.

ABOUT THE AUTHOR

Skip Press has written more than nine biographies of famous people. In addition, he has published fiction and nonfiction books and magazine articles for young adults. Many of his stories have appeared in *Boy's Life* and *Disney Adventures*. Among his nonfiction works is *The Kuwaiti Oil Fires*, an environmental look at the Persian Gulf War. Press's work has received national recognition in print and on video, radio, stage, screen, and television.

Press is a member of the Dramatists Guild and other national writing societies. He also teaches in the UCLA Extension Writer's Program. Press and his family live in California.

ABOUT THE LESSONS

The lessons that follow "Mark Twain: The Early Years" focus on the sources Skip Press used to gather facts about Mark Twain before writing Twain's biography and on the interpretations he applied to the facts he chose to include.

Before writing the biography, Press did extensive research into his subject's life. He then had to decide which sources were most reliable and which facts he would include in the biography. In addition to selecting the facts to include, the biographer must show the significance of those facts. This involves interpreting the facts—suggesting which facts are most important and what they really reveal about the subject's life.

WRITING: DEVELOPING A BIOGRAPHY

At the end of this unit, you will write a part of a biography about an adult you know. The suggestions below will help you get started:

- Think of an adult about whom you would like to write a biography—someone who means a great deal to you, or perhaps someone who has inspired you in some way. He or she could be a relative, a friend, a teacher, or simply someone whom you admire. Write down that person's name.
- Ask yourself these questions about the person you have chosen as your subject: Why is this person important to me? Why do I think this person would make a good subject for a biography? What is special about this person? Is it something he or she has done or accomplished? Does he or she have a personality or a particular talent or job that is special? Write two or three sentences explaining why you think this person is special.
- Develop a description of your subject. On a sheet of paper, create a cluster diagram like the example shown on page 138. Think of as many details as you can that describe your subject and fill in the diagram with those details. What does your subject look like? What is his or her personality like? What does he or she do? What notable experiences has your subject had? Has this person any special achievements? What are your own feelings about him or her?

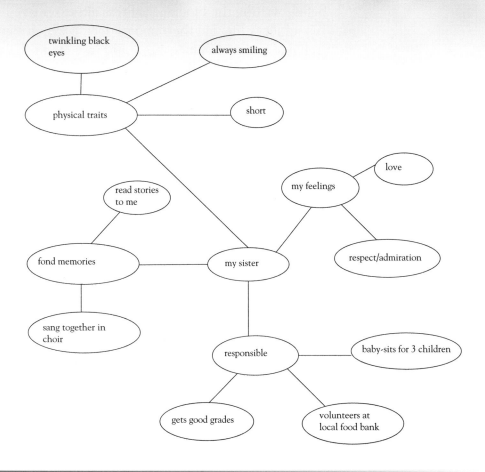

AS YOU READ

Think about these questions as you read the selection. They will help you take note of the sources Press used in gathering facts and how he interpreted some of those facts.

- At what point in the biography does Press use Twain's own words to help tell the story? What other sources of information does Press use?
- In what ways does Press make connections between Twain's life and his novels and stories?
- What experiences and events in Twain's childhood does Press emphasize? What point is he making by emphasizing those facts?

Mark Twain: The Early Years

from *The Importance of Mark Twain* by Skip Press

Chapter 1
In with the Comet

It is a strange coincidence that Mark Twain was born while Halley's Comet was in the North American sky and that he died upon its return, seventy-five years later, just as he had predicted. He was born Samuel Langhorne Clemens, on November 30, 1835, in the small town of Florida, Missouri, to Jane and John Marshall Clemens. Little Sam came two months prematurely. When he arrived, Orion was ten years old, Pamela eight, Margaret seven, and Benjamin three. The new baby was named Samuel, after his grandfather on his father's side, and Langhorne, after one of his father's friends from Virginia.

John Clemens was a lawyer and shopkeeper. He was a tall man, thin and unusually pale, who looked older than his thirty-six years. His deep-set gray eyes revealed a fearless nature. One story about his legendary daring was that while at church, he handed the minister a notice about the loss of his cow to be read from the pulpit on Sunday morning. When the minister forgot about the notice, John went to the front of the church and read the note to the congregation himself. Perhaps his father's courage rubbed off on young Sam, who never seemed afraid to try anything.

Mark Twain described his father as "Silent, austere, of perfect probity [high ideals] and high principle; ungentle of manner toward his children, but always a gentleman in his phrasing—and never punished them—a look was enough, and more than enough." Sadly, Twain said that he never remembered seeing or hearing his father laugh.

In contrast to his father's stern disposition, Twain described his mother, Jane, as having "the heart of a young girl." When she was being courted by John Clemens, Jane Lampton was reputed to have been the best dancer in all of Kentucky and was celebrated for her beauty, grace, and wit. "She was of a sunshiny disposition," her son wrote, "and her long life was mainly a holiday to her."

Twain remained close to his mother throughout her life. As a boy, though, he gave her a fair share of worries. Late in her life they had this conversation about his childhood:

"You gave me more uneasiness than any child I had," she said. "I suppose you were afraid I wouldn't live," he suggested. "No; afraid you *would!*" she joked.

In his early years Sam was a frail child, and his mother was constantly feeding him cod liver oil and home remedies to improve his health. The doctor was summoned for him often. Once Sam caught measles on purpose (probably to get attention), and the family thought he was going to die.

Sam was also an independent and strong-willed child who ran away from home often. In these ways Sam closely resembled Twain's later character Tom Sawyer.

Down on the Farm

Jane Lampton Clemens's brother, John Quarles, had a farm near Florida, Missouri, which was a source of delight for young Sam. Even after the family moved away from Florida, his mother would bring him to the farm every summer. At the farm, Sam played with Tabitha, a cousin his own age, whom he called Puss. A slave girl named Mary attended the children, but she was only six years older, so she was more like a playmate. The children spent their days wading in a wide brook with deep pools, playing on swings hung from trees in the pasture, and picking their fill of the blackberries that grew wild along the fences. Just beyond the apple and peach orchards were the slave quarters, where the children visited daily with a white-haired old black woman who told them stories of how to ward off spells and witches. She claimed to be a thousand years old and to have talked with Moses himself. In fact, she said that the bald spot on her head came from fright when she saw the pharaoh drown.

Sam's favorite black person on the farm, however, was a slave named Uncle Dan'l (Daniel). Kind-hearted and dependable, Dan'l became the model for Jim in *Huckleberry Finn*.

Days on Uncle John's farm were heavenly for young Sam. Evenings brought lavish Southern meals of homegrown vegetables and wild game and stories shared around the dinner table. On breezy summer nights the family dined in an outdoor pavilion. As fall approached and the evenings grew chilly, they gathered around the wide, blazing fireplace inside the two-story house. Musical entertainment, group singing, and stories were the main forms of entertainment. The storytelling atmosphere no doubt went a long way toward influencing young Sam to become a teller of tales.

Hannibal and the River

In 1839 John Clemens moved his family forty miles east of Florida, Missouri, to the town of Hannibal. Their relocation was probably hastened by the death of Sam's sister Margaret, at the age of nine, from "bilious fever." Moving from the location of her death may have helped the family forget their loss somewhat.

Hannibal was serene and beautiful. It was circled with bluffs like Holliday's Hill on the north and Lover's Leap on the south. It was also a port on the Mississippi River, and the steamboat traffic passing by the town excited young Sam. "When I was a boy," he said in *Life on the Mississippi*, "there was but one permanent ambition among my comrades. That was to be a steamboatman."

Perhaps because of its beauty and importance as a river port, Hannibal's citizens considered their town second only to St. Louis among Missouri towns. It was just a village, but a big city compared to Florida, and it exposed Sam to aspects of society he hadn't seen before.

In Hannibal, John Clemens became a jack-of-all-trades, keeping store, serving as justice of the peace, president of the Library Association, and chairman of the Committee on Roads. He also practiced law. John had many professions, not because he was overly ambitious, but because he had to do many things simply to try to make a living. John's ultimate plan, however, was to become rich.

Before coming to Missouri, he and his family had lived in Fentress County, Tennessee, where he acquired seventy-five thousand acres of land for about a penny an acre. He hoped to mine the land for coal, copper, or iron, but that never happened. In the Clemens family "the Tennessee land" was a constant source of discussion but never produced a penny. Twain later dramatized the family's hopes for the land in his book *The American Claimant*, but the only profits Sam saw from this land were from writing about it in the novel; he made scarcely a penny from any inheritance. His father's unfulfilled dreams regarding the land prompted him to comment:

> It is good to begin life poor; it is good to begin life rich—these are wholesome; but to begin it poor and *prospectively* rich! The man who has not experienced it cannot imagine the curse of it.

Once during their years in Hannibal, the family was offered $250 for the land, far less than what it was worth. As usual, they needed money, so even this offer was considered. Sam's brother Orion described it this way:

> If we had received that two hundred and fifty dollars, it would have been more than we ever made, clear of expenses,

out of the whole of the Tennessee land, after forty years of worry to three generations.

Hannibal as Inspiration

Living in a bigger city and observing his father's law practice exposed young Sam to crime—even murder. Once Sam saw a slave killed just because his owner did not like the way the slave completed a task. He saw a murder committed only a few yards from his house on Hill Street, while another time he saw a widow use a musket to kill a rowdy stranger who threatened her. One night when he was eight, Sam discovered the body of a murdered man in his father's office. These unusual experiences all became fodder for later books. For example, the stranger killed by the widow became part of Injun Joe's revenge in *Tom Sawyer*. The drunks, murderers, and people who mistreated black people in *Huckleberry Finn* were also townspeople from Hannibal.

The murder of the slave that Sam witnessed was just one example of an attitude that prevailed throughout the town of Hannibal. Hannibal was essentially a Southern town in manner and disposition, which meant that most people were prejudiced against blacks. Local superstition told children to be afraid of black people. Runaway slaves were generally considered to be as dangerous as wild beasts and were to be treated accordingly.

Sam saw prejudice displayed in his own household as well. Although the Clemens family was relatively poor, they managed to hire two black servants: Jennie, a servant who came with the family from Florida, and Uncle Ned, a handyman who helped around the house. When Jennie talked back, Mrs. Clemens called her high-spirited and a source of trouble. Sam began to question the rightness of slavery at a young age, though he dared not do so publicly. It is no accident that Jim in *Huckleberry Finn* is represented as a thinking, caring human being who simply wants to lead a life of freedom. When *Huckleberry Finn* was written, no author had ever treated black and white characters as equals in a novel, as Twain did with Jim and Huck Finn.

Boyhood Adventures

Despite the darker elements of life in Hannibal, Sam found plenty of friends and lots of places to have fun. Over the years they explored every corner of Hannibal and the surrounding area. All of the places made famous in *The Adventures of Tom Sawyer* and *The Adventures of Huckleberry Finn* were based on Hannibal. For example, Tom Sawyer and Becky Thatcher's experience in "McDougal's Cave," is based on a real Hannibal location, Dr. McDowell's limestone cave. The steamboats, the rafts, the island in the river where Huck and Tom and Jim hide out are all real, and we can rest assured that young Sam Clemens and his childhood buddies explored them all.

Most colorful of all Sam's playmates was his best friend, Tom Blankenship. Tom had freedoms few boys enjoyed: he came and went from home as he pleased and spent the majority of his time on the river, fishing and hunting. Tom even claimed to know spells and incantations.[1] Compared to other boys, he was like a wild thing and the most exciting companion a boy could have. Twain immortalized Tom as Huck Finn. In fact, Huck's house, as described in the novel, is a vivid depiction of Tom's boyhood home.

The real-life adventures of Sam and Tom and their friends John Briggs and Will Bowen provide the basis for many stories in *Tom Sawyer* and *Huckleberry Finn*. In fact, the relationship of Huck Finn and Jim was inspired by a real-life incident. Ben Blankenship, Tom's older brother, discovered a runaway slave from Monroe County, Missouri, hiding outside Hannibal. Instead of turning the man in for the fifty dollar reward that the poor boy could definitely have used, Ben fed the man all summer. Finally some woodchoppers discovered the slave's hideout and chased him through a marsh, where the unfortunate fugitive drowned. In *Huckleberry Finn*, however, Mark Twain allows Jim to experience a happier fate when Huck Finn and Tom Sawyer help Jim escape his captors.

---

[1] set of words spoken as a magic charm or to cast a magic spell

Sam Gets Some Schooling

Like Tom Sawyer, Sam Clemens hated school. Sam attended three different one-room schoolhouses while his father was alive, quitting eventually at the age of thirteen. His education began at the age of four and a half in a makeshift school run by Mrs. Elizabeth Horr, the wife of Hannibal's cooper (barrel maker). For twenty-five cents a week, she taught a dozen or so students of varying ages prayers, the Bible, and McGuffey's Readers (nineteenth-century basic education books). Then came study with an Irishman named Cross, and study with J. D. Dawson in 1847 when Sam was twelve. Dawson was the model for Mr. Dobbins in *Tom Sawyer*, and probably just as boring to young Sam.

Although schoolwork was not a priority for him, young Sam excelled at spelling. In Cross's and Dawson's classes, he regularly received the medal given for winning the spelling bees that were usually held once a week.

Death and Lost Hopes

As Sam struggled with school, his family struggled with personal finances and tragedy. Despite all his jobs, John Clemens failed to prosper in Hannibal. His resolve to improve things was shaken in 1842, when young Benjamin "took sick" and died (the actual cause of death is unknown). Another major disappointment came when Sam's older brother Orion was forced to leave his father's employ at the family store in Hannibal and become a printer's apprentice for the Hannibal *Journal* newspaper. The family felt that Orion's pursuit of a trade was a social step downward and only made the family's woes seem more severe.

In 1847, after going bankrupt, John Clemens died of pneumonia at the age of forty-nine. Everyone in the family now had to contribute to the group's survival. For twelve-year-old Sam, that meant working as a printer's "devil," or apprentice, alongside his brother at the *Journal* after school. This was the beginning of a ten-year career in newspapers that would include being a full-time apprentice, Orion's assistant editor, and a journeyman printer[2] around the country.

---

[2] a worker who has learned a trade and works for another person, usually by the day; a free-lance worker

A Writer Is Born

As Sam learned the printer's trade at the *Journal*, he began writing stories. He wrote about what he knew best—Hannibal. Sam had committed to memory every detail about Hannibal, good and bad, so writing stories about the town was relatively easy. In 1851 he succeeded in publishing two short nonfiction stories about Hannibal in Philadelphia's *Saturday Evening Post*. A year later at the age of sixteen, under the signature "S.L.C.," Boston's humor magazine *The Carpet-Bag* published "The Yankee Frightening the Squatter." In the same month, May 1852, he again wrote about Hannibal for the *American Courier* in Philadelphia, but this time he wrote something purely imaginary about Indians who had once visited Hannibal:

> But where now are the children of the forest? Hushed is the war-cry—no more does the light canoe cut the crystal waters of the Mississippi; but the remnant of those once powerful tribes are torn asunder and scattered abroad, and now they wander far, far from the homes of their childhood and the graves of their fathers.

Unfortunately, Sam was not paid for any of the stories. Still, these early publications allowed him to dream of greater success and fueled his desire to wander far from the home of his childhood. It was one thing to dream of the world, however, and quite another to really go out into it. Yet leave he did. In June 1853 he departed from Hannibal, but only after swearing on the Bible to his mother that he would keep away from cards and drinking. Sam's first destination was St. Louis, not all that far from Hannibal. Luckily for generations of readers to come, he had other destinations in mind, and other adventures too.

Chapter 2
Life on the Mississippi

Eighteen-year-old Sam, already trained as a printer and editor at the Hannibal newspaper, set out to make a living as a typesetter. His first stop was St. Louis, where his sister Pamela had moved after marrying a well-to-do merchant named William A. Moffett. Sam got a job in the composing room of the St. Louis *Evening News*, staying only long enough to earn enough money to reach New York City, where the Crystal Palace World's Fair was in progress. In a letter to Pamela, we see the beginnings of Clemens's descriptive powers:

> From the gallery [second floor] you have a glorious sight— the flags of the different countries represented, the lofty dome, glittering jewelry, gaudy tapestry, etc., with the busy crowd passing to and fro—'tis a perfect fairy palace—beautiful beyond description. . . . The visitors to the Palace average 6,000 daily—double the population of Hannibal. The price of admission being 50 cents, they take in about $3,000.

Sam had arrived in New York with a few dollars in his pocket and a ten-dollar bill sewn inside the lining of his coat. He got a job at a printing establishment for four dollars a week, and room and board at a house on Duane Street. After expenses he was able to save about fifty cents a week.

He stayed only a few months in New York. Anxious to see the world, he soon moved to Philadelphia and got a job at the *Inquirer*, a daily newspaper. He was convinced he could survive anywhere, and he liked Philadelphia much more than New York. He was fascinated by the city, which was much larger than Hannibal, and its historical sites, including the graves of Benjamin and Deborah Franklin, were of great interest to Sam. Franklin's life greatly impressed Sam, and it is interesting that their lives seemed similar. As Albert Bigelow Paine[3] put it:

> Each learned the printer's trade; each worked in his brother's printing office and wrote for the paper; each left quietly and went to New York, and from New York to Philadelphia, as a journeyman printer; each in due season became a world figure, many-sided, human, and of incredible popularity.

---

[3] Mark Twain's biographer and companion

Although Sam submitted a few poems to the Philadelphia *Ledger,* which were turned down, he generally forgot about writing until Orion, who had bought a newspaper office in Muscatine, Iowa, urged Sam to contribute. A letter to Orion explained Sam's temporary abandonment of writing:

> I will try to write for [Orion's] paper occasionally, but I fear my letters will be very uninteresting, for this incessant night work dulls one's ideas amazingly. . . . I believe I am the only person in the *Inquirer* office that does not drink. One young fellow makes $18 for a few weeks [of work], and gets on a grand "bender" [drunk] and spends every cent of it.

Working as a typesetter was hard, demanding work that required great attention to detail, and Sam found little enjoyment in it. He did not start drinking to forget his woes as some of his friends did, but he was too mentally drained by his job to do much more than see the sights in his free hours.

Sam began to grow restless and homesick. In January 1854 he quit his typesetting job and made a short trip to Washington, D.C., went back to Philadelphia to briefly work for two papers, then returned to New York. By late summer he could stand being away from home no longer. He took a train to Muscatine, where Orion and most of the Clemens family were living.

Orion wanted Sam to work for him. Having experienced Orion's financial ups and downs before, however, Sam declined. Instead, he went to St. Louis to work on the *Evening News.* Orion married on the spur of the moment and moved to Keokuk, Iowa. Between the summer and winter of 1855, Sam visited Orion, and his brother offered Sam five dollars a week and room and board to work as a journeyman printer. This time Sam accepted the job and worked for his brother for most of two years.

Dreams of Adventure

Working with his brother did not quiet Sam's desire for adventure, however. While in Keokuk, Sam read Lieutenant Herndon's description of his survey of the upper Amazon River, including tales of natives who could stay awake for days by eating coca leaves (cocaine is derived from coca leaves). Sam did not take the drug—he only read about it. Although it sounds terrible (considering what we know today about the drug), Sam dreamed of becoming rich by harvesting coca for North American distribution. At the time, coca was considered an herb with magical properties. To achieve his goal of becoming rich off cocaine, Sam had to raise the money for a trip to South America. As if guided by a divine hand, a solution came floating on the wind. In early November 1857, Sam was walking down Main Street in Keokuk when he grabbed a bit of paper as it flew past him. It was a fifty-dollar bill. He had no idea where this startling find had flown from. In an article called "The Turning Point of My Life," written many years later, he said, "I advertised the find and left for the Amazon the same day."

The statement is not exactly true—he stayed around longer than that—but it was still quite a stroke of luck. No one claimed the money, though Sam admitted he didn't describe it very specifically. He decided that this was truly a sign that he should pursue his South American journey as soon as possible. He first visited his mother, who now lived in St. Louis. While there, he got an idea to make more money from his adventures when he returned to Keokuk and made a deal with George Rees at a Keokuk newspaper, the *Saturday Post*. Rees agreed to buy Sam's descriptions of his South American journey for five dollars a letter, a good sum in those days.

Sam Clemens, Cub Pilot

Sam sold only two letters that described his proposed journey before taking a job at a Cincinnati printing office. By the spring of 1857, Sam was twenty-one and had saved enough money to go to South America. He boarded the steamer *Paul Jones* at Cincinnati, Ohio, which would take him to New Orleans, where he could board the ship that would take him to South America. While on the way to Louisiana, Sam had time to think. Instead of resolving to continue with his dream of becoming a coca baron, he decided to pursue his boyhood ambition of becoming a master river pilot. Once again, luck was with him.

Sam approached Horace Bixby, the pilot of the *Paul Jones*, in the pilothouse one morning, and told him of his desire to become a steamboat pilot. It turned out that Bixby and Sam had friends in common—the Bowen brothers, William, Sam, and Bart—now all river pilots. William, in fact, had done his first steering under Bixby. Bixby liked Sam's slow drawl and easy manner, and Sam's honest reply to the pilot's questions amused him. The two hit it off, and, because Bixby had a sore foot that day, he let Sam take the wheel. After a while he offered a deal: he would take Sam on as a "cub," or learner, if Sam would pay him five hundred dollars. Sam countered with an offer of one hundred dollars cash and the rest when he earned it. Bixby agreed. He began teaching Sam immediately, which gave him a chance to nurse his sore foot.

When they reached New Orleans, Sam discovered that no boats were leaving for South America any time soon. He considered this a sign that fate had intervened in his destiny. He went back to St. Louis on the steamboat, borrowed enough money from his brother-in-law, William Moffett, to complete his first payment to Bixby, then returned to New Orleans.

Sam had originally "supposed all that a pilot had to do was to keep his boat in the river." He quickly found out how difficult the job could be. Bixby impressed upon his cub that navigating the twelve hundred miles of rapidly shifting water that made up the Mississippi could be treacherous. He instructed Sam to get a notebook and take notes every time he gave him an instruction. Sam later recalled this training as enhancing his already sharp memory. In *Life on the Mississippi* he reflected:

I think a pilot's memory is about the most wonderful thing in the world. . . . Give a man a tolerably fair memory to start with, and piloting will develop it into a very colossus [giant] of capability. . . . Astonishing things can be done with the human memory if you will devote it faithfully to one particular line of business.

The Strange Death of Henry Clemens

While Sam learned his craft quickly, he experienced a severe emotional blow. In 1858 his brother Henry was killed while crewing on the steamboat *Pennsylvania* on which Sam also worked as a steersman. The pilot of the *Pennsylvania* was a tyrannical, foul-mouthed man named Brown. One day while they were all three in the pilothouse, Brown hit Henry after Brown himself had been chewed out by the captain for not acting on an order that Henry had relayed. In defense of his brother, Sam knocked Brown down and beat him up. Because Sam worked under Brown, this was a serious offense and could have resulted in Sam's being fired. But the captain also hated Brown and arranged for Sam to follow on another boat back to St. Louis, where he would take over Brown's pilot job.

The *Pennsylvania* never made it to St. Louis. Four of its eight boilers blew up near Memphis, and over 150 people died. Henry was thrown free, relatively uninjured. He chose to swim back, however, to try to save others. Unfortunately, he died in a Memphis hospital from injuries incurred in the rescue attempt.

When Sam came for the body, he discovered that the ladies of Memphis—who had tried to nurse the young, handsome Henry back to health—had made up a fund and bought a metallic liner for Henry's wooden coffin. When Sam entered the room, he saw Henry in the coffin, with white flowers on his chest. A woman entered the room and placed a single red rose directly in the middle of the other flowers. Sam experienced a terrible sense of déjà vu. Months before, Sam had had a vivid dream in which he pictured this exact scene. Sam's awful dream was complete; the incident renewed his lifelong interest in the supernatural.

Sam Clemens, River Pilot

Sam managed to press on in spite of the loss and was granted his pilot's license on April 9, 1859. Fellow river pilot and friend Horace Bixby told an interviewer years later that Sam passed the apprenticeship in only eighteen months. Other accounts say it took two years. Either way, it was a relatively short period of time, considering the intricacies of the Mississippi and the enormous amount of detail a pilot had to remember. Soon Sam was making nearly $250 a month, as much as a justice of the Supreme Court, or the vice president of the United States. Even better, he did not have to pay for lodging or food while he was on the river. He was able to send money home to his mother and even to loan some to Orion.

Because of the thousands of twists and turns of the Mississippi, with underwater shoals and wrecked boats to be wary of, all pilots kept a log book. The river was constantly changing, so new notations had to be made all the time. Sam, however, used his notebooks for more than just river notations. In one he wrote out an exercise in French, from the writings of French philosopher Voltaire. Another notation prophesied[4] Clemens's future:

> How to Take Life.—Take it just as though it was—as it is—an earnest, vital, and important affair. Take it as though you were born to the task of performing a merry part in it—as though the world had awaited . . . your coming. Take it as though it was a grand opportunity to do and achieve, to carry forward great and good schemes; to help and cheer a suffering, weary, it may be heartbroken, brother. Now and then a man stands aside from the crowd, labors earnestly, steadfastly, confidently, and straight-away becomes famous for wisdom, intellect, skill, greatness of some sort. The world wonders, admires, idolizes, and it only illustrates what others may do if they take hold of life with a purpose. The miracle, or the power that elevates the few, is to be found in their industry, application, and perseverance under the promptings of a brave, determined spirit.

Sam Goes After Mark Twain

Sam was popular as a pilot, regarded as safe, and as such was given large and difficult boats. He gathered quite a reputation as

---

[4] made a prediction

a storyteller too. Horace Bixby remembered that "Sam was always scribbling when not at the wheel." The only memorable thing Sam published during his piloting days, though, was a satire of an old pilot named Isaiah Sellers who regularly contributed to the New Orleans *Picayune* under the name Mark Twain. Sellers was known to exaggerate his abilities as a pilot and his length of service. The young pilots loved to mock his stories. Sam signed his satirical piece of fiction Sergeant Fathom. His fellow pilot Bart Bowen loved it and got it printed in the paper *True Delta* in May 1859.

The piece was widely read and enjoyed. Its mockery of Mark Twain was so easily recognizable and so humiliating that Sellers never wrote another paragraph for the *Picayune*. Sam felt bad about the effect his story had on Sellers. When he later took up the name Mark Twain himself, it was partly in deference[5] to the old man he had thoughtlessly wounded.

Visit with a Psychic
Once Sam had mastered piloting, his life entered a somewhat carefree period. He made enough money to afford extravagant ten-dollar dinners. He took his mother, his cousin Ella Creel, and another young woman on a tour of New Orleans. Still, despite the prospect of being set for life, Sam was uncertain of his future. Henry's death had shown him that a promising young life could end unexpectedly. Thus, early in 1861 he visited a famous New Orleans psychic known as Madame Capprell. He then reported to Orion in a letter dated February 6 that the clairvoyant had told Sam that Orion should devote himself to his business and to politics with all his might and that Orion could hold government office. She told Sam that a turning point in his life occurred in "1840-7-3, which was it?" (His father had died in 1847.) Then she said the following:

> You might have distinguished yourself as an orator, or as an editor; you have written a great deal; you write well—but

_____
[5] respect or esteem due a superior or an elder

you are rather out of practice; no matter—you will be in practice some day.

Sam had no way of knowing how right she would be. In the letter to Orion, he wrote that he was "under the decided impression that going to the fortune-teller's was just as good as going to the opera, and cost a trifle more." In other words, it was merely entertainment.

The clairvoyant was wrong about one major item. She predicted that Sam would retire from piloting in ten years. Instead, his career ended only two months later, with the outbreak of the Civil War. The river pilots were as divided on the issue of North versus South as anyone in the United States. Traffic on the Mississippi and other major rivers could no longer flow freely— it was now tightly controlled by military forces of both sides. Horace Bixby took the Union side and became chief of the Union River Service. When Bixby made that choice, Sam felt he had to quit. There was always the possibility he would be forced to pilot a Union gunboat, and Sam loved the South too much to let that happen. Not ready to join either the Confederacy or the Union immediately, he boarded a steamer named *Uncle Sam* and decided to go home and think it over. The *Uncle Sam* was fired upon by Union troops in St. Louis, then examined by Union forces and passed. It was the last steamboat to make the trip from New Orleans on a commercial journey until after the Civil War, and Sam Clemens was certain his piloting days were over. Now, whether he liked it or not, he would have to pick sides in a war that he didn't really believe in.

REVIEWING AND INTERPRETING

Record your answers to these questions in your personal literature notebook. Follow the directions for each part.

REVIEWING   Try to complete each of these sentences without looking back at the selection.

Recalling Facts   **1.** Mark Twain was born
a. the same year his father died.
b. during the Civil War.
c. on a small farm in southern Florida.
d. in the same year that Halley's Comet was in the North American sky.

Understanding Main Ideas   **2.** The main reason Twain wanted to be financially successful was because he
a. wanted to travel to South America.
b. saw how his father constantly struggled to make a living.
c. wanted to move to St. Louis.
d. wanted to pay for his training as a riverboat pilot.

Identifying Sequence   **3.** Twain first began to write stories
a. before he moved to Hannibal.
b. when he worked at the *Journal* with his brother Orion.
c. before his father died in 1847.
d. when he worked as a pilot on the Mississippi.

Finding Supporting Details   **4.** Twain renewed his lifelong interest in the supernatural when he
a. realized he had dreamed of Henry's death months before.
b. caught a 50-dollar bill as it flew past him.
c. assumed that fate intervened because there were no boats going to South America.
d. was granted his pilot's license in 1859.

Getting Meaning from Context

5. "These unusual experiences all became *fodder* for later books." In this context fodder means
  a. coarse food for cattle.
  b. impressions.
  c. readily available material.
  d. provisions.

INTERPRETING   To complete these items, you may look back at the selection if you'd like.

Making Inferences

6. You can infer that Twain felt closest to
  a. Uncle John.
  b. his father.
  c. his mother.
  d. his sister Pamela.

Generalizing

7. Which pair of adjectives best describe young Mark Twain?
  a. shy and withdrawn
  b. stubborn and independent
  c. hostile and hardworking
  d. distant and unfriendly

Recognizing Fact and Opinion

8. Based on the biography, which of the following statements is an opinion?
  a. Twain was born Samuel Langhorne Clemens.
  b. John Clemens died of pneumonia at the age of forty-nine.
  c. Twain based the character of Huck Finn on a childhood friend.
  d. Days on Uncle John's farm were heavenly for young Sam.

Identifying Cause and Effect

9. Twain finally went to work for his brother Orion's newspaper because
  a. Twain knew that his brother needed his help.
  b. Orion was eager for Twain to become a writer.
  c. Twain thought he could contribute essays to the paper.
  d. Orion offered Twain room and board and five dollars a week.

Drawing Conclusions   **10.** After reading these two chapters, you can conclude that Twain
   a. was always looking for new adventures.
   b. wanted to settle down and work at one newspaper.
   c. enjoyed being a typesetter.
   d. always dreamed of becoming a writer.

Now check your answers with your teacher. Study the items you answered incorrectly. What skills were they checking? Talk to your teacher about ways to work on those skills.

Bibliography: Sources and Interpretations

Autobiographies and biographies are among the most popular forms of nonfiction. A *biography* is a story of a real person's life written by someone else. An *autobiography* is a story of a real person's life written by that person. The word *biography* comes from the Greek roots *bio*, meaning "life," and *graph*, meaning "writing." The *subject* of a biography is the person whose life story is being told.

Biographies contain facts and details about real people and events. In his biography Skip Press includes many facts and details about Mark Twain's childhood and his early adult years. To write a comprehensive account of Twain's life, Press had to learn as much as possible about him. A biographer's job is usually easier if the subject is still living: He or she can interview the subject directly. The biographer can also talk to friends and relatives of the subject. Because Mark Twain died more than 80 years ago, Press had to rely on diaries, letters, autobiographical writings, other people's biographies of Twain, and Twain's own published works for information.

In addition to researching these sources of information, Press had to evaluate the sources and decide which ones were reliable and which were questionable. Even people who knew or had knowledge of Twain have given different descriptions of him and the events in his life. A good biographer must carefully judge each source and then choose the sources that he or she thinks are the most reliable.

Once the biographer has facts and details, he or she must do more than just list the information about a person's life. A good biographer interprets the facts about his or her subject for you. An *interpretation* is one person's view of certain words, events, or actions. Biographers, and all nonfiction writers, interpret facts by explaining their meaning and evaluating their importance. To help you understand the life of the subject and the many aspects of a subject's personality, the biographer sorts through the facts and decides which are the most important. What events, people, or conditions had an impact on the subject's life? What forces motivated the subject? What were the turning points in the subject's life? By focusing on the answers to these questions, the biographer is able to explain the subject's life.

In the lessons that follow, you will look at the kinds of sources Skip Press used to gather information about Mark Twain's life and the ways he interpreted that information:

1. **Primary and Secondary Sources**   Before writing a biography, the author researches the subject's life. That research includes information gathered from two kinds of sources—primary and secondary sources.

2. **Interpretation and Theme**   Once a biographer researches the available sources and decides which facts to include, he or she establishes a theme—the underlying message or central idea of a piece of writing. The theme develops from the author's interpretation of the facts of the subject's life.

3. **Interpretation and Main Ideas and Supporting Details**   A biographer organizes the facts of a subject's life in a meaningful way. As the writer studies the facts and the arrangement of events, he or she interprets those facts and events and forms certain opinions about the subject's life. The writer offers those interpretations as main ideas and then supports those ideas with examples and details.

LESSON ① PRIMARY AND SECONDARY SOURCES

If you were asked to write a research paper about Mark Twain, where would you begin your research? One of the most readily available reference sources is an encyclopedia. An encyclopedia would give you an overview of Twain's life: when and where he was born and died, a list of his works, a bibliography of biographies and works written about Twain. You might decide to read a biography of Twain to help you with your research. Biographies and encyclopedias are secondary sources. A *secondary source* is information that is based on the writings or evidence of people other than the subject or the author. Because Mark Twain is considered an important American writer, there were many biographies available to Press. But by using only other writers' biographies, Press risked repeating errors and passing on someone else's interpretations of Twain's life. Therefore, Press also used primary sources.

If you were to read Twain's journal or his letters to his family and friends, you would be researching a *primary source*—information that comes directly from the subject's own experience or observation. The author of a primary source has actually seen or participated in the events or observations he or she is describing.

To develop a complete picture of Mark Twain, Press used both primary and secondary sources.

Primary Sources   The most important reason for using primary sources in a biography is to create an accurate picture of the subject. By reading Twain's own words, you can learn what Twain was really like. In the first two chapters of *The Importance of Mark Twain*, which you have just read, Press uses quotations from Twain's letters and Twain's book *Life on the Mississippi*. These primary sources give you a sense of what life was like for Twain as a young boy. In the following excerpt note how Press effectively uses Twain's own words to help complete the picture of his parents:

> Mark Twain described his father as "Silent, austere, of perfect probity [high ideals] and high principle; ungentle of manner toward his children, but always a gentleman in his phrasing—and never punished them—a look was enough, and more than enough." . . .
>
> In contrast to his father's stern disposition, Twain described his mother, Jane, as having "the heart of a young girl." When she was being courted by John Clemens, Jane Lampton was reputed to have been the best dancer in all of Kentucky and was celebrated for her beauty, grace, and wit.

"She was of a sunshiny disposition," her son wrote, "and her long life was mainly a holiday to her."

Imagine that Press said, "Twain's father was stern, but his mother had a lighthearted attitude toward life." You would be able to form an image of Twain's parents, but the addition of Twain's own words creates a much more vivid image, as well as a more believable one. You can believe Press's description of Twain's parents because you can read exactly what Twain said about them.

Secondary Sources   In order to collect sufficient information about their subjects, biographers usually must use secondary sources of information. This is particularly true, as mentioned earlier, when the subject has been dead for a long time. In these first two chapters from *The Importance of Mark Twain*, Press uses at least two secondary sources of information. One of these is Albert Bigelow Paine's biography of Twain. Paine was a friend of Twain's. He not only wrote an account of Twain's life but also recorded Twain's own words. Even though Paine's biography is a secondary source, the passages in which Paine quotes Twain's actual words are from a primary source.

The other important secondary source that Press researched was a biography about Twain written by Justin Kaplan. Kaplan is one of the foremost Twain scholars and has written many works about him. Both Kaplan's and Paine's biographies of Twain contain primary sources of information from letters and other writings by Twain himself.

EXERCISE ⟨1⟩

Read this passage from the selection. Sam's brother Orion had urged Sam to contribute to the newspaper he bought, and Sam sends a letter in reply. Use what you have learned in this lesson to answer the questions.

I will try to write for [Orion's] paper occasionally, but I fear my letters will be very uninteresting, for this incessant night work dulls one's ideas amazingly. . . . I believe I am the only person in the *Inquirer* office that does not drink. One young fellow makes $18 for a few weeks [of work], and gets on a grand "bender" [drunk] and spends every cent of it.

1. Did Press make use here of a primary or secondary source of information? From what source is the quote taken?

2. Why is this source of information important to an understanding of Twain's feelings about his job at the *Inquirer*?

Now check your answers with your teacher. Review this lesson if you don't understand why an answer was incorrect.

WRITING ON YOUR OWN

In this exercise you will use what you learned in this lesson to help you gather facts about the subject of your biography. Follow these steps:

- Remember, your biography will cover only a part of your subject's life. You could write about your subject's early life—up through high school. Or you could write about his or her adult years—the years after high school.
- Begin to gather information. To get the most accurate information, use your primary source—the subject himself or herself. Arrange an interview. Come prepared with questions that will help you develop an accurate account of the subject's life during the time period you chose. For example, you might ask your subject for an opinion of his or her high-school education. Or you might ask why your subject chose the career he or she did. Take careful notes during the interview. Put quotation marks around any of the exact quotes from your subject that you may wish to use.

• To supplement information obtained from your primary source and to get other viewpoints and opinions about your subject, explore some secondary sources. Talk to relatives, friends, and acquaintances who know the subject well. See whether any print sources are available. Perhaps there have been articles in the local newspaper about your subject. Perhaps a relative or friend has a letter from your subject that is appropriate and that he or she would be willing to share with you. Take notes to record the information you gather from secondary sources.

LESSON 2 — INTERPRETATION AND THEME

Have you ever filled out a job application, a survey, or a medical form? On each of those forms, you give facts about yourself and your life. You might be asked when and where you were born, how many people are in your family, your age or weight, and your hobbies. These are all facts about you. But what does the person reading the forms *really* know about you or what you think? These facts don't help to explain *who* you are.

If a biographer wrote only the facts about a subject, you would be in much the same position as the person reading your forms. So to help you better understand the life of the subject, the biographer interprets the facts for you.

How does a biographer interpret the facts? As biographers do their research, they usually begin to see a general trend or idea that seems to run through the subject's life. They may find themselves asking, What makes this subject so important, or creative, or talented? They may begin to see that events in a subject's childhood affected what he or she did as an adult. The writer's interpretation of the facts becomes the main theme—the underlying message—of the biography.

The title of Press's biography, *The Importance of Mark Twain*, suggests that his main theme is that Mark Twain was an important figure and that Press will explain in the biography what made Twain an important figure. Press will interpret the events and influences in Twain's life in order to help the reader to understand how Sam Clemens, poor boy from Missouri became Mark Twain, the extraordinarily talented writer.

In the opening paragraph of the biography, Press lets the reader know right away that there was something unusual, even extraordinary, about Twain.

> It is a strange coincidence that Mark Twain was born while Halley's Comet was in the North American sky and that he died upon its return, seventy-five years later, just as he had predicted.

Sometimes the writer will introduce one or more related themes in addition to the main theme. A related theme revealed by Press through his interpretation of the facts is that Twain was a careful observer of life.

> I think a pilot's memory is about the most wonderful thing in the world. . . . Give a man a tolerably fair memory to start with, and piloting will develop it into a very colossus [giant] of capability. . . . Astonishing things can be done with the human memory if you will devote it faithfully to one particular line of business.

Press also wants the reader to understand that Twain, like most good writers, wrote about what he knew best. In fact, he often included his own experiences in his fiction. Tom Blankenship, Twain's best friend, was the model for the wild and adventurous Huck Finn. Press shows how part of Twain's success as a writer was his ability to turn childhood experiences into adventurous, humorous stories and novels.

EXERCISE 〈2〉

Read this passage from the selection. Use what you have learned in this lesson to answer the questions that follow it.

Sam saw prejudice displayed in his own household as well. Although the Clemens family was relatively poor, they managed to hire two black servants: Jennie, a servant who came with the family from Florida, and Uncle Ned, a handyman who helped around the house. When Jennie talked back, Mrs. Clemens called her high-spirited and a source of trouble. Sam began to question the rightness of slavery at a young age, though he dared not do so publicly. It is no accident that Jim in *Huckleberry Finn* is represented as a thinking, caring human being who simply wants to lead a life of freedom. When *Huckleberry Finn* was written, no author had ever treated black and white characters as equals in a novel, as Twain did with Jim and Huck Finn.

1. From all the facts that Press had available to him, why do you think he choose to include these events in Twain's life? What does this passage tell you about Twain's character?

2. How do the facts in this passage support the theme that Twain was a careful observer of life?

Now check your answers with your teacher. Review this lesson if you don't understand why an answer was incorrect.

WRITING ON YOUR OWN

In this exercise you will use what you have learned in this lesson to help you interpret the facts you have gathered about your subject and to develop a theme for your biography. Follow these steps:

• Review the details you filled in on your cluster diagram from Writing: Developing a Biography and the information you gathered from primary and secondary sources, from Writing on Your Own 1.

- After reviewing your own description of the subject, the subject's own words, the descriptions and opinions of the subject from people who knew him or her, and any print information you may have found, see whether you can identify an underlyimg message or idea that seems to emerge from all that information. It might be that the subject is a caring, generous person; a dedicated and inspiring teacher or coach; a talented artist, writer, or performer; a person who makes everyone feel better because of his or her warm, friendly personality; a parent or relative who continually makes sacrifices to help you. This underlying message, or central idea, is your theme. Using a sentence or two, write a theme for your biography.
- Review again the facts that you gathered. Decide which facts support the theme you have chosen. On a separate sheet of paper, list only those pieces of information that support your theme.

LESSON ③   INTERPRETATION AND MAIN IDEAS AND SUPPORTING DETAILS

A biographer must organize the facts of a subject's life in a meaningful way. When writing a biography, most biographers use chronological order—the order in which events happen in time—as their method of organization. Press begins his biography with Twain's birth and early adult life and ends the book with Twain's death.

As he researched, Press developed certain views and opinions about Twain's life. In each chapter of the biography, Press includes his interpretations of Twain's life by presenting main ideas and then selecting evidence or examples to support those ideas.

In the two chapters you have just read, Press presents a number of ideas about Twain. Among the most important ideas is that Twain had an irrepressible sense of adventure. He could not wait to experience more of the world and see what it had to offer. Press supports this idea throughout these two chapters. He begins by telling you that Twain was "an independent and strong-willed child who often ran away from home." He reinforces the idea of Twain's adventurous boyhood by suggesting that it is not surprising that Twain wrote *Huckleberry Finn* and *Tom Sawyer*. Twain's real childhood became the inspiration for many of his books. Press shows how the riverboat traffic on the Mississippi also piqued Twain's desire to travel.

Another main idea that Press introduces is that Twain had a desire to be a financial success. Twain himself lends support to this idea in the following passage:

> It is good to begin life poor; it is good to begin life rich—these are wholesome; but to begin it poor and *prospectively* rich! The man who has not experienced it cannot imagine the curse of it.

Press also supports this idea by showing how hard Twain's father works to support the family and Twain's own struggle to make money. At first Twain does not want to work for his brother; he has seen Orion's "financial ups and downs." But he finally takes the job when he is offered room, board, and five dollars a week.

When reading a biography, look for the author's main ideas. Also note whether the writer has supported his or her ideas with sufficient evidence or examples.

EXERCISE ◇3◇

Read the following passage from the selection. Use what you have learned in this lesson to answer the questions.

Working with his brother did not quiet Sam's desire for adventure, however. While in Keokuk, Sam read Lieutenant Herndon's description of his survey of the upper Amazon

River, including tales of natives who could stay awake for days by eating coca leaves (cocaine is derived from coca leaves). Sam did not take the drug—he only read about it. Although it sounds terrible (considering what we know today about the drug), Sam dreamed of becoming rich by harvesting coca for North American distribution. At the time, coca was considered an herb with magical properties. To achieve his goal of becoming rich off cocaine, Sam had to raise the money for a trip to South America. As if guided by a divine hand, a solution came floating on the wind. In early November 1857, Sam was walking down Main Street in Keokuk when he grabbed a bit of paper as it flew past him. It was a fifty-dollar bill. He had no idea where this startling find had flown from. In an article called "The Turning Point of My Life," written many years later, he said "I advertised the find and left for the Amazon the same day."

1. How does this passage support Press's main idea that Twain had an irrepressible sense of adventure?

2. How does this passage support Press's main idea that Twain wanted to be financially successful?

Now check your answers with your teacher. Review this lesson if you don't understand why an answer was incorrect.

 WRITING ON YOUR OWN 3

In this exercise you will use what you have learned in this lesson to select main ideas and supporting details for your biography. Follow these steps:

• Review the list of facts you wrote for Writing on Your Own 2, which supported the theme of your biography. Look for main ideas in those pieces of information. For example, if your theme were that your uncle is a helpful, generous person, you might write one main idea this way: "My uncle Juan always finds time to help others." Then you would look at the facts to find details that support that main idea. Examples that would support that main idea might be as follows: he helps me with my homework; one day I saw him helping a neighbor repair a flat tire; he helped my brother move and then bought pizza for everyone.

• Use a graphic organizer like the one below to help you organize your main ideas. Try to fill out an organizer for at least three main ideas that support your theme, writing the main idea in the box at the top and the supporting details in the boxes below it.

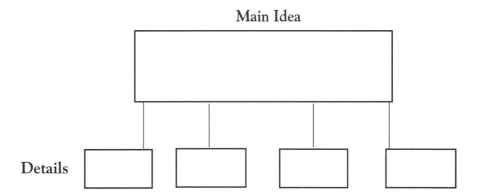

DISCUSSION GUIDES

1. Many people with whom Mark Twain came into contact in his early years had an influence on his life in some way. Working with a small group look back at the selection and find out in what way each of the following people influenced his life: John Clemens, Orion Clemens, Uncle Dan'l (Daniel), Tom Blankenship, and Horace Bixby. Prepare a report explaining who each person is and in what way each influenced Twain's life. Present your report to the class.

2. Working with a partner, prepare an imaginary interview with Mark Twain. Both of you should read further about Mark Twain so that the one acting as interviewer can ask interesting, appropriate questions. Decide for yourselves from reading this selection and any other research you may do what attitude Twain might have had toward each question. After sufficient practice, conduct the interview before the class. Allow time for discussion and questions from your classmates.

3. Twain turned his experiences as a riverboat pilot into his book *Life on the Mississippi*. He based many of the stories in *Tom Sawyer* and *Huckleberry Finn* on his real-life adventures and his boyhood friends. Later, he based his book *The Innocents Abroad* on the edited journal and letters he wrote about his trip to the Mediterranean area and the Holy Land. In a small group discuss what you think would have happened if Twain had gone to South America. Do you think he would have been satisfied with his life as a coca baron? Discuss why you think he would or would not have been satisfied. Share your group's opinions with the class.

WRITE A BIOGRAPHY

In this unit you have seen how a biographer gathers facts about his or her subject from both primary and secondary sources, interprets those facts to develop a theme, and then organizes them into main ideas and details that support the theme. Now you will write a part of a biography about your chosen subject.

Follow these steps to complete your biography. If you have questions about the writing process, refer to Using the Writing Process (page 250).

- Gather and review the following pieces of writing you did for this unit: 1) a cluster diagram with details describing your subject; 2) the notes you took in gathering facts from primary and secondary sources; 3) the theme and list of ideas you selected that support the theme; 4) graphic organizers for at least three main ideas with supporting details.
- Write an opening paragraph for your biography. Identify who your subject is and describe him or her, using details from your cluster diagram. You might state your theme at the end of this paragraph.
- Use the graphic organizers you created to write a paragraph for each main idea. Include the details that support the main idea. Arrange the paragraphs to give the facts of your subject's life in chronological order.
- Write a concluding paragraph that briefly summarizes the main points in your subject's life. You may want to close with an anecdote that relates directly to the theme.
- Reread your draft. Do all the parts work smoothly together? Do the descriptions, events, and experiences you wrote about support the theme? Have you given an accurate account of the subject's life? Revise your draft accordingly.
- With a small group, share one another's biographies. Each member of the group may wish to read his or her biography aloud. Others may offer comments and suggestions.
- Proofread your biography for errors in spelling, grammar, punctuation, and capitalization. Make a final copy and save it in your writing portfolio.

Author's Viewpoint

Adventures of a Young Printer

♦

from *Autobiography* by Benjamin Franklin

INTRODUCTION

BUILDING BACKGROUND

Benjamin Franklin was one of the 56 signers of the Declaration of Independence on July 4, 1776, and one of the 39 delegates who wrote and signed the nation's constitution in Philadelphia in 1787. Franklin's *Autobiography* has been one of the most popular books in English for more than 130 years. Franklin started writing his *Autobiography* in 1771, before the American Revolution, and finished it in 1788, after the colonies had declared and won their independence.

Long before Benjamin Franklin signed the Declaration of Independence or the Constitution of the United States, he was concerned about the welfare of his fellow citizens. In Philadelphia, Franklin founded the colonies' first public lending library, first volunteer fire company, and first fire-insurance company. Two hundred years before environmental pollution became an issue, Franklin supported the cleaning and paving of city streets and the planting of trees to purify city air.

Benjamin Franklin organized a volunteer militia, or a citizen army, in Pennsylvania. He was deputy postmaster general for the early colonies. During the American Revolution, Franklin served as the nation's ambassador to Europe. After the United

The boy in this early engraving titled *Learning to Be a Printer* has been identified as Benjamin Franklin.

States won independence, he organized the new nation's postal system. He founded the first Pennsylvania charity hospital as well as an academy that later became the University of Pennsylvania. He was also the first president of the Pennsylvania Society for Promoting the Abolition of Slavery.

In addition to his many civic interests, Franklin devoted much time to scientific pursuits, especially to exploring the nature of electricity. (Everyone has heard the story of how Franklin flew a kite in a storm to prove that electricity was present in lightning.) It has been said that Franklin found electricity a curiosity and left it a science. Franklin's curiosity about how things worked inspired many of his inventions, and two of them, bifocal glasses and the Franklin stove, are still in use today.

A famous historian described Benjamin Franklin as "a universal genius" and "the embodiment of what we like to call the American spirit." Although he gave no fiery speeches and fought in no battles, Benjamin Franklin played as large a part as any elected official or military officer in shaping the early years of the United States of America.

The excerpt you will read from Benjamin Franklin's *Autobiography* begins during his apprenticeship in his brother's printing shop in Boston. In it Franklin describes how he escaped from his apprenticeship and started a new life in Philadelphia.

ABOUT THE AUTHOR

Benjamin Franklin was born in poor circumstances in Boston in 1706. When he died in Philadelphia in 1790, he was known and admired around the world and recognized as one of the new nation's most honored and respected citizens. Benjamin was the 15th of 17 children and the youngest son. His father, Josiah, was a candle and soap maker who struggled hard to support his large family. Josiah sent Ben to grammar school, intending to train him for the ministry. But when Josiah Franklin learned how costly such an education was and how poorly paid many ministers were, he withdrew the boy from school. He then put Ben to work in his own shop.

Young Ben disliked his father's trade. He longed to go to sea, but his father opposed the boy's wish. Josiah searched for a trade that Ben would enjoy. Knowing Ben's love of reading, Josiah settled on the printing trade. Ben's older brother, James, was a printer, so the boy became an apprentice in his brother's shop. In those days an apprentice was legally bound to a master for a specific number of years. While an apprentice learned his trade, he was given food and lodging by his master. He could not leave his master until his apprenticeship legally ended. At the age of 12, Ben signed papers obliging him to work for his brother James until he was 21 years old.

Franklin grew increasingly unhappy with his situation. In "Adventures of a Young Printer," he describes how, at the age of 17, he ran away from Boston and eventually reached Philadelphia. In Philadelphia young Franklin opened his own printing shop, which he turned into a prosperous business.

ABOUT THE LESSONS

The lessons that follow "Adventures of a Young Printer" focus on Benjamin Franklin's viewpoint. Every writer is affected by the historical period in which he or she lives. In addition, a writer's own experiences, values, and opinions also influence his or her viewpoint. A person's viewpoint affects how he or she sees the world as well as how that person writes about events.

As you will see, Benjamin Franklin's viewpoint was greatly influenced by his early years in Boston as well as by his experiences establishing his independence in Philadelphia. You will also see how Franklin's personal experiences and the values and opinions he developed as a young man affected his viewpoint many years later, when he wrote his autobiography.

WRITING: EXPRESSING YOUR VIEWPOINT

At the end of the unit, you will write a short essay expressing your viewpoint about an experience from your own childhood. The suggestions below will help you get started:

- Think of several events or experiences that occurred when you were quite young—things that made a strong impression on you or changed you in some way. It could be your first day at kindergarten or preschool, the first time you rode a bicycle by yourself, or the first time you helped a parent or some other adult with an important task.
- Choose one of these experiences to write about in this unit. On a separate sheet of paper, make a graphic organizer like the one below. Fill in as many details as you can recall about your experience. Keep the graphic organizer at hand. As you work on the Writing on Your Own exercises which follow, more details may come to mind. Add them to the organizer as you go along.

What happened?	When did it happen?	Who was involved?	Where did it happen?

- Using your graphic organizer, draft a paragraph briefly describing your experience: what happened, when it happened, who was involved, and where it happened.
- As the writing exercises progress, you will rewrite and expand this paragraph to express your viewpoint about this important experience in your life.

AS YOU READ   Think about these questions as you read the autobiography.
They will help you identify Franklin's viewpoint.

- How did conditions in the colonies affect Franklin's life when he was a young man?
- How does Franklin, the mature writer, feel about himself as a young man? What does he say about his youthful relationship with his brother James?
- From the excerpt what can you tell about the things that Franklin considers important?

Adventures of a Young Printer

from *Autobiography* by Benjamin Franklin

My brother had, in 1720 or 21, begun to print a newspaper. It was the second that appeared in America, and was called the *New England Courant*. The only one before it was the *Boston News-Letter*. I remember his being dissuaded by some of his friends from the undertaking, as not likely to succeed, one newspaper being, in their judgment, enough for America. At this time (1771) there are not less than five-and-twenty. He went on, however, with the undertaking, and after having worked in composing the types[1] and printing off the sheets, I was employed to carry the papers through the streets to the customers.

He had some ingenious men among his friends, who amused themselves by writing little pieces for this paper, which gained it credit and made it more in demand, and these gentlemen often visited us. Hearing their conversations, and their accounts of the approbation[2] their papers were received with, I was excited to try my hand among them; but, being still a boy, and suspecting that my brother would object to printing anything of mine in his paper if he knew it to be mine, I contrived to disguise my hand and, writing an anonymous paper, I put it in at night under

---
[1] printer's language meaning to set metal letters in position for printing

[2] approval

the door of the printing-house. It was found in the morning and communicated to his writing friends when they called in as usual. They read it, commented on it in my hearing, and I had the exquisite pleasure of finding it met with their approbation, and that, in their different guesses at the author, none were named but men of some character among us for learning and ingenuity. I suppose now that I was rather lucky in my judges, and that perhaps they were not really so very good ones as I then esteemed them.

Encouraged, however, by this, I wrote and conveyed in the same way to the press several more papers which were equally approved; and I kept my secret till my small fund of sense for such performances was pretty well exhausted, and then I discovered[3] it, when I began to be considered a little more by my brother's acquaintance, and in a manner that did not quite please him, as he thought, probably with reason, that it tended to make me too vain. And perhaps this might be one occasion of the differences that we began to have about this time. Though a brother, he considered himself as my master, and me as his apprentice, and accordingly expected the same services from me as he would from another, while I thought he demeaned me too much in some he required of me, who from a brother expected more indulgence. Our disputes were often brought before our father, and I fancy I was either generally in the right, or else a better pleader, because the judgment was generally in my favor. But my brother was passionate, and had often beaten me, which I took extremely amiss; and, thinking my apprenticeship very tedious, I was continually wishing for some opportunity of shortening it, which at length offered in a manner unexpected.*

One of the pieces in our newspaper on some political point, which I have now forgotten, gave offense to the Assembly.[4] He was taken up, censured, and imprisoned for a month, by the speaker's

*I fancy his harsh and tyrannical treatment of me might be a means of impressing me with that aversion to arbitrary power that has stuck to me through my whole life.

---

[3] revealed

[4] the governing body of Massachusetts Bay Colony

warrant, I suppose because he would not discover his author. I too was taken up and examined before the council; but, though I did not give them any satisfaction, they contented themselves with admonishing me, and dismissed me, considering me, perhaps, as an apprentice who was bound to keep his master's secrets.

During my brother's confinement, which I resented a good deal, notwithstanding our private differences, I had the management of the paper; and I made bold to give our rulers some rubs in it, which my brother took very kindly, while others began to consider me in an unfavorable light, as a young genius that had a turn for libeling[5] and satire. My brother's discharge was accompanied with an order of the House (a very odd one), that "James Franklin should no longer print the paper called the *New England Courant*."

There was a consultation held in our printing-house among his friends what he should do in this case. Some proposed to evade the order by changing the name of the paper; but my brother seeing inconveniences in that, it was finally concluded on as a better way to let it be printed for the future under the name of *Benjamin Franklin*; and to avoid the censure of the Assembly, that might fall on him as still printing it by his apprentice, the contrivance was that my old indenture should be returned to me, with a full discharge on the back of it, to be shown on occasion; but to secure to him the benefit of my service, I was to sign new indentures for the remainder of the term, which were to be kept private. A very flimsy scheme it was; however, it was immediately executed, and the paper went on accordingly under my name for several months.

At length, a fresh difference arising between my brother and me, I took upon me to assert my freedom, presuming that he would not venture to produce the new indentures. It was not fair in me to take this advantage, and this I therefore reckon one of the first errata[6] of my life; but the unfairness of it weighed little

---

[5] injuring a person's reputation by publicly speaking or writing unfavorably about that person

[6] errors; printers use the term to indicate mistakes in printed work;

with me when under the impressions of resentment for the blows his passion too often urged him to bestow upon me, though he was otherwise not an ill-natured man; perhaps I was too saucy and provoking.

When he found I would leave him, he took care to prevent my getting employment in any other printing-house of the town, by going round and speaking to every master, who accordingly refused to give me work. I then thought of going to New York, as the nearest place where there was a printer; and I was then rather inclined to leave Boston when I reflected that I had already made myself a little obnoxious to the governing party, and, from the arbitrary proceedings of the Assembly in my brother's case, it was likely I might, if I stayed, soon bring myself into scrapes; and further, that my indiscreet disputations[7] about religion began to make me pointed at with horror by good people as an infidel or atheist. I determined on the point, but my father now siding with my brother, I was sensible that, if I attempted to go openly, means would be used to prevent me. My friend Collins, therefore, undertook to manage a little for me. He agreed with the captain of a New York sloop[8] for my passage, under the notion of my being a young acquaintance of his, that had got a naughty girl with child, whose friends would compel me to marry her, and therefore I could not appear or come away publicly. So I sold some of my books to raise a little money, was taken on board privately, and as we had a fair wind, in three days I found myself in New York, near three hundred miles from home, a boy of but seventeen, without the least recommendation to, or knowledge of, any person in the place, and with very little money in my pocket.

My inclinations for the sea were by this time worn out, or I might now have gratified them. But, having a trade, and supposing myself a pretty good workman, I offered my service to the printer in the place, old Mr. William Bradford, who had been the first printer in Pennsylvania, but removed from thence upon

[7] arguments

[8] a one-masted sailing ship

the quarrel of George Keith. He could give me no employment, having little to do and help enough already; but, says he, "My son at Philadelphia has lately lost his principal hand, Aquila Rose, by death; if you go thither, I believe he may employ you." Philadelphia was one hundred miles further; I set out, however, in a boat for Amboy, leaving my chest and things to follow me round by sea.

In crossing the bay, we met with a squall that tore our rotten sails to pieces, prevented our getting into the Kill,[9] and drove us upon Long Island. In our way, a drunken Dutchman, who was a passenger too, fell overboard; when he was sinking, I reached through the water to his shock pate,[10] and drew him up, so that we got him in again. His ducking sobered him a little, and he went to sleep, taking first out of his pocket a book, which he desired I would dry for him. It proved to be my old favorite author, Bunyan's *Pilgrim's Progress*, in Dutch, finely printed on good paper, with copper cuts,[11] a dress better than I had ever seen it wear in its own language. I have since found that it has been translated into most of the languages of Europe, and suppose it has been more generally read than any other book, except perhaps the Bible. Honest John[12] was the first that I know of who mixed narration and dialogue, a method of writing very engaging to the reader, who in the most interesting parts finds himself, as it were, brought into the company and present at the discourse. Defoe in his *Crusoe*, his *Moll Flanders, Religious Courtship, Family Instructor*, and other pieces, has imitated it with success; and Richardson has done the same in his *Pamela*, etc.[13]

---

[9] a Dutch word meaning a channel or stream

[10] the thick hair on the top of the head

[11] illustrations made by printing pictures engraved on copper plates

[12] John Bunyan, author of Pilgrim's Progress; The book is an allegory, or symbolic story, in which the central character, Christian, journeys from the City of Destruction to the Celestial City.

[13] Daniel Defoe (1660–1731) and Samuel Richardson (1689–1761), important British novelists

When we drew near the island, we found it was at a place where there could be no landing, there being a great surf on the stony beach. So we dropped anchor, and swung round towards the shore. Some people came down to the water edge and hallowed to us, as we did to them; but the wind was so high, and the surf so loud, that we could not hear so as to understand each other. There were canoes on the shore, and we made signs, and hallowed that they should fetch us; but they either did not understand us, or thought it impracticable, so they went away, and night coming on, we had no remedy but to wait till the wind should abate,[14] and in the mean time the boatman and I concluded to sleep if we could; and so crowded into the scuttle,[15] with the Dutchman, who was still wet, and the spray, beating over the head of our boat, leaked through to us, so that we were soon almost as wet as he. In this manner we lay all night, with very little rest; but, the wind abating the next day, we made a shift to reach Amboy before night, having been thirty hours on the water, without victuals or any drink but a bottle of filthy rum, the water we sailed on being salt.

In the evening I found myself very feverish, and went into bed; but having read somewhere that cold water drank plentifully was good for a fever, I followed the prescription, sweat plentifully most of the night; my fever left me, and in the morning, crossing the ferry, I proceeded on my journey on foot, having fifty miles to Burlington, where I was told I should find boats that would carry me the rest of the way to Philadelphia.

It rained very hard all the day; I was thoroughly soaked, and by noon a good deal tired; so I stopped at a poor inn, where I stayed all night, beginning now to wish I had never left home. I cut so miserable a figure, too, that I found, by the questions asked me, I was suspected to be some runaway servant, and in danger of being taken up on that suspicion. However, I proceeded the next day, and got in the evening to an inn, within

---

[14] decrease

[15] a small opening with a lid

eight or ten miles of Burlington, kept by one Dr. Brown. He entered into conversation with me while I took some refreshment, and, finding I had read a little, became very sociable and friendly. Our acquaintance continued as long as he lived. He had been, I imagine, an itinerant doctor, for there was no town in England or country in Europe of which he could not give a very particular account. He had some letters,[16] and was ingenious, but much of an unbeliever, and wickedly undertook some years after to travesty the Bible in doggerel[17] verse, as Cotton[18] had done Virgil.[19] By this means he set many of the facts in a very ridiculous light, and might have hurt weak minds if his work had been published; but it never was.

At his house I lay that night, and the next morning reached Burlington, but had the mortification to find that the regular boats were gone a little before my coming, and no other expected to go till Tuesday, this being Saturday; wherefore I returned to an old woman in the town, of whom I had bought gingerbread to eat on the water, and asked her advice. She invited me to lodge at her house till passage by water should offer; and, being tired with my foot traveling, I accepted the invitation. She, understanding I was a printer, would have had me stay at that town and follow my business, being ignorant of the stock necessary to begin with. She was very hospitable, gave me a dinner of ox-cheek with great good will, accepting only of a pot of ale in return; and I thought myself fixed till Tuesday should come. However, walking in the evening by the side of the river, a boat came by, which I found was going towards Philadelphia, with several people in her. They took me in, and, as there was no wind, we rowed all the way; and about midnight, not having yet seen the city, some of the company were confi-

---

[16] could read and write

[17] bad poetry, often written for comic effect

[18] Cotton Mather (1663–1728), a New England Puritan minister who was well known for his fiery sermons

[19] a poet of ancient Rome, whose works were studied by students learning Latin in Franklin's day

dent we must have passed it, and would row no farther; the others knew not where we were; so we put towards the shore, got into a creek, landed near an old fence, with the rails of which we made a fire, the night being cold (in October), and there we remained till daylight. Then one of the company knew the place to be Cooper's Creek, a little above Philadelphia, which we saw as soon as we got out of the creek, and arrived there about eight or nine o'clock on the Sunday morning, and landed at the Market Street wharf.

I have been the more particular in this description of my journey, and shall be so of my first entry into that city, that you may in your mind compare such unlikely beginnings with the figure I have since made there. I was in my working dress, my best clothes being to come round by sea. I was dirty from my journey; my pockets were stuffed out with shirts and stockings; I knew no soul nor where to look for lodging. I was fatigued with traveling, rowing, and want of rest; I was very hungry; and my whole stock of cash consisted of a Dutch dollar and about a shilling in copper. The latter I gave the people of the boat for my passage, who at first refused it, on account of my rowing; but I insisted on their taking it, a man being sometimes more generous when he has but a little money than when he has plenty, perhaps through fear of being thought to have but little.

Then I walked up the street, gazing about, till near the market-house I met a boy with bread. I had made many a meal on bread, and, inquiring where he got it, I went immediately to the baker's he directed me to, in Second Street, and asked for biscuit, intending such as we had in Boston; but they, it seems, were not made in Philadelphia. Then I asked for a three-penny loaf, and was told they had none such. So, not considering or knowing the difference of money, and the greater cheapness nor the names of his bread, I bade him give me three-penny-worth of any sort. He gave me, accordingly, three great puffy rolls. I was surprised at the quantity, but took it, and, having no room in my pockets, walked off with a roll under each arm, and eating the other. Thus I went up Market Street as far as Fourth Street, passing by the door of Mr. Read, my future wife's father; when she, standing at the door, saw me, and thought I made, as I certainly did, a most awkward, ridiculous appearance. Then I turned and went down Chestnut Street and part of Walnut Street, eating my roll all the way, and, coming round, found myself again at Market Street wharf, near the boat I came in, to which I went for a draught of the river water; and, being filled with one of my rolls, gave the other two to a woman and her child that came down the river in the boat with us, and were waiting to go farther.

Thus refreshed, I walked again up the street, which by this time had many clean-dressed people in it, who were all walking the same way. I joined them, and thereby was led into the great meeting-house of the Quakers near the market. I sat down among them, and, after looking round awhile and hearing nothing said, being very drowsy through labor and want of rest the preceding night, I fell fast asleep, and continued so till the meeting broke up, when one was kind enough to rouse me. This was, therefore, the first house I was in, or slept in, in Philadelphia.

Walking down again toward the river and looking in the faces of people, I met a young Quaker man, whose countenance I liked and accosting him, requested he would tell me where a stranger could get lodging. We were then near the sign of the Three Mariners. "Here," says he, "is one place that entertains strangers, but it is not a reputable house; if thee wilt walk with me, I'll show thee a better." He brought me to the Crooked Billet in Water Street. Here I got a dinner; and while I was eating it several sly questions were asked me, as it seemed to be suspected from my youth and appearance that I might be some runaway.

After dinner my sleepiness returned, and, being shown to a bed, I lay down without undressing, and slept till six in the evening, was called to supper, went to bed again very early, and slept soundly till next morning. Then I made myself as tidy as I could and went to Andrew Bradford the printer's. I found in the shop the old man his father, whom I had seen at New York, and who, traveling on horseback, had got to Philadelphia before me. He introduced me to his son, who received me civilly, gave me a breakfast, but told me he did not at present want a hand, being lately supplied with one; but there was another printer in town, lately set up, one Keimer, who perhaps might employ me; if not, I should be welcome to lodge at his house, and he would give me a little work to do now and then till fuller business should offer.

The old gentleman said he would go with me to the new printer; and when we found him, "Neighbor," says Bradford, "I have brought to see you a young man of your business; perhaps you may want such a one." He asked me a few questions, put a composing stick in my hand to see how I worked, and then said he would employ me soon, though he had just then nothing for me to do; and, taking old Bradford, whom he had never seen before, to be one of the town's people that had a good will for him, entered into a conversation on his present undertaking and prospects; while Bradford, not discovering that he was the other printer's father, on Keimer's saying he expected soon to get the greatest part of the business into his own hands, drew him on by artful questions, and starting little doubts, to explain all his views, what interest he relied on, and in what manner he intended to proceed. I, who stood by and heard all, saw immediately that one of them was a crafty old sophister,[20] and the other a mere novice.[21] Bradford left me with Keimer, who was greatly surprised when I told him who the old man was.

Keimer's printing-house, I found, consisted of an old shattered press, and one small, worn-out font[22] of English, which he was then using himself, composing an elegy[23] on Aquila Rose, before mentioned, an ingenious young man, of excellent character, much respected in the town, clerk of the Assembly, and a pretty poet. Keimer made verses too, but very indifferently. He could not be said to write them, for his manner was to compose them in the types directly out of his head. So there being no copy, but one pair of cases, and the elegy likely to require all the

---

[20] deceiver

[21] beginner, inexperienced person

[22] an assortment of printing type all one size and style

[23] a poem written in honor of someone who has died

letter, no one could help him. I endeavored to put his press (which he had not yet used, and of which he understood nothing) into order fit to be worked with; and, promising to come and print off his elegy as soon as he should have got it ready, I returned to Bradford's, who gave me a little job to do for the present, and there I lodged and dieted. A few days after, Keimer sent for me to print off the elegy. And now he had got another pair of cases, and a pamphlet to reprint, on which he set me to work.

These two printers I found poorly qualified for their business. Bradford had not been bred to it, and was very illiterate; and Keimer, though something of a scholar, was a mere compositor, knowing nothing of presswork.[24] He had been one of the French prophets,[25] and could act their enthusiastic agitations. At this time he did not profess any particular religion, but something of all on occasion; was very ignorant of the world, and had, as I afterward found, a good deal of the knave in his composition. He did not like my lodging at Bradford's while I worked with him. He had a house, indeed, but without furniture, so he could not lodge me; but he got me a lodging at Mr. Read's, before mentioned, who was the owner of his house; and, my chest and clothes being come by this time, I made rather a more respectable appearance in the eyes of Miss Read than I had done when she first happened to see me eating my roll in the street.

---

[24] one who knows how to set type but does not know how to operate the printing press

[25] a group of religious zealots in London in the early 1700s; members preached the end of the world, spoke in tongues, and had fainting fits; The group was outlawed in England in 1709, but stories of its excesses and emotionalism circulated in the colonies.

REVIEWING AND INTERPRETING

Record your answers to these questions in your personal literature notebook. Follow the directions for each part.

REVIEWING

Try to complete each of these sentences without looking back at the selection.

Recalling Facts

1. When Benjamin Franklin's future wife first saw him, he was
   a. stepping off a ferry boat.
   b. calling on her father.
   c. carrying a puffy roll under each arm.
   d. running his own printing shop.

Understanding Main Ideas

2. Benjamin Franklin left Boston to
   a. see what the other colonies were like.
   b. find work in his trade.
   c. achieve his dream of going to sea.
   d. learn a trade.

Identifying Sequence

3. Which of the following events happened last?
   a. Franklin arrived in Philadelphia.
   b. Franklin's brother was arrested.
   c. Franklin began to work for the printer Keimer.
   d. Franklin was seen by his future wife.

Getting Meaning from Context

4. "He had been, I imagine, an itinerant doctor, for there was no town in England or country in Europe of which he could not give a very particular account." In this context itinerant means
   a. traveling.
   b. wealthy.
   c. bad.
   d. unhappy.

Finding Supporting Details

5. An example of Benjamin Franklin's generosity was that he
a. gave away two rolls he had bought.
b. sold his books at a loss.
c. printed the Aquila Rose elegy for Keimer.
d. wrote articles for his brother's newspaper.

INTERPRETING To complete these items, you may look back at the selection if you'd like.

Making Inferences

6. What inference can you make about newspapers in the colonies at the time Franklin was an apprentice printer?
a. There were no newspapers in the colonies.
b. Printing presses were controlled directly by the British government.
c. Only Boston and Philadelphia had newspapers.
d. Freedom of the press was not a guaranteed right.

Generalizing

7. Benjamin Franklin traveled from Boston to Philadelphia mostly by
a. horse.
b. boat.
c. foot.
d. train.

Identifying Cause and Effect

8. Benjamin Franklin took a job with Keimer because
a. Keimer was the only printer in Philadelphia.
b. his brother liked Keimer.
c. Keimer was the only printer who had work for him to do.
d. Keimer was the best printer in town.

Drawing Conclusions

9. Even though Franklin did not always agree with his brother, he resented James's imprisonment because Benjamin
a. had to do more work.
b. did not get paid while James was in prison.
c. disliked the injustice of the Assembly's action.
d. was blamed for getting his brother into trouble.

Recognizing Fact and
Opinion

10. On the basis of the excerpt, which of the following statements is an opinion?
   a. James Franklin owned the second newspaper in the colonies.
   b. Keimer owned an old, shattered press.
   c. On his trip to Philadelphia, Benjamin Franklin saved a man's life.
   d. Benjamin Franklin was a proud, rebellious young man.

Now check your answers with your teacher. Study the items you answered incorrectly. What skills were they checking? Talk to your teacher about ways to work on those skills.

Author's Viewpoint

You learned in Unit 5 that an *autobiography* is the story of a real person's life written by that person. People usually have one or more reasons for writing their autobiographies. They may want to explain how they reached a certain position in life or why they were successful. They may want to share their ideas with others, ensure themselves a place in history, or justify their actions.

Benjamin Franklin did not write his autobiography to boast about his many achievements. His purpose in writing it was largely instructive. Franklin had educated himself through reading and study and he had learned important lessons from the experiences life provided him. He hoped that by writing his autobiography he could pass on what he had learned to others.

Franklin began writing the story of his life in 1771, when he was 65 years old. He addressed the book to his 41-year-old son William. Franklin began his *Autobiography* by saying that he had always been interested in obtaining information about his ancestors, and he imagined that his children might be interested in their father's life.

In the *Autobiography* Franklin described both his successes and what he called his *errata*, a Latin word meaning errors. Even though Franklin's stated purpose was to leave an account of his life for his family, you can assume that he also knew that a far larger audience would read his words. By the early 1770s, Franklin was well known in the colonies and in Europe. Whatever he wrote was of interest to many people.

Because the author of an autobiography is writing about him- or herself, the author's viewpoint has a major affect on what the author tells you and how he or she tells it to you. *Viewpoint* refers to the feelings, opinions, and experiences that affect a writer's outlook on life. Viewpoint affects not only how the writer understands the facts he or she presents to you but also which facts he or she includes in a piece of writing. Two people can interpret the same facts or experiences in very different ways. For example, a person who is not confident might interpret a public speaking assignment as a very threatening situation. Someone who is self-confident might interpret the same assignment as an exciting challenge. In talking to you about the assignment, the first person would probably focus on such things as the size of the audience, forgetting his or her notes, or mispronouncing words. The second person would probably tell you about what a great opportunity this was to present his or her ideas and opinions to many people at once. The situation would be the same for these two people, but their viewpoints could not be more different.

When you read nonfiction—and especially autobiography—it is important for you to be aware that all the facts and opinions you are reading are an expression of the writer's own individual perspective. When you read an autobiography, you might expect it to contain the complete truth about the writer's life. After all, who knows more about the life than the person who lived it? Yet an autobiography seldom reveals everything about the writer's life. For example, a writer might leave out incidents that would reveal unflattering information. Even writers who try to tell the whole truth see reality from their own particular viewpoints.

In his *Autobiography*, Benjamin Franklin wanted to reveal his mistakes as well as his accomplishments. He tried to give a balanced account of his life. Still, he did not have room to include everything that happened to him. The events he did choose to describe are told from his own viewpoint. In this lesson you will examine the ways in which viewpoint affected Franklin's *Autobiography*.

Many factors contribute to an author's viewpoint and, in turn, affect what he or she says to you and how he or she says it. In this unit we will talk about three of these elements:

1. **Viewpoint and Frame of Reference**.   Writers are affected by the social and historical conditions that surround them. These environmental factors determine the kind of experiences a writer has and how he or she thinks or feels about those experiences. In other words, they determine a writer's frame of reference.

2. **Viewpoint and Age.** A writer's age has a major affect on his or her writing. A young child or a teenager sees and thinks differently from the way an adult or an elderly person does. The older a writer is, the more knowledge and experiences he or she has to affect what he or she has to say.

3. **Viewpoint and Personal Values.** A writer's beliefs and opinions affect what he or she writes. Everyone has some religious and moral or ethical beliefs that affect his or her viewpoint. An individual also has opinions about the relative importance of various aspects of his or her of life—work, play, family life, money, social and political activities, and so forth. These values also affect a writer's viewpoint.

LESSON 1 — VIEWPOINT AND FRAME OF REFERENCE

Like everyone else, writers are affected by the times in which they live. *Frame of reference* refers to the social and historical conditions in which a writer lives. Every writer is influenced by the attitudes and outlook of the society and the historical period in which he or she lives. Some authors may criticize or reject these attitudes. Others may strongly agree with and support these attitudes. Some authors may not even consciously think about these attitudes either way; all the same, they are affected by them. Every writer's frame of reference influences his or her viewpoint in some way.

Benjamin Franklin was born in Boston in 1706, less than 100 years after the first English colonists had settled there. Boston was the largest city in the Massachusetts Bay Colony, one of the 13 American colonies ruled by Britain. Massachusetts was founded by Puritans, whose strong religious beliefs ruled their daily lives. As a boy growing up in Boston, Franklin was aware of the power wielded by the leaders of the Puritan movement. A second important factor in understanding Franklin's frame of reference is the attitude during this time toward school and work. Unless they belonged to the wealthy upper classes, boys and girls finished their education and began working to earn a living usually by the time they were 10. Frequently, they were indentured as servants or apprentices, just as young Franklin had been. A third important factor influencing Franklin's frame of reference in "Adventures of a Young Printer" is transportation. As you have seen in Franklin's description of his journey to Philadelphia, in the early 1700s transportation in the colonies was still relatively dangerous and primitive. Franklin's journey to Philadelphia represented a new beginning and a major break with his past—psychologically and emotionally he was a long way from home.

As you read the following passage, think about how young Franklin's frame of reference is reflected in the experiences he describes.

> Though a brother, he considered himself as my master, and me as his apprentice, and accordingly expected the same services from me as he would from another, while I thought he demeaned me too much in some he required of me, who from a brother expected more indulgence. Our disputes were often brought before our father, and I fancy I was either generally in the right, or else a better pleader, because the judgment was generally in my favor. But my brother was passionate, and had often beaten me, which I took extremely amiss; and, thinking my apprenticeship very tedious, I was continually wishing for some opportunity of shortening it, which at length offered in a manner unexpected.

This passage comes immediately after Franklin's description of how he anonymously published several articles in his brother's newspaper and is praised for their quality. Young Benjamin feels that his brother should give him special treatment because of his talent and because they are brothers. These feelings conflict with Ben's humble (and legal) position as his brother's indentured apprentice, and he objects, but he does not complain that the idea of being indentured itself is bad. Indenturing is part of the social situation in which Franklin lives, and he reluctantly accepts it.

EXERCISE ⟨1⟩

Read this passage in which Benjamin describes making plans to leave his brother. Use what you have learned in this lesson to answer the questions that follow it..

> During my brother's confinement, which I resented a good deal, notwithstanding our private differences, I had the management of the paper; and I made bold to give our rulers some rubs in it, which my brother took very kindly, while others began to consider me in an unfavorable light, as a young genius that had a turn for libeling and satire. My brother's discharge was accompanied with an order of the House (a very odd one), that "James Franklin should no longer print the paper called the *New England Courant* ."

1. Franklin says that he "resented a good deal" his brother's confinement. What does this tell you about his attitude toward his brother's arrest and imprisonment?

2. What do you think Franklin's own opinion was about the fact that others began to consider him in "an unfavorable light?"

Now check your answers with your teacher. Review this lesson if you don't understand why an answer was incorrect.

WRITING ON YOUR OWN ⟨1⟩

In this exercise you will use what you learned in this lesson to rewrite and expand your description of a childhood experience so that it reflects your frame of reference at the time the event happened. Follow these steps:

- Reread the description of your childhood experience that you wrote for Writing: Expressing Your Viewpoint.
- Try to recall as much as you can about your attitudes and feelings at the time the experience happened. Write down several sentences that express how you felt as these events were happening. For example, if you were describing your first day at kindergarten, you might write, *I was very worried about being away from my mother for an entire day. I hid in a corner and cried for the first hour. When I finally noticed all the drawing materials in the classroom art corner, I couldn't wait to try the fingerpaints. At lunch time I was too excited to eat.*
- Rewrite and expand the paragraph you wrote for Writing: Expressing Your Viewpoint to include your feelings about the experience as it happened.

LESSON 2 — VIEWPOINT AND AGE

Although Benjamin Franklin was writing about the experiences in this selection nearly 50 years after they happened, at some points his narrative reflects his viewpoint of the events as they happened at the time—he tells you what he thought and felt as the experiences happened. When Franklin wrote his autobiography, however, he was 65. He had been a successful businessman, scientist, and statesman for many years. As he was writing, he was also seeing things from the viewpoint of a mature, older man reflecting on a long, eventful life.

You can see both of Franklin's viewpoints at work near the beginning of "Adventures of a Young Printer," when he describes the reaction of his brother's friends to the first anonymous article he submitted to his brother's newspaper.

They read it, commented on it in my hearing, and I had the exquisite pleasure of finding it met with their approbation, and that, in their different guesses at the author, none were named but men of some character among us for learning and ingenuity. I suppose now that I was rather lucky in my judges, and that perhaps they were not really so very good ones as I then esteemed them.

Franklin describes the "exquisite pleasure" he felt at the time when he heard his writing praised. From the viewpoint of the age at which he is writing about the experience, however, he recognizes that his work was not so praiseworthy after all and that his brother's friends were not really as "learned" or "ingenious" as he thought they were at the time.

The age of a writer often affects what he or she chooses to include in an autobiography. For example, when remembering his successful life, Franklin could afford to admit some of his youthful mistakes. He knows that his reputation is securely established and can not be harmed by such admissions. A newly famous person might not feel so secure about his or her position as Franklin does, and that person might not want to admit having made mistakes. Looking back after 50 years, for example, Franklin is comfortable about admitting that he took advantage of the secrecy of his indenture papers to leave his brother. He is even prepared to reconsider and revise his earlier description of his brother's poor treatment of him.

EXERCISE ⟨2⟩

Read this passage from the selection. Use what you have learned in this lesson to answer the questions that follow it.

> I have been the more particular in this description of my journey, and shall be so of my first entry into that city, that you may in your mind compare such unlikely beginnings with the figure I have since made there. I was in my working dress, my best clothes being to come round by sea. I was dirty from my journey; my pockets were stuffed out with shirts and stockings; I knew no soul nor where to look for lodging. I was fatigued with traveling, rowing, and want of rest; I was

very hungry; and my whole stock of cash consisted of a Dutch dollar and about a shilling in copper. The latter I gave the people of the boat for my passage, who at first refused it, on account of my rowing; but I insisted on their taking it, a man being sometimes more generous when he has but a little money than when he has plenty, perhaps through fear of being thought to have but little.

1. As an old man writing about his entry into Philadelphia, Franklin refers to his "unlikely beginnings." Do you think he saw himself in the same way at that time?

2. Do you think the last sentence of this passage reflects Benjamin Franklin's viewpoint as a young man, or is it his later interpretation of his actions when he was writing about the experience?

Now check your answers with your teacher. Review this lesson if you don't understand why an answer was incorrect.

 WRITING ON YOUR OWN

In this exercise you will use what you learned in this lesson to rewrite and expand your description of a childhood experience by expressing how your viewpoint has changed as you have grown older. Follow these steps:

- Reread the description of your experience that you wrote for Writing on Your Own 1.
- Imagine yourself as you are today, observing your younger self and the events as they happened. Write down several sentences that express your thoughts as you watch this experience unfold from your present perspective. If you are describing your first day at kindergarten, for example, you might write, *I realize now that my mother was probably more upset about leaving me at the classroom door than I was*

about leaving her. Looking back, I realize how cleverly the teacher coaxed me out of my tears by directing my attention to the art supplies.

• Expand and rewrite your description from Writing on Your Own 1 to include your present viewpoint of yourself and this experience from your past. If you have not done so already, you will probably need to divide your description into more than one paragraph at this point.

LESSON 3 VIEWPOINT AND PERSONAL VALUES

Personal values are the things that an individual person considers most important in life. What a person considers to be a part of his or her values varies from person to one another. Personal values often include issues such as religious, moral, or ethical beliefs. Values can also include opinions or beliefs about social, political, or economic relationships between people. One person may consider ecological awareness an important personal value, while another may put personal financial success or security for his or her family ahead of a concern for others or the environment.

Whatever a writer's personal values are, they have a major affect on the style and content of what he or she writes. As you can tell from this selection, Benjamin Franklin's earliest years in Boston were spent in a highly religious, politically repressive environment. While he was still in Boston, he recognized his own intelligence and talent, and he was determined to make something of himself. When Franklin left Boston for Philadelphia, he carried some of the values he had learned with him. He was also seeking a place where he could live according to other, equally important values, which had brought him into conflict with the political and religious leaders in Boston. For example, he was looking for greater personal freedom and tolerance.

Read the following passage in which Franklin describes his

meeting with Dr. Brown while he was traveling to Philadelphia. Think about what it tells you about the author's personal values.

> Our acquaintance continued as long as he lived. He had been, I imagine, an itinerant doctor, for there was no town in England or country in Europe of which he could not give a very particular account. He had some letters, and was ingenious, but much of an unbeliever, and wickedly undertook some years after to travesty the Bible in doggerel verse, as Cotton had done Virgil. By this means he set many of the facts in a very ridiculous light, and might have hurt weak minds if his work had been published; but it never was.

Earlier Franklin had written that some people in Boston thought he was an infidel or an atheist. In this passage he suggests that while he may have slightly unusual religious opinions or beliefs, he still thinks of the Bible as something that should not be made fun of. You should notice also that he refers to the "facts" in the Bible, implying that he sees it as a document that gives accurate factual information.

EXERCISE ⟨3⟩

Read this passage from the selection. Use what you have learned in this lesson to answer the questions that follow it.

> He asked me a few questions, put a composing stick in my hand to see how I worked, and then said he would employ me soon, though he had just then nothing for me to do; and, taking old Bradford, whom he had never seen before, to be one of the town's people that had a good will for him, entered into a conversation on his present undertaking and prospects; while Bradford, not discovering that he was the other printer's father, on Keimer's saying he expected soon to get the greatest part of the business into his own hands, drew

him on by artful questions, and starting little doubts, to explain all his views, what interest he relied on, and in what manner he intended to proceed. I who stood by and heard all, saw immediately that one of them was a crafty old sophister, and the other a mere novice. Bradford left me with Keimer, who was greatly surprised when I told him who the old man was.

1. What does this passage imply about Benjamin Franklin's values or beliefs?

2. Do you think Franklin would have revealed to Keimer how Mr. Bradford had tricked him if Keimer had not already said he would give Franklin a job?

Now check your answers with your teacher. Review this lesson if you don't understand why an answer is incorrect.

 WRITING ON YOUR OWN

In this exercise you will use what you learned in this lesson to rewrite and expand your description of a childhood experience by showing how this experience has affected your personal values. Follow these steps:

• Reread the description of your childhood experience that you wrote for Writing on Your Own 2.
• Think for a few moments about the reasons that you chose this particular experience to write about. Make notes about your reasons: Ask yourself why this experience has remained in your memory. What made it a significant experience for you? Did it teach you a lesson that you have always remembered? Did it change something important in the way you see life or in the way you see yourself?
• Expand and rewrite your paragraphs from Writing on Your Own 2 to include your reflections on how this experience

affected you or changed you in some way. If you are writing about your first experience in kindergarten, for example, you might say that you think your interest in expressing your feelings through painting began then. Or you might say that it was your kindergarten teacher's kindness and sympathy that started you thinking that someday you might want to be a teacher.

DISCUSSION GUIDES

1. With a partner, discuss why James Franklin discharged Ben's first indenture papers. Do you think he took advantage of Ben by writing new indenture papers that were to be kept secret? Do you think Ben was fair to his brother later on when he took advantage of the secrecy of the papers to leave for Philadelphia? Share your opinions with your class.

2. In "Adventures of a Young Printer," Ben Franklin describes his impressions of the printer Keimer, his first employer in Philadelphia. With a partner discuss what kind of relationship you think developed between Franklin and Keimer. What details support your opinion? Share your predictions with the class.

3. According to Ben Franklin, his brother James felt that Ben should be treated like any other apprentice. Ben thought, however, that his brother should be more indulgent toward him because of their family connection. Organize a class debate in which one group supports Ben's position and the other supports James's view.

WRITE AN ESSAY EXPRESSING YOUR VIEWPOINT

In this unit you have learned how a writer's viewpoint is influenced by his or her frame of reference, age, and personal values. Now you will use what you have learned to write a brief essay reflecting on how a childhood experience affected your present viewpoint about yourself or the world around you.

Follow these steps to complete your essay. If you have any questions about the writing process, refer to Using the Writing Process (page 250).

- Gather and review the following pieces of writing you did for this unit: 1) the graphic organizer from Writing: Expressing Your Viewpoint; 2) paragaphs expressing how you felt; 3) paragraphs written from your present perspective; and 4) paragraphs including your personal reflections.
- Now you will write a brief essay about how a childhood experience is reflected in your present viewpoint of the world.
- Begin by writing an introductory paragraph that describes part of your present viewpoint—an attitude, a belief, or a value that is an important part of the person you are today.
- Next develop the body of your essay. Show how this early experience led to your present viewpoint. If there are descriptive details in your graphic organizer that you have not included yet, try to work them into the essay now. If more supporting details come to mind as you are writing, add them as well.
- Finally, write a conclusion for your essay. You may restate the main idea of the essay—how this experience changed your viewpoint—or you may end by speculating how your present viewpoint could be altered by future experiences.
- Proofread your essay for errors in spelling, grammar, punctuation, and capitalization. Make a final copy and save it in your writing portfolio. You may wish to put a copy of your essay away for rereading several years from now. It might be interesting to see whether your viewpoint changed during that time.
- Share your essay with the class, if you wish.

UNIT 7

Persuasion

Letter from Birmingham Jail

◆

by Martin Luther King, Jr.

INTRODUCTION

BUILDING BACKGROUND

Martin Luther King, Jr., opposed established racist policies through nonviolent forms of protest and campaigned tirelessly for civil rights for every citizen of the United States.

In January 1963, the Reverend Martin Luther King, Jr., traveled to Birmingham, Alabama. He was the head of the Southern Christian Leadership Conference (SCLC), the largest civil rights action group in the South. King and his staff had come to lead black citizens in protests against what he called "the most thoroughly segregated city in the country." King's plan was to use boycotts and sit-ins to put pressure on the city's merchants, who would in turn put pressure on city officials to desegregate all the city's public facilities. The SCLC published and distributed a pamphlet listing the demonstrators' demands: All lunch counters, restrooms, and drinking fountains in department and variety stores must be desegregated. African Americans must be hired in local businesses and industry. A biracial committee must be established to work out a schedule for desegregation in other areas of city life.

Groups of black citizens began sit-ins at area department stores, demanding service. As soon as they were arrested and taken away to jail, others took their places. The City of Birmingham responded to these actions by obtaining a court injunction that barred King and his associates from conducting further public demonstrations. King immediately held a press conference and announced that he would go to jail himself rather than stop the demonstrations. King led a parade of 50 volunteers through downtown Birmingham. He and his group were immediately arrested and jailed for disobeying the court's injunction.

While King was in the Birmingham jail, a statement appeared in the Birmingham *News* to the effect that the protesters' actions were "unwise and untimely" and that they were being led by "outsiders." The statement went on to praise the Birmingham police for their "restraint" in dealing with the lawbreakers, and it urged black citizens of Birmingham not to participate in the disturbances. It was signed by eight prominent local clergymen, all of them white.

Deeply upset by this attack from those he thought should most understand and support his motives, King began writing a response to these critics. Using a pen smuggled to him by one of his lawyers, he wrote at first on the margins of the newspaper in which the statement appeared. He continued the letter on scraps of toilet paper and then on some writing paper given to him by another prisoner. King's calm, reasonable defense of himself and his movement has become a classic document, as important as his famous "I Have A Dream" speech.

ABOUT THE AUTHOR

Martin Luther King, Jr., won the Nobel Prize for Peace in 1964 for his nonviolent struggle against racial oppression. King was born in 1929. The son, grandson, and great-grandson of Baptist ministers, he entered the clergy himself in 1954. He had been at his first job as pastor of the Dexter Avenue Baptist Church in Montgomery, Alabama, for less than a year when he was thrust into national attention by his leadership of the Montgomery bus boycott. He was only 26 years old at the time. For the next 13 years, King was almost continually in the public eye, leading the fight to achieve legal, social, and economic equality for African

Americans. On April 4, 1968, King was assassinated in Memphis, Tennessee, where he had gone to support a strike by the city's black sanitation workers.

ABOUT THE LESSONS

The lessons that follow "Letter from Birmingham Jail" focus on the techniques writers use to persuade their audience to accept a particular course of action or way of thinking about something. "Letter from Birmingham Jail" is an essay in the form of an open letter. An *open letter* is written directly to a particular recipient, but it is also printed or published so that it can be read by a much larger audience. By using the open-letter technique, a writer can make a statement or present an argument to a particular person or group, and at the same time can attempt to gain support for his or her argument from the readers who make up the larger audience.

In his open letter King wants to persuade his readers of the rightness of his actions. One way a writer persuades you of something is to present relevant supporting information and strong, logical reasons for his or her actions or opinions. Another method of persuasion is to appeal to your emotions. King very effectively uses both kinds of appeal in his essay: he offers rational arguments, *and* he appeals to your emotions.

WRITING: DEVELOPING A PERSUASIVE ARGUMENT

At the end of this unit, you will write a persuasive essay. The suggestions below will help you get started:

- Imagine that an international corporation has announced plans to build a giant amusement park on an abandoned military airfield near the small town where you live. Think about the possible positive and negative effects that might come from this development.

- Make a list of all the possible effects of the amusement park on your life and the lives of your friends and family, on jobs, on local businesses, and on the general quality of life where you live. Think about the many ways that the park would change things where you live. After considering all the effects, decide whether you are in favor of the amusement park or opposed to it.
- Write down who your readers will be. Will you write an open letter to the editor of the local newspaper? Will you write to the specific group that wants to build the park? What can you say to persuade these readers to agree with you about the amusement park?

AS YOU READ

Think about the following questions as you read King's letter. They will help you will see how King appeals to his readers' reason and their emotions in trying to gain their support for his actions and beliefs.

- How does King describe the clergymen in the beginning of his letter. How does he describe himself?
- What arguments does King offer to show the clergymen that they are mistaken?
- What words and phrases does King use to appeal to his readers' emotions?

You will note that there is a numeral at the beginning of each paragraph of King's letter. The numerals will help you locate specific paragraphs in the letter when you need to do so.

Letter from Birmingham Jail

◆

by Martin Luther King, Jr.

April 16, 1963

My Dear Fellow Clergymen:

1   While confined here in the Birmingham city jail, I came across your recent statement calling my present activities "unwise and untimely." Seldom do I pause to answer criticism of my work and ideas. If I sought to answer all the criticisms that cross my desk, my secretaries would have little time for anything other than such correspondence in the course of the day, and I would have no time for constructive work. But since I feel that you are men of genuine good will and that your criticisms are sincerely set forth, I want to try to answer your statement in what I hope will be patient and reasonable terms.

2   I think I should indicate why I am here in Birmingham, since you have been influenced by the view which argues against "outsiders coming in." I have the honor of serving as president of the Southern Christian Leadership Conference, an organization operating in every southern state, with headquarters in Atlanta, Georgia. We have some eighty-five affiliated organizations across the South, and one of them is the Alabama Christian Movement for Human Rights. Frequently we share staff, educational and financial resources with our affiliates. Several months ago the affiliate here in Birmingham asked us to be on call to engage in a nonviolent direct-action program if

such were deemed necessary. We readily consented, and when the hour came we lived up to our promise. So I, along with several members of my staff, am here because I was invited here. I am here because I have organizational ties here.

3   But more basically, I am in Birmingham because injustice is here. Just as the prophets of the eighth century B.C. left their villages and carried their "thus saith the Lord" far beyond the boundaries of their home towns, and, just as the Apostle Paul left his village of Tarsus and carried the gospel of Jesus Christ to the far corners of the Greco-Roman world, so am I compelled to carry the gospel of freedom beyond my own home town. Like Paul, I must constantly respond to the Macedonian[1] call for aid.

4   Moreover, I am cognizant[2] of the interrelatedness of all communities and states. I cannot sit idly by in Atlanta and not be concerned about what happens in Birmingham. Injustice anywhere is a threat to justice everywhere. We are caught in an inescapable network of mutuality, tied in a single garment of destiny. Whatever affects one directly, affects all indirectly. Never again can we afford to live with the narrow, provincial "outside agitator" idea. Anyone who lives inside the United States can never be considered an outsider anywhere within its bounds.

5   You deplore the demonstrations taking place in Birmingham. But your statement, I am sorry to say, fails to express a similar concern for the conditions that brought about the demonstrations. I am sure that none of you would want to rest content with the superficial kind of social analysis that deals merely with effects and does not grapple with underlying causes. It is unfortunate that demonstrations are taking place in Birmingham, but it is even more unfortunate that the city's white power structure left the Negro community with no alternative.

---

[1] St. Paul is credited in the Bible with converting the land of Macedonia from paganism to Christianity.

[2] fully informed; aware

6   In any nonviolent campaign there are four basic steps: collection of the facts to determine whether injustices exist; negotiation; self-purification; and direct action. We have gone through all these steps in Birmingham. There can be no gainsaying[3] the fact that racial injustice engulfs this community. Birmingham is probably the most thoroughly segregated city in the United States. An ugly record of brutality is widely known. Negroes have experienced grossly unjust treatment in the courts. There have been more unsolved bombings of Negro homes and churches in Birmingham than in any other city in the nation. These are the hard brutal facts of the case. On the basis of these conditions, Negro leaders sought to negotiate with the city fathers. But the latter consistently refused to engage in good-faith negotiation.

7   Then, last September, came the opportunity to talk with leaders of Birmingham's economic community. In the course of the negotiations, certain promises were made by the merchants—for example, to remove the stores' humiliating racial signs. On the basis of these promises, the Reverend Fred Shuttlesworth and the leaders of the Alabama Christian Movement for Human Rights agreed to a moratorium on all demonstrations. As the weeks and months went by, we realized that we were the victims of a broken promise. A few signs, briefly removed, returned; the others remained.

8   As in so many past experiences, our hopes had been blasted, and the shadow of deep disappointment settled upon us. We had no alternative except to prepare for direct action, whereby we would present our very bodies as a means of laying our case before the conscience of the local and the national community. Mindful of the difficulties involved, we decided to undertake a process of self-purification. We began a series of workshops on nonviolence, and we repeatedly asked ourselves: "Are you able to accept blows without retaliating?" "Are you able to endure the ordeal of jail?" We decided to schedule our direct-action program for the Easter season, realizing that except for

[3] denying; describing as false

Christmas, this is the main shopping period of the year. Knowing that a strong economic-withdrawal program would be the by-product of direct action, we felt that this would be the best time to bring pressure to bear on the merchants for the needed change.

9   Then it occurred to us that Birmingham's mayoralty election was coming up in March, and we speedily decided to postpone action until after election day. When we discovered that the Commissioner of Public Safety, Eugene "Bull" Connor,[4] had piled up enough votes to be in the run-off, we decided again to postpone action until the day after the run-off so that the demonstrations could not be used to cloud the issues. Like many others, we waited to see Mr. Connor defeated, and to this end we endured postponement after postponement. Having aided in this community need, we felt that our direct-action program could be delayed no longer.

10   You may well ask: "Why direct action? Why sit-ins, marches and so forth? Isn't negotiation a better path?" You are quite right in calling for negotiation. Indeed, this is the very purpose of direct action. Nonviolent direct action seeks to create such a crisis and foster such a tension that a community which has constantly refused to negotiate is forced to confront the issue. It seeks so to dramatize the issue that it can no longer be ignored. My citing the creation of tension as part of the work of the non-violent-resister may sound rather shocking. But I must confess that I am not afraid of the word "tension." I have earnestly opposed violent tension, but there is a type of nonviolent ten-sion which is necessary for growth. Just as Socrates[5] felt that it was necessary to create a tension in the mind so that individuals could rise from the bondage of myths and half-truths to the unfettered[6] realm of creative analysis and objective appraisal, so

---

[4] police chief in Birmingham who attracted national attention when newspapers and television showed him leading his police force in attacking unarmed black protesters with clubs and dogs.

[5] one of the best known and widely read ancient Greek philosophers

[6] unrestrained

must we see the need for nonviolent gadflies[7] to create the kind of tension in society that will help men rise from the dark depths of prejudice and racism to the majestic heights of understanding and brotherhood.

11   The purpose of our direct-action program is to create a situation so crisis-packed that it will inevitably open the door to negotiation. I therefore concur with you in your call for negotiation. Too long has our beloved Southland been bogged down in a tragic effort to live in monologue rather than dialogue.

12   One of the basic points in your statement is that the action that I and my associates have taken in Birmingham is untimely. Some have asked: "Why didn't you give the new city administration time to act?" The only answer that I can give to this query is that the new Birmingham administration must be prodded about as much as the outgoing one, before it will act. We are sadly mistaken if we feel that the election of Albert Boutwell as mayor will bring the millennium[8] to Birmingham. While Mr. Boutwell is a much more gentle person than Mr. Connor, they are both segregationists, dedicated to maintenance of the status quo. I have hope that Mr. Boutwell will be reasonable enough to see the futility of massive resistance to desegregation. But he will not see this without pressure from devotees of civil rights. My friends, I must say to you that we have not made a single gain in civil rights without determined legal and nonviolent pressure. Lamentably, it is an historical fact that privileged groups seldom give up their privileges voluntarily. Individuals may see the moral light and voluntarily give up their unjust posture; but, as Reinhold Niebuhr[9] has reminded us, groups tend to be more immoral than individuals.

13   We know through painful experience that freedom is never voluntarily given by the oppressor; it must be demanded by the oppressed. Frankly, I have yet to engage in a direct-action

---

[7] people who engage in constant, provocative criticism

[8] a thousand-year period described in the Bible during which Christ will rule the world

[9] an important modern Christian theologian (1892–1971)

campaign that was "well-timed" in the view of those who have
not suffered unduly from the disease of segregation. For years
now I have heard the word "Wait!" It rings in the ear of every
Negro with piercing familiarity. This "Wait" has almost always
meant "Never." We must come to see, with one of our distinguished jurists, that "justice too long delayed is justice denied."

14   We have waited for more than 340 years for our constitutional and Godgiven rights. The nations of Asia and Africa are
moving with jetlike speed toward gaining political independence, but we still creep at horse-and-buggy pace toward gaining
a cup of coffee at a lunch counter. Perhaps it is easy for those
who have never felt the stinging darts of segregation to say,
"Wait." But when you have seen vicious mobs lynch your mothers and fathers at will and drown your sisters and brothers at
whim; when you have seen hate-filled policemen curse, kick and
even kill your black brothers and sisters; when you see the vast
majority of your twenty million Negro brothers smothering in
an airtight cage of poverty in the midst of an affluent society;
when you suddenly find your tongue twisted and your speech
stammering as you seek to explain to your six-year-old daughter
why she can't go to the public amusement park that has just
been advertised on television, and see tears welling up in her
eyes when she is told that Funtown is closed to colored children,
and see ominous clouds of inferiority beginning to form in her
little mental sky, and see her beginning to distort her personality
by developing an unconscious bitterness toward white people;
when you have to concoct[10] an answer for a five-year-old son
who is asking: "Daddy, why do white people treat colored people
so mean?"; when you take a cross-country drive and find it necessary to sleep night after night in the uncomfortable corners of
your automobile because no motel will accept you; when you are
humiliated day in and day out by nagging signs reading "white"
and "colored"; when your first name becomes "nigger," your
middle name becomes "boy" (however old you are) and your last
name becomes "John," and your wife and mother are never

_____

[10] to make up

given the respected title "Mrs."; when you are harried by day and haunted by night by the fact that you are a Negro, living constantly at tiptoe stance, never quite knowing what to expect next, and are plagued with inner fears and outer resentments; when you are forever fighting a degenerating sense of "nobodiness"—then you will understand why we find it difficult to wait. There comes a time when the cup of endurance runs over, and men are no longer willing to be plunged into the abyss of despair. I hope, sirs, you can understand our legitimate and unavoidable impatience.

15   You express a great deal of anxiety over our willingness to break laws. This is certainly a legitimate concern. Since we so diligently urge people to obey the Supreme Court's decision of 1954 outlawing segregation in the public schools, at first glance it may seem rather paradoxical for us consciously to break laws. One may well ask: "How can you advocate breaking some laws and obeying others?" The answer lies in the fact that there are two types of laws: just and unjust. I would be the first to advocate obeying just laws. One has not only a legal but a moral responsibility to obey just laws. Conversely,[11] one has a moral responsibility to disobey unjust laws. I would agree with St. Augustine[12] that "an unjust law is no law at all."

16   Now, what is the difference between the two? How does one determine whether a law is just or unjust? A just law is a man-made code that squares with the moral law or the law of God. An unjust law is a code that is out of harmony with the moral law. To put it in the terms of St. Thomas Aquinas:[13] An unjust law is a human law that is not rooted in eternal law and natural law. Any law that uplifts human personality is just. Any law that degrades human personality is unjust. All segregation statutes are unjust because segregation distorts the soul and damages the personality. It gives the segregator a false sense of

---

[11] reversed in position; opposite

[12] the religious and philosophical writings of St. Augustine (354–430) form the basis of both Catholic and Protestant teaching

[13] noted Italian philosopher and Dominican friar (c. 1225–1274)

superiority and the segregated a false sense of inferiority. Segregation, to use the terminology of the Jewish philosopher Martin Buber,[14] substitutes an "I-it" relationship for an "I-thou" relationship and ends up relegating persons to the status of things. Hence segregation is not only politically, economically and sociologically unsound, it is morally wrong and sinful. Paul Tillich[15] has said that sin is separation. Is not segregation an existential[16] expression of man's tragic separation, his awful estrangement,[17] his terrible sinfulness? Thus it is that I can urge men to obey the 1954 decision of the Supreme Court, for it is morally right; and I can urge them to disobey segregation ordinances, for they are morally wrong.

17   Let us consider a more concrete example of just and unjust laws. An unjust law is a code that a numerical or power majority group compels a minority group to obey but does not make binding on itself. This is *difference* made legal. By the same token, a just law is a code that a majority compels a minority to follow and that it is willing to follow itself. This is *sameness* made legal.

18   Let me give another explanation. A law is unjust if it is inflicted on a minority, that, as a result of being denied the right to vote, had no part in enacting or devising the law. Who can say that the legislature of Alabama which set up that state's segregation laws was democratically elected? Throughout Alabama all sorts of devious methods are used to prevent Negroes from becoming registered voters, and there are some counties in which even though Negroes constitute a majority of the population, not a single Negro is registered. Can any law enacted under such circumstances be considered democratically structured?

19   Sometimes a law is just on its face and unjust in its application. For instance, I have been arrested on a charge of parading without a permit. Now, there is nothing wrong in having an

---

[14] a Jewish philosopher and educator (1878–1965) widely regarded as one of the great thinkers of the 20th century

[15] a prominent Protestant theologian (1886–1965)

[16] referring to existence or the real world

[17] distance or removal from someone or something

ordinance which requires a permit for a parade. But such an ordinance becomes unjust when it is used to maintain segregation and to deny citizens the First-Amendment privilege of peaceful assembly and protest.

20   I hope you are able to see the distinction I am trying to point out. In no sense do I advocate evading or defying the law, as would the rabid segregationist. That would lead to anarchy.[18] One who breaks an unjust law must do so openly, lovingly, and with a willingness to accept the penalty. I submit that an individual who breaks a law that conscience tells him is unjust, and who willingly accepts the penalty of imprisonment in order to arouse the conscience of the community over its injustice, is in reality expressing the highest respect for law.

21   Of course, there is nothing new about this kind of civil disobedience. It was evidenced sublimely in the refusal of Shadrach, Meshach, and Abednego[19] to obey the laws of Nebuchadnezzar, on the ground that a higher moral law was at stake. It was practiced superbly by the early Christians, who were willing to face hungry lions and the excruciating pain of chopping blocks rather than submit to certain unjust laws of the Roman Empire. To a degree, academic freedom is a reality today because Socrates practiced civil disobedience. In our own nation, the Boston Tea Party represented a massive act of civil disobedience.

22   We should never forget that everything Adolf Hitler did in Germany was "legal" and everything the Hungarian freedom fighters did in Hungary was "illegal." It was "illegal" to aid and comfort a Jew in Hitler's Germany. Even so, I am sure that, had I lived in Germany at the time, I would have aided and comforted my Jewish brothers. If today I lived in a Communist country where certain principles dear to the Christian faith are suppressed, I would openly advocate disobeying that country's antireligious laws.

---

[18] a situation in which there is no rule or authority

[19] In the Bible the Babylonian King Nebuchadnezzar ordered these three men into a fiery furnace because they would not renounce their Christian faith. They walked on the burning coals and emerged unharmed.

23   I must make two honest confessions to you, my Christian and Jewish brothers. First, I must confess that over the past few years I have been gravely disappointed with the white moderate. I have almost reached the regrettable conclusion that the Negro's great stumbling block in his stride toward freedom is not the White Citizen's Counciler or the Ku Klux Klanner, but the white moderate, who is more devoted to "order" than to justice; who prefers a negative peace which is the absence of tension to a positive peace which is the presence of justice; who constantly says: "I agree with you in the goal you seek, but I cannot agree with your methods of direct action"; who paternalistically believes he can set the timetable for another man's freedom; who lives by a mythical concept of time and who constantly advises the Negro to wait for a "more convenient season." Shallow understanding from people of good will is more frustrating than absolute misunderstanding from people of ill will. Lukewarm acceptance is much more bewildering than outright rejection.

24   I had hoped that the white moderate would understand that law and order exist for the purpose of establishing justice and that when they fail in this purpose they become the dangerously structured dams that block the flow of social progress. I had hoped that the white moderate would understand that the present tension in the South is a necessary phase of the transition from an obnoxious negative peace, in which the Negro passively accepted his unjust plight, to a substantive and positive peace, in which all men will respect the dignity and worth of human personality. Actually, we who engage in nonviolent direct action are not the creators of tension. We merely bring to the surface the hidden tension that is already alive. We bring it out in the open, where it can be seen and dealt with. Like a boil that can never be cured so long as it is covered up but must be opened with all its ugliness to the natural medicines of air and light, injustice must be exposed, with all the tension its exposure creates, to the light of human conscience and the air of national opinion before it can be cured.

25   In your statement you assert that our actions, even though peaceful, must be condemned because they precipitate[20] vio-

---

[20] to cause to happen

lence. But is this a logical assertion? Isn't this like condemning a robbed man because his possession of money precipitated the evil act of robbery? Isn't this like condemning Socrates because his unswerving commitment to truth and his philosophical inquiries precipitated the act by the misguided populace in which they made him drink hemlock? Isn't this like condemning Jesus because his unique God-consciousness and never-ceasing devotion to God's will precipitated the evil act of crucifixion? We must come to see that, as the federal courts have consistently affirmed, it is wrong to urge an individual to cease his efforts to gain his basic constitutional rights because the quest may precipitate violence. Society must protect the robbed and punish the robber.

26   I had also hoped that the white moderate would reject the myth concerning time in relation to the struggle for freedom. I have just received a letter from a white brother in Texas. He writes: "All Christians know that the colored people will receive equal rights eventually, but it is possible that you are in too great a religious hurry. It has taken Christianity almost two thousand years to accomplish what it has. The teachings of Christ take time to come to earth." Such an attitude stems from a tragic misconception of time, from the strangely irrational notion that there is something in the very flow of time that will inevitably cure all ills. Actually, time itself is neutral; it can be used either destructively or constructively. More and more I feel that the people of ill win have used time much more effectively than have the people of good will. We will have to repent in this generation not merely for the hateful words and actions of the bad people but for the appalling silence of the good people. Human progress never rolls in on wheels of inevitability; it comes through the tireless efforts of men willing to be coworkers with God, and without this hard work, time itself becomes an ally of the forces of social stagnation. We must use time creatively, in the knowledge that the time is always ripe to do right. Now is the time to make real the promise of democracy and transform our pending national elegy into a creative psalm of brotherhood. Now is the time to lift our national policy from the quicksand of racial injustice to the solid rock of human dignity.

27   You speak of our activity in Birmingham as extreme. At first I was rather disappointed that fellow clergymen would see my nonviolent efforts as those of an extremist. I began thinking about the fact that I stand in the middle of two opposing forces in the Negro community. One is a force of complacency, made up in part of Negroes who, as a result of long years of oppression, are so drained of self-respect and a sense of "somebodiness" that they have adjusted to segregation; and in part of a few middle-class Negroes who, because of a degree of academic and economic security and because in some ways they profit by segregation, have become insensitive to the problems of the masses. The other force is one of bitterness and hatred, and it comes perilously close to advocating violence. It is expressed in the various black nationalist groups that are springing up across the nation, the largest and best-known being Elijah Muhammad's Muslim movement. Nourished by the Negro's frustration over the continued existence of racial discrimination, this movement is made up of people who have lost faith in America, who have absolutely repudiated Christianity, and who have concluded that the white man is an incorrigible "devil."

28   I have tried to stand between these two forces, saying that we need emulate neither the "do-nothingism" of the complacent nor the hatred and despair of the black nationalist. For there is the more excellent way of love and nonviolent protest. I am grateful to God that, through the influence of the Negro church, the way of nonviolence became an integral part of our struggle.

29   If this philosophy had not emerged, by now many streets of the South would, I am convinced, be flowing with blood. And I am further convinced that if our white brothers dismiss as rabble-rousers" and "outside agitators" those of us who employ nonviolent direct action, and if they refuse to support our nonviolent efforts, millions of Negroes will, out of frustration and despair, seek solace and security in black-nationalist ideologies—a development that would inevitably lead to a frightening racial nightmare.

30   Oppressed people cannot remain oppressed forever. The yearning for freedom eventually manifests itself, and that is what

has happened to the American Negro. Something within has reminded him of his birthright of freedom, and something without has reminded him that it can be gained. Consciously or unconsciously, he has been caught up by the *Zeitgeist*,[21] and with his black brothers of Africa and his brown and yellow brothers of Asia, South America and the Caribbean, the United States Negro is moving with a sense of great urgency toward the promised land of racial justice. If one recognizes this vital urge that has engulfed the Negro community, one should readily understand why public demonstrations are taking place. The Negro has many pent-up resentments and latent[22] frustrations, and he must release them. So let him march; let him make prayer pilgrimages to the city hall; let him go on freedom rides—and try to understand why he must do so. If his repressed emotions are not released in nonviolent ways, they will seek expression through violence; this is not a threat but a fact of history. So I have not said to my people: "Get rid of your discontent." Rather, I have tried to say that this normal and healthy discontent can be channeled into the creative outlet of nonviolent direct action. And now this approach is being termed extremist.

31   But though I was initially disappointed at being categorized as an extremist, as I continued to think about the matter I gradually gained a measure of satisfaction from the label. Was not Jesus an extremist for love: "Love your enemies, bless them that curse you, do good to them that hate you, and pray for them which despitefully use you, and persecute you." Was not Amos[23] an extremist for justice: "Let justice roll down like waters and righteousness like an ever-flowing stream." Was not Paul an extremist for the Christian gospel: "I bear in my body the marks of the Lord Jesus." Was not Martin Luther[24] an extremist: "Here

---

[21] a German word meaning "the spirit of a time period or a generation"

[22] something that is present but repressed or concealed

[23] a Biblical prophet

[24] religious reformer and founder of the Protestant Reformation—the beginnings of the Protestant religion (1483–1546)

I stand; I cannot do otherwise, so help me God." And John Bunyan:[25] "I will stay in jail to the end of my days before I make a butchery of my conscience" And Abraham Lincoln: "This nation cannot survive half slave and half free." And Thomas Jefferson: "We hold these truths to be self-evident, that all men are created equal. . . ." So the question is not whether we will be extremists, but what kind of extremists we will be. Will we be extremists for hate or for love? Will we be extremists for the preservation of injustice or for the extension of justice? In that dramatic scene on Calvary's hill three men were crucified. We must never forget that all three were crucified for the same crime—the crime of extremism. Two were extremists for immorality, and thus fell below their environment. The other, Jesus Christ, was an extremist for love, truth and goodness, and thereby rose above his environment. Perhaps the South, the nation and the world are in dire need of creative extremists.

32   I had hoped that the white moderate would see this need. Perhaps I was too optimistic; perhaps I expected too much. I suppose I should have realized that few members of the oppressor race can understand the deep groans and passionate yearnings of the oppressed race, and still fewer have the vision to see that injustice must be rooted out by strong, persistent and determined action. I am thankful, however, that some of our white brothers in the South have grasped the meaning of this social revolution and committed themselves to it. They are still all too few in quantity, but they are big in quality. Some—such as Ralph McGill, Lillian Smith, Harry Golden, James McBride Dabbs, Ann Braden and Sarah Patton Boyle[26]—have written about our struggle in eloquent and prophetic terms. Others have marched with us down nameless streets of the South. They have languished in filthy, roach-infested jails, suffering the abuse and brutality of policemen who view them as "dirty nigger-lovers." Unlike so many of their moderate brothers and

[25] Protestant preacher and the author of *Pilgrim's Progress*

[26] southern journalists, writers, and public figures who spoke openly for integration and equal rights

sisters, they have recognized the urgency of the moment and sensed the need for powerful "action" antidotes to combat the disease of segregation.

33   Let me take note of my other major disappointment. I have been so greatly disappointed with the white church and its leadership. Of course, there are some notable exceptions. I am not unmindful of the fact that each of you has taken some significant stands on this issue. I commend you, Reverend Stallings, for your Christian stand on this past Sunday, in welcoming Negroes to your worship service on a nonsegregated basis. I commend the Catholic leaders of this state for integrating Spring Hill College several years ago.

34   But despite these notable exceptions, I must honestly reiterate that I have been disappointed with the church. I do not say this as one of those negative critics who can always find something wrong with the church. I say this as a minister of the gospel, who loves the church; who was nurtured in its bosom; who has been sustained by its spiritual blessings and who will remain true to it as long as the cord of life shall lengthen.

35   When I was suddenly catapulted into the leadership of the bus protest in Montgomery, Alabama, a few years ago, I felt we would be supported by the white church. I felt that the white ministers, priests and rabbis of the South would be among our strongest allies. Instead, some have been outright opponents, refusing to understand the freedom movement and misrepresenting its leaders; all too many others have been more cautious than courageous and have remained silent behind the anesthetizing security of stained-glass windows.

36   In spite of my shattered dreams, I came to Birmingham with the hope that the white religious leadership of this community would see the justice of our cause and, with deep moral concern, would serve as the channel through which our just grievances could reach the power structure. I had hoped that each of you would understand. But again I have been disappointed.

37   I have heard numerous southern religious leaders admonish their worshipers to comply with a desegregation decision because it is the law, but I have longed to hear white ministers

declare: "Follow this decree because integration is morally right and because the Negro is your brother." In the midst of blatant injustices inflicted upon the Negro, I have watched white churchmen stand on the sideline and mouth pious[27] irrelevancies and sanctimonious[28] trivialities. In the midst of a mighty struggle to rid our nation of racial and economic injustice, I have heard many ministers say: "Those are social issues, with which the gospel has no real concern." And I have watched many churches commit themselves to completely other-worldly religion which makes a strange, un-Biblical distinction between body and soul, between the sacred and the secular.

38   I have traveled the length and breadth of Alabama, Mississippi and all the other southern states. On sweltering summer days and crisp autumn mornings I have looked at the South's beautiful churches with their lofty spires pointing heavenward. I have beheld the impressive outlines of her massive religious-education buildings. Over and over I have found myself asking: "What kind of people worship here? Who is their God? Where were their voices when the lips of Governor Barnett dripped with words of interposition and nullification? Where were they when Governor Wallace gave a clarion call for defiance and hatred? Where were their voices of support when bruised and weary Negro men and women decided to rise from the dark dungeons of complacency to the bright hills of creative protest?"

39   Yes, these questions are still in my mind. In deep disappointment I have wept over the laxity of the church. But be assured that my tears have been tears of love. There can be no deep disappointment where there is not deep love. Yes, I love the church. How could I do otherwise? I am in the rather unique position of being the son, the grandson and the great-grandson of preachers. Yes, I see the church as the body of Christ. But, oh! How we have blemished and scarred that body through social neglect and through fear of being nonconformists.

------

[27] reverent, religious, devout

[28] pretended religiousness

40   There was a time when the church was very powerful—in the time when the early Christians rejoiced at being deemed worthy to suffer for what they believed. In those days the church was not merely a thermometer that recorded the ideas and principles of popular opinion; it was a thermostat that transformed the mores of society. Whenever the early Christians entered a town, the people in power became disturbed and immediately sought to convict the Christians for being "disturbers of the peace" and "outside agitators." But the Christians pressed on, in the conviction that they were "a colony of heaven," called to obey God rather than man. Small in number, they were big in commitment. They were too God-intoxicated to be "astronomically intimidated." By their effort and example they brought an end to such ancient evils as infanticide and gladiatorial contests.

41   Things are different now. So often the contemporary church is a weak, ineffectual voice with an uncertain sound. So often it is an archdefender of the status quo. Far from being disturbed by the presence of the church, the power structure of the average community is consoled by the church's silent—and often even vocal—sanction of things as they are.

42   But the judgment of God is upon the church as never before. If today's church does not recapture the sacrificial spirit of the early church, it will lose its authenticity, forfeit the loyalty of millions, and be dismissed as an irrelevant social club with no meaning for the twentieth century. Every day I meet young people whose disappointment with the church has turned into outright disgust.

43   Perhaps I have once again been too optimistic. Is organized religion too inextricably bound to the status quo to save our nation and the world? Perhaps I must turn my faith to the inner spiritual church, the church within the church, as the true *ekklesia*[29] and the hope of the world. But again I am thankful to God that some noble souls from the ranks of organized religion

[29] a Greek word denoting the spirit of the church as distinguished from its physical form or structure

have broken loose from the paralyzing chains of conformity and joined us as active partners in the struggle for freedom. They have left their secure congregations and walked the streets of Albany, Georgia, with us. They have gone down the highways of the South on tortuous rides for freedom. Yes, they have gone to jail with us. Some have been dismissed from their churches, have lost the support of their bishops and fellow ministers. But they have acted in the faith that right defeated is stronger than evil triumphant. Their witness has been the spiritual salt that has preserved the true meaning of the gospel in these troubled times. They have carved a tunnel of hope through the dark mountain of disappointment.

44   I hope the church as a whole will meet the challenge of this decisive hour. But even if the church does not come to the aid of justice, I have no despair about the future. I have no fear about the outcome of our struggle in Birmingham, even if our motives are at present misunderstood. We will reach the goal of freedom in Birmingham and all over the nation, because the goal of America is freedom. Abused and scorned though we may be, our destiny is tied up with America's destiny. Before the pilgrims landed at Plymouth, we were here. Before the pen of Jefferson etched the majestic words of the Declaration of Independence across the pages of history, we were here. For more than two centuries our forebears labored in this country without wages; they made cotton king; they built the homes of their masters while suffering gross injustice and shameful humiliation—and yet out of a bottomless vitality they continued to thrive and develop. If the inexpressible cruelties of slavery. could not stop us, the opposition we now face will surely fail. We will win our freedom because the sacred heritage of our nation and the eternal will of God are embodied in our echoing demands.

45   Before closing I feel impelled to mention one other point in your statement that has troubled me profoundly. You warmly commended the Birmingham police force for keeping "order" and "preventing violence." I doubt that you would have so warmly commended the police force if you had seen its dogs sinking their teeth into unarmed, nonviolent Negroes. I doubt

that you would so quickly commend the policemen if you were to observe their ugly and inhumane treatment of Negroes here in the city jail; if you were to watch them push and curse old Negro women and young Negro girls; if you were to see them slap and kick old Negro men and young boys; if you were to observe them as they did on two occasions, refuse to give us food because we wanted to sing our grace together. I cannot join you in your praise of the Birmingham police department.

46   It is true that the police have exercised a degree of discipline in handling the demonstrators. In this sense they have conducted themselves rather "nonviolently" in public. But for what purpose? To preserve the evil system of segregation. Over the past few years I have consistently preached that nonviolence demands that the means we use must be as pure as the ends we seek. I have tried to make clear that it is wrong to use immoral means to attain moral ends. But now I must affirm that it is just as wrong, or perhaps even more so, to use moral means to preserve immoral ends. Perhaps Mr. Connor and his policemen have been rather nonviolent in public, as was Chief Pritchett in Albany, Georgia, but they have used the moral means of nonviolence to maintain the immoral end of racial injustice. As T. S. Eliot[30] has said: "The last temptation is the greatest treason: To do the right deed for the wrong reason."

47   I wish you had commended the Negro sit-inners and demonstrators of Birmingham for their sublime courage, their willingness to suffer and their amazing discipline in the midst of great provocation. One day the South will recognize its real heroes. They will be the James Merediths, with the noble sense of purpose that enables them to face jeering and hostile mobs, and with the agonizing loneliness that characterizes the life of the pioneer. They will be old, oppressed, battered Negro women, symbolized in a seventy-two-year-old woman in Montgomery, Alabama, who rose up with a sense of dignity and with her people decided not to ride segregated buses, and who responded with ungrammatical profundity to one who inquired about her weariness: "My feet is tired,

---

[30] Nobel Prize-winning poet (1888–1965)

but my soul is at rest." They will be the young high school and college students, the young ministers of the gospel and a host of their elders, courageously and nonviolently sitting in at lunch counters and willingly going to jail for conscience' sake. One day the South will know that when these disinherited children of God sat down at lunch counters, they were in reality standing up for what is best in the American dream and for the most sacred values in our Judaeo-Christian heritage, thereby bringing our nation back to those great wells of democracy which were dug deep by the founding fathers in their formulation of the Constitution and the Declaration of Independence.

48   Never before have I written so long a letter. I'm afraid it is much too long to take your precious time. I can assure you that it would have been much shorter if I had been writing from a comfortable desk, but what else can one do when he is alone in a narrow jail cell, other than write long letters, think long thoughts and pray long prayers?

49   If I have said anything in this letter that overstates the truth and indicates an unreasonable impatience, I beg you to forgive me. If I have said anything that understates the truth and indicates my having a patience that allows me to settle for anything less than brotherhood, I beg God to forgive me.

50   I hope this letter finds you strong in the faith. I also hope that circumstances will soon make it possible for me to meet each of you, not as an integrationist or a civil-rights leader but as a fellow clergyman and a Christian brother. Let us all hope that the dark clouds of racial prejudice will soon pass away and the deep fog of misunderstanding will be lifted from our fear-drenched communities, and in some not too distant tomorrow the radiant stars of love and brotherhood will shine over our great nation with all their scintillating beauty.

Yours for the cause of Peace and Brotherhood,
Martin Luther King, Jr.

REVIEWING AND INTERPRETING

Record your answers to these questions in your personal literature notebook. Follow the directions for each part.

REVIEWING Try to complete each of these sentences without looking back at the selection.

Recalling Facts
1. Martin Luther King, Jr., was arrested and jailed for
a. violent acts.
b. parading without a permit.
c. entering a white neighborhood.
d. attacking a policeman.

Understanding Main Ideas
2. King's letter
a. accuses eight Birmingham clergymen of racism.
b. argues that he had not broken any laws.
c. urges his followers not to fight for his freedom.
d. explains the motives behind his actions.

Identifying Sequence
3. King wrote that the first basic step in a nonviolent campaign is
a. direct action.
b. self-purification.
c. collection of facts.
d. negotiation.

Finding Supporting Details
4. Which statement supports King's position that black Americans should no longer be expected to "wait?"
a. "A law is unjust if it is inflicted on a minority."
b. "Perhaps the South, the nation, and the world are in dire need of creative extremists."
c. "I have consistently preached that nonviolence demands that the means we use must be as pure as the ends we seek."
d. "We know through painful experience that freedom is never voluntarily given by the oppressor."

Getting Meaning from Context

5. "The yearning for freedom eventually manifests itself, and that is what has happened to the American Negro." In this sentence, *manifests* means
a. expands.
b. reveals.
c. destroys.
d. overcomes.

INTERPRETING   To complete these items, you may look back at the selection if you'd like.

Making Inferences

6. King wrote this letter
a. to demand that the eight clergymen assist him.
b. to explain his actions and motives to a larger audience.
c. because he thought he could get better treatment while in the jail.
d. to threaten Birmingham city officials.

Generalizing

7. "Letter from Birmingham Jail" can best be described as
a. an apology.
b. a defense.
c. an accusation.
d. a report.

Recognizing Fact and Opinion

8. Which of the following is a statement of fact?
a. "There can be no gainsaying the fact that racial injustice engulfs this community."
b. "We know from painful experience that freedom is never voluntarily given by the oppressor."
c. "In the course of the negotiations, certain promises were made by the merchants—for example, to remove the stores' humiliating racial signs."
d. "As the weeks and months went by, we realized that we were the victims of a broken promise."

Identifying Cause and Effect

9. Which of the following did Martin Luther King, Jr., believe would happen if nonviolent protest were unsuccessful?
   a. Black Americans would be doomed to another 340 years without their rights.
   b. Black Americans would adopt the violent methods of black-nationalist groups.
   c. Segregation would spread to other parts of the United States.
   d. The nation's economy would decline.

Drawing Conclusions

10. From his letter, you can conclude that King
   a. felt his religious faith was being attacked.
   b. accepted the punishment for his actions in Birmingham.
   c. was concerned that he was losing his followers.
   d. expected to be pardoned and released from jail.

Now check your answers with your teacher. Study the items you answered incorrectly. What skills are they checking? Talk with your teacher about ways to work on these skills.

Persuasion

You learned in Unit 2 that persuasion is one of the four basic types of nonfiction writing. (The other three types are description, narration, and exposition.) *Persuasion* is writing that uses reasons, arguments, and logic to make a point and lead the reader to a logical conclusion. The conclusions in a persuasive essay express the writer's opinions or views about the subject of the essay. The writer tries to convince the reader to accept his or her views about that subject. The word *essay*, in fact, comes from the French word "to try."

In "Letter from Birmingham Jail," Martin Luther King, Jr., has two goals: First, he seeks to persuade the eight clergymen— and others who oppose him—to understand and accept his motives and his actions. Second, he seeks to inspire his followers to continue their fight while he is imprisoned.

There are many persuasive writing techniques writers use to develop their arguments and to appeal to their readers' emotions. In the lessons that follow, we will talk about three of those techniques:

1. **Developing and Organizing a Rational Argument** In a persuasive essay the writer proposes certain actions or beliefs that he or she wants the reader to accept. The writer's arguments are based on evidence and reasoning that will lead to acceptance of his or her conclusions. The arguments are presented in the order in which the writer thinks they will be most persuasive.

2. **Appeals to Reason** Rational arguments are based on facts the writer presents and the logical connections the writer makes between the facts.

3. **Appeals to Emotion** Unlike rational arguments that try to change how one thinks about an issue, emotional appeals are intended to change how one feels about the issue.

**DEVELOPING AND ORGANIZING A RATIONAL ARGUMENT**

In persuasive writing an argument is the method the writer uses to lead you to a conclusion; it is how the writer persuades the audience to take an action or accept certain ideas or beliefs. Persuasive arguments develop from a basic conflict. The conflict may come from a difference in ideas, attitudes, or opinions. To resolve this conflict, the writer presents a *proposition*—a belief or action that the writer wants the audience to support. To be effective, the writer's argument must provide facts and opinions as evidence to support the proposition.

The basic proposition of "Letter from Birmingham Jail" is not stated directly, but it might be summarized as follows: *Immediate positive steps must be taken to end segregation.* This unstated general proposition is clearly implied by the several specific propositions that Martin Luther King, Jr., states directly in his essay. King organized his essay as a response to eight clergymen's newspaper statement. The clergymen charged him and others with being outsiders who had no business interfering in Birmingham's problems. They said that he had chosen a bad time for his activities. And they said that his activist methods were wrong—that patience, not pressure, was the way for black citizens to gain their rights. The first three specific propositions King argues for in "Letter from Birmingham Jail" are direct responses to these statements by the clergymen.

When a writer is organizing a persuasive essay, he or she must consider the most effective order in which to present the propositions and their supporting arguments. How a persuasive writer organizes his essay is frequently determined by the audience for the essay. In "Letter from Birmingham Jail," King is responding directly to statements made by the clergymen. After King states each of his propositions in response to the clergymen's criticisms and presents his arguments, he offers two other propositions of his own. He describes these propositions as "confessions" of two "disappointments"—two situations that he argues must be changed. The first proposition is presented in paragraph 23:

I must make two honest confessions to you, my Christian and Jewish brothers. First, I must confess that over the past few years I have been gravely disappointed with the white moderate. I have almost reached the regrettable conclusion that the Negro's greatest stumbling block in his stride toward freedom is not the White Citizen's Counciler or the Ku Klux Klanner, but the white moderate, who is more devoted to "order" than to justice; who prefers a negative peace which is the absence of tension to a positive peace which is the presence of justice; who constantly says: "I agree with you in the goal you seek, but I cannot agree with your methods of direct action"; who paternalistically believes he can set the timetable for another man's freedom; who lives by a mythical concept of time and who constantly advises the Negro to wait for a more "convenient season." Shallow understanding from people of good will is more frustrating than absolute misunderstanding from people of ill will. Lukewarm acceptance is more bewildering than outright rejection.

King is saying that the greatest stumbling block to freedom for black Americans is not really those who directly oppose integration. Instead it is the white moderates, who say they are in favor of integration but do not take active steps to make it happen. King's second proposition is stated in paragraph 33:

Let me take note of my other major disappointment. I have been so greatly disappointed with the white church and its leadership. Of course there are some notable exceptions. I am not unmindful of the fact that each of you has taken some significant stands on this issue. I commend you, Reverend Stallings, for your Christian stand on this past Sunday, in welcoming Negroes to your worship service on a nonsegregated basis. I commend the Catholic leaders of this state for integrating Spring Hill College several years ago.

Here King is accusing white churches and their leaders of ignoring their own deepest religious principles when they directly oppose his freedom movement or try to ignore it.

EXERCISE

Use what you have learned in this lesson to answer the following questions about how Martin Luther King, Jr., organizes and presents his arguments in "Letter from Birmingham Jail."

1. The Birmingham clergymen's statement made three criticisms of King and his activities.What is King's proposition in response to one of these criticisms? What are his arguments in support of this proposition?

2. In organizing his essay, which criticism from the clergymen does King respond to first? Why do you think he decides to present arguments for this proposition before the others?

Check your answers with your teacher. Review this lesson if you don't understand why an answer was incorrect.

 ## WRITING ON YOUR OWN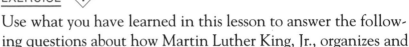

In this exercise you will use what you have learned in this lesson to develop your argument. Follow these steps:

• Review your list of positive and negative effects of the amusement park that you wrote for Writing: Developing a Persuasive Argument. Rewrite the effects as statements, or propositions. For example, if you are in favor of the park, your propositions might include *The park will increase tax income for the town; the park will create jobs; the park will attract more customers for town merchants.* If you oppose the park, your propositions might include *The park will increase the cost to the town for sanitation and fire and police services;*

the park will increase traffic and attract crowds of strangers, making the town a less pleasant place to live; the park will damage environmentally sensitive wetlands areas.

- Read your propositions and think about how you will support each one. Think about the audience for the persuasive essay you are going to write. What would be the most effective order in which to present your propositions to this audience? What proposition will they think is most important? Which arguments do you think they will find most persuasive? Do you want to begin with your strongest points or build up to them at the end of your argument?

APPEALING TO REASON

Writers use two basic methods to develop rational, persuasive arguments: inductive reasoning or deductive reasoning. Martin Luther King, Jr., uses both methods of reasoning in "Letter from Birmingham Jail" to persuade you that his motives are good and that his actions are reasonable and necessary.

Inductive Reasoning   *Inductive reasoning* is the process of becoming convinced that a number of examples, all leading toward the same general conclusion, do in fact justify accepting that general conclusion. Another term for inductive reasoning is *generalizing*. A *generalization* is an idea or statement that emphasizes the general characteristics rather than the specific details of a subject. For example, if all of the zebras you had ever seen, alive or in pictures, had black stripes, you might conclude, All zebras have black stripes. You would have arrived at that generalization through inductive reasoning.

You should keep in mind, however, that a generalization based on inductive reasoning can only be a *probable* conclusion. No matter how much reliable evidence supports an inductive conclusion, only one negative example is necessary to prove that it is incorrect. (You might one day see a zebra with brown stripes—there are some.) You should also realize that writers do not always present their inductive reasoning in a straightforward sequence, first listing all the examples in order and then stating a general conclusion. The examples and conclusion may come in any order and there may be more than one conclusion. When you are reading a persuasive essay, it is important to look for the generalization. Then it is important to see whether all the examples support that generalization.

In the sixth paragraph of his essay, King makes the following generalization: "There can be no gainsaying the fact that racial injustice engulfs this community. Birmingham is probably the most thoroughly segregated city in the United States." These two sentences are inductive conclusions. They are based on the facts that King offers in the sixth and seventh paragraphs in his letter. Reread those paragraphs. As you can see, if the evidence he offers is true, there can be little doubt about the accuracy of King's generalizations. Racial injustice *does* engulf this community.

Deductive Reasoning   In contrast to inductive reasoning, *deductive reasoning* begins with one or more generalizations and moves to a conclusion that is a specific example of the general statements. If the general statements are true, then logically an individual example of the statements must also be true. For example:

General statement: *All fish breath through gills.*
General statement: *A salmon is a fish.*
Conclusion: *Salmon breath through gills.*

Many of the strongest arguments Martin Luther King, Jr., makes in this essay are based on deductive reasoning. First, he makes a general statement that he expects his readers to accept as true. Then he applies this statement to the situation in Birmingham to show that his actions follow logically from this statement. One of the charges the eight clergymen made in their statement was that King and his group were "outsiders"—people who lived elsewhere and who had no right to interfere with how things were done in Birmingham. King's proposition is that he and his group *should* be in Birmingham, and he makes several arguments for this proposition. The fourth paragraph of his essay offers one of these arguments based on deductive reasoning.

> Moreover, I am cognizant of the interrelatedness of all communities and states. I cannot sit idly by in Atlanta and not be concerned about what happens in Birmingham. Injustice anywhere is a threat to justice everywhere. We are caught in an inescapable network of mutuality, tied in a single garment of destiny. Whatever affects one directly, affects all indirectly. Never again can we afford to live with the narrow, provincial "outside agitator" idea. Anyone who lives inside the United States can never be considered an outsider anywhere within its bounds.

If the clergymen, and you as the reader, accept that communities and states are interrelated—that "injustice anywhere is a threat to justice everywhere"—then it logically follows that what happens to black citizens in Birmingham indirectly affects every other citizen of the state and the nation.

EXERCISE ⟨2⟩

Use what you have learned in this lesson to answer the following questions about the appeals to reason that King uses in this essay.

1. In one of the first four paragraphs of this essay, King talks about the interrelatedness of all communities. He offers two additional general statements in those paragraphs as support for his presence in Birmingham. What are they?

2. In paragraph 12 King states that the clergymen have called his actions "untimely." What arguments does he offer against this criticism? Does he use inductive or deductive reasoning?

Now check your answers with your teacher. Review this lesson if you don't understand why an answer was incorrect.

WRITING ON YOUR OWN

In this exercise you will use what you have learned in this lesson to continue the development of your argument. Follow these steps:

- Reread the list of propositions you wrote for Writing On Your Own 1. Can you think of any additional propositions. Think about the evidence and reasoning you will use to support each of your propositions. Which propositions can best be supported using inductive reasoning and which will use deductive reasoning?
- Copy the graphic organizer on page 242 onto a sheet of paper. For each proposition on your list, use either the inductive or deductive reasoning graph, depending on how you choose to argue your ideas. Look at the examples that have been provided in the organizers. They will help you understand how inductive and deductive arguments are developed. Use the graphic organizers to develop and organize your evidence and reasoning in support of each of your propositions. Create a separate organizer for each inductive or deductive reason.
- Write a paragraph presenting the reasoning for each of your propositions.

LESSON 3 APPEALING TO EMOTIONS

Appeals to reason try to change the way you *think* about an issue; appeals to emotion try to influence the way you *feel* about the issue. Emotional appeals may appeal to your religious or other personal beliefs, your morals, or your ethics. Writers also make emotional appeals by stirring up your emotions— making you feel sadness, happiness, pride, love, or anger. If you have ever heard a recording or seen a film of a speech by Martin Luther King, Jr., you know that King was an extraordinarily moving speaker. As a Southern Baptist minister, he had much practice in preaching sermons that appealed both to his

Inductive Reasoning

Proposition: The park will damage our town's environment.

Example:
The land for the theme park is located next to a wetland.
Example:
This is the last wetland in the area that provides nesting for water birds.
Example:
Wetlands act as a water filtration system, keeping our water clean.
Conclusion:
The park will damage our environment.

Deductive Reasoning

Proposition: The park will create new jobs.

General Statement:
The unemployment rate in our town is high.
General Statement:
The park will provide five hundred new jobs.
Conclusion:
The park will help employ people in our town.

listeners' thoughts and emotions. Although King wrote "Letter from Birmingham Jail" as a rational defense of his beliefs and actions, the persuasiveness of his essay is also greatly enhanced by his appeals to his readers' emotions.

King uses a variety of techniques to appeal to the emotions in "Letter from Birmingham Jail." In this lesson you will learn about how he uses tone, allusions, and aphorisms to appeal to the emotions in support of his propositions.

Tone   You will recall that *tone* is a writer's attitude toward his or her subject or audience. The reader infers a writer's tone from *how* the writer expresses himself or herself and from *what* details the writer offers. Given the circumstances in which King is writing this open letter and his subject, it is not hard to generalize that his attitude toward his subject is very serious. His attitude toward his audience, however, is more complex. While King strongly disagrees with what the clergymen have written, he does not want to attack them too vigorously. He wants to *persuade* them, not *defeat* them. No matter how angry he may feel, he does not give his anger free rein.

As you read this opening paragraph from King's essay, think about the tone he is creating—his attitude toward his readers.

> While confined here in the Birmingham city jail, I came across your recent statement calling my present activities "unwise and untimely." Seldom do I pause to answer criticism of my work and ideas. If I sought to answer all the criticisms that cross my desk, my secretaries would have little time for anything other than such correspondence in the course of the day, and I would have no time for constructive work. But since I feel that you are men of genuine good will and that your criticisms are sincerely set forth, I want to try to answer your statement in what I hope will be patient and reasonable terms.

Notice how quickly King establishes his own status. He is telling the clergymen that he is not an insignificant person. They cannot lecture him on what he should and should not do.

King subtly shows that he is a busy and important man: he has more than one secretary, and he and they are usually too busy with "constructive" work to answer criticisms. Next King flatters his readers: they are "men of genuine good will," he says, and he thinks their criticisms are "sincerely set forth." By this King implies that despite his differences with the clergymen's thinking, he assumes that their intentions are good.

In the last sentence of the paragraph, King tells the clergymen that he will "try" to answer their statements with patience and reason, implying that this is not easy, given how much he disagrees with them. The very fact that King says he is going to appeal to the clergymen's reason is itself an appeal to emotion. Again he compliments his readers by assuming that they are reasonably intelligent men, who can understand and accept logical arguments. By using a reasonable tone, King has encouraged the clergymen to listen to his arguments—and by using a more dignified tone than his accusers, he has also appealed to the larger audience who will read his open letter.

King's reasonable and patient tone counters his critics' superior stance. In the first part of the essay, he contrasts the clergymen's unreasonable statements with his own logical beliefs and actions. Once he has done that, he can claim the superior position for himself. In the latter part of the essay he tells the clergymen that he is "disappointed" in them and people like them, who speak as though they have good will but do not act on their words.

Allusion   An *allusion* is a reference to a well-known person, place, thing, or event. The writer expects you to recognize the reference and to infer how it applies to his or her subject. In "Letter from Birmingham Jail," Martin Luther King, Jr., makes many allusions to people and events from the Bible and from American history, as well as references to well-known literary figures and philosophers.

At two points King compares himself and his activities to the Greek philosopher Socrates and his method of teaching by question and answer rather than lectures. This method forced students to examine closely what they knew and what they believed.

> Just as Socrates felt that it was necessary to create a tension in the mind so that individuals could rise from the bondage of myths and half-truths to the unfettered realm of creative analysis and objective appraisal, so must we see the need for nonviolent gadflies to create the kind of tension in society that will help men rise from the dark depths of prejudice and racism to the majestic heights of understanding and brotherhood.

Notice that King not only compares himself to the famous philosopher and teacher but also compares his method of teaching with Socrates' method. King reasons that if it was right for Socrates to create tension by asking questions, then his own, similar actions must also be right.

Aphorism   An *aphorism* is a concise, polished statement of a thought or principle. It makes a strong point in a memorable way. Writers frequently quote such concise statements made by other writers and speakers. Examples of aphorisms are *The truth is never pure and rarely simple* and *If wishes were horses, beggars might ride*. Aphorisms that have become popular expressions become proverbs. These proverbs were once aphorisms *A stitch in time saves nine* and *A rolling stone gathers no moss*.

King uses an aphorism in paragraph 13, when he quotes a "distinguished jurist" who said that "justice too long delayed is justice denied." Reading such an aphorism is often very emotionally satisfying because it offers a great deal of wisdom in a few easily remembered words.

In addition to quoting aphorisms by others, King also created his own powerful aphorisms. One of the strong emotional appeals of "Letter from Birmingham Jail" comes from the powerful aphorisms he creates to drive home his propositions and make them stick in your mind long after you have read them.

For example in paragraph 23 of his essay, King begins his argument about the lack of support coming from white moderates. After stating his disappointment at the beginning of the paragraph, King presents a long sentence giving examples of white moderates' failures. Then he ends with two aphorisms that powerfully summarize his disappointment: "Shallow understanding from people of good will is more frustrating than absolute misunderstanding from people of ill will. Lukewarm acceptance is much more bewildering than outright rejection."

EXERCISE ⟨3⟩

Read this passage from King's letter. Use what you have learned in this lesson to answer the questions that follow it.

> Human progress never rolls in on wheels of inevitability; it comes through the tireless efforts of men willing to be co-workers with God, and without this hard work, time itself becomes an ally of the forces of social stagnation. We must use time creatively, in the knowledge that the time is always ripe to do right. Now is the time to make real the promise of democracy and transform our pending national elegy into a creative psalm of brotherhood. Now is the time to lift our national policy from the quicksand of racial injustice to the solid rock of human dignity.

1. What techniques does King use in this passage to appeal to your emotions? Briefly describe each.

2. King makes allusions to more than 20 people and events in "Letter from Birmingham Jail." What are some of these allusions? Choose one of these allusions and explain how that allusion adds to the emotional appeal of his argument.

Now check your answers with your teacher. Review this lesson if you don't understand why an answer was incorrect.

WRITING ON YOUR OWN 〈3〉

In this exercise you will use what you learned in this lesson to add appeals to emotions to your argument.

* Reread the paragraphs you wrote for Writing On Your Own 2. Which propositions about the amusement park do you think might have an emotional appeal to your readers? Issues that might ignite strong feelings include *money, the environment,* and *lifestyle* or *living conditions.* Think about your readers. What tone or attitude do you think will appeal to them? Should you flatter them or challenge them? Should you excite and inspire them, or try to persuade them to think or act calmly and reasonably?

* Draft an opening paragraph for your argument. It should establish the tone that you will use in the rest of the essay.

* Next, think about which propositions in your argument might gain emotional support from an allusion to some well-known person, place, or thing. Remember, because the subject you are writing about is a local issue, referring to local places or events, or quoting local people, can be effective allusions. Rewrite your paragraphs to include your allusions.

* Finally, look at each of the sentences in your paragraphs that states a proposition, a general statement, or a conclusion. Revise or rewrite as many of these as you can to make them concise, polished statements of the points you are making. Reread some of the aphorisms Martin Luther King, Jr., created in his essay and try to use one.

DISCUSSION GUIDES

1. Form a small group and have each member reread paragraphs 15–22, in which King defines the difference between "just" and "unjust" laws. After the reading discuss the following: King writes that "one has a moral responsibility to disobey unjust laws." Do you agree? Do you think citizens have the *right* to disobey laws that they believe are unjust? If you do, would you also say that citizens have a *responsibility* to disobey unjust laws? Each member of the group should have an opportunity to express his or her opinion.

2. Working in a small group, choose one paragraph from King's essay that you think is particularly effective. Each member of the group should rewrite the paragraph using his or her own words. Share your rewritten versions and discuss how and why they are more or less effective than the original.

3. Divide into several small groups. Each group should review the various propositions King offers in his essay and the arguments he presents to support each proposition. Which of King's arguments does your group think is the weakest or least persuasive? Discuss the flaws or weaknesses of King's argument and determine what he might have done to strengthen the argument by appealing either to reason or emotions. Compare and contrast your group's conclusions with those of the other groups.

WRITE A PERSUASIVE ESSAY

In this unit you have seen how Martin Luther King Jr., used rational arguments and emotional appeals in his essay to persuade others to understand and accept his motives and actions. Now you will write a persuasive essay that is for or against the building of an amusement park in your town.

Follow these steps to complete your essay. If you have any questions about the writing process, refer to Using the Writing Process (page 250).

- Gather and review all of the writing exercises you did for this unit: 1) a list of all the positive and negative effects that might come from the development of an amusement park in your town; 2) a rewrite of each of the possible effects as statements, or propositions; 3) paragraphs presenting your reasoning (inductive or deductive) for each of your propositions; 4) a draft of an opening paragraph for your argument and rewrites of your previously written paragraphs that include allusions and aphorisms.

- Begin by revising the draft of the opening paragraph that you wrote in Writing On Your Own 3. In addition to establishing the tone of your persuasive essay and stating who your audience is, your introductory paragraph or paragraphs should clearly state what topic or issue you are writing about.

- Arrange the paragraphs you wrote in Writing On Your Own 2 and 3 in the order in which you will present your propositions. If you have more than one argument for a single proposition, decide on the order in which you will present them.

- Ask a classmate, friend, or family member to read your essay. Ask the reader whether your arguments are convincing. If not, ask the reader why he or she felt they aren't convincing enough. You may then wish to revise your essay to strengthen and better support your arguments.

- Proofread your persuasive essay for spelling, grammar, punctuation, and capitalization. Make a final copy and save it in your writing portfolio.

USING THE WRITING PROCESS

This reference section explains the major steps in the writing process. It will help you complete the writing exercises in this book. Read the information carefully so you can understand the process thoroughly. Whenever you need a quick review of important things to think about when you write, refer to the handy checklist on page 256.

Most tasks worth doing have several steps. For example, houses can be built only after the builder follows a number of complicated, logical steps. Moviemakers must go through a series of steps before releasing a film. Even a task as simple as making a peanut butter and jelly sandwich requires that the sandwich maker perform specific steps in order. So it should be no surprise that anyone who wants to write a good story, play, poem, report, or article must follow certain steps too. Taken together, the steps a writer follows are called the *writing process*. This writing process is divided into three main stages: prewriting, writing, and revising. Each stage is important for good writing.

STAGE 1: Prewriting

Prewriting consists of all the preparation you do before you put a single word down on paper. There are many decisions that you must make in order to make your writing as interesting, logical, and easy to read as possible. Here are the steps you should take before you begin to write:

1. **Decide on your audience.** Who will read your writing? Will your audience be your teacher? Will it be readers of the school newspaper? Or will your audience be family or friends? Your writing will change, depending on who you think your audience will be.

2. **Decide on your purpose.** Why are you writing? Do you want to teach your audience something? Do you want to entertain them? Do you want to change someone's mind about an issue? Think about your purpose before you begin to write.

3. **Think about possible topics.** What are some topics that interest you? Make a list of topics that you are familiar with and might like to write about. Make another list of topics that interest you and that you want to learn about.

   One technique that helps some writers at this stage is *brainstorming.* When you brainstorm, you let your mind wander freely. Without judging your ideas first, scribble them down as they come to you—even if they seem silly or far-fetched. Good ideas often develop from unusual thoughts.

   If you're having trouble coming up with ideas by yourself, brainstorm with a partner or a group of classmates. Jot down everyone's ideas as they say them. Brainstorm-ing alone or with others should give you a long list of possible writing topics.

4. **Choose and narrow your topic.** Once you have chosen a topic, you will probably find that it is impossible to cover every aspect of it in one piece of writing. Say, for example, you have chosen to write about the possibility of life on other planets. In a single piece, you could not possibly include everything that has been researched about extraterrestrial life. Therefore, you must choose one or two aspects to focus on, such as alleged sightings in the United States or worldwide organizations that study extraterrestrial life. Otherwise, you might overload your writing with too many ideas. Concentrate on telling about a few things thoroughly and well.

5. **Research your topic.** You probably have had experience using an encyclopedia, the library, or the Internet to look up information for factual reports. But even when you write fictional stories, you often need to do some research. In a story set during the Civil War, for example, your characters wouldn't use pocket cameras or wear suits of armor. In order to make your story as accurate and believable as possible, you would have to research how Americans lived and dressed during the years of the Civil War.

   To conduct your research, you may want to use books, magazines, newspapers, reference works, or electronic sources. Some topics may require you to interview knowledge-able people. For realistic stories set in the present time, you may find that the best research is simple observation of every-day life. Thorough research will help ensure that your facts and details are accurate.

6. **Organize your research.** Once you have the facts, ideas, and details, you need to decide how to arrange them. Which order will you choose? No matter what you are writing, it is always helpful to begin with a written plan. If you are writing a story, you probably will tell it in time order. Make a list of the major story events, arranged from first to last.

Arranging details in time order is not the only way to orga-nize information, however. Some writers start by making *lists* (informal outlines) of the facts and ideas they have gathered. Then they rearrange the items on their lists until they have the order that will work well in their writing.

Other writers make formal *outlines,* designating the most important ideas with roman numerals (I, II, III, IV, and so on) and related details with letters and numerals (A, B, C; 1, 2, 3; a, b, c; and so on). An outline is a more formal version of a list, and like the items in a list, the items in an outline can be rearranged until you decide on a logical order. Both out-lines and lists help you organize and group your ideas.

Mapping or *clustering* is another helpful technique used by many writers. With this method, you write a main idea in the center of a cluster and then surround it with facts and ideas connected to that idea. Following is an example of a cluster map:

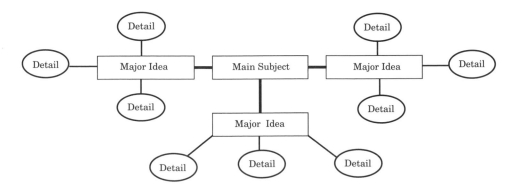

STAGE 2: Writing

1. **Get started.** Begin your writing with an introductory sentence or paragraph. A good introduction can become a guide for the rest of your piece. For ideas on good opening sentences, take a look at some of your favorite stories or magazine articles.

   Your introduction should give your audience a hint about what is coming next. If you are writing a story, your introduction should set the tone and mood. It should reveal the narrator's point of view, and it may introduce the main characters, the setting, and your purpose for writing. Do the best you can with your introduction, but remember that, if you wish to, you can always change it later.

2. **Keep writing.** Get your thoughts down as quickly as possible, referring to your prewriting notes to keep you on track. Later, when you are done with this *rough draft,* you will have a chance to revise and polish your work to make it as clear and accurate as possible. For right now, however, don't stop for spelling, grammar, or exact wording problems. Come as close as you can to what you want to say but don't let yourself get bogged down in details.

STAGE 3: Revising

Now you're ready to revise your work. Careful revision includes editing and reorganizing that can make a big difference in the final product. You may wish to get feedback from your classmates or your teacher about how to revise your work.

1. **Revise and edit your work.** When you are revising and editing, ask yourself these questions:

   • *Did I follow my prewriting plan?* Reread your entire first draft. Compare it to your original plan. Did you skip anything important? If you added an idea, did it work logically with the rest of your plan? Even if you decide that your prewriting plan is no longer what you want, it may include ideas you don't want to lose.

- *Is my writing clear and logical?* Does one idea follow the other in a sensible order? Do you want to change the order or add ideas to make the organization clearer?
- *Is my language clear and interesting?* Have you chosen exact verbs, nouns, and adjectives? For example, have you used forms of the verb *to be (is, are, being, become)* more often than you should? If so, replace them or change your sentence to make them unnecessary. Include precise action words such as *raced, hiked, zoomed,* and *hurried* in place of the overused verb *went.* Instead of using vague nouns such as *water* and *green,* choose exact ones such as *cascade* or *pond* and *lime.* Replace common adjectives such as *beautiful* and *nice* with precise ones such as *elegant, gorgeous,* and *lovely.*
- *Is my writing clear and to the point?* Take out words that repeat the same ideas. For example, don't use both *liberty* and *freedom.* These words are synonyms. Choose one word or the other.

2. **Proofread for errors in spelling, grammar, capitalization, and punctuation.** Anyone reading your writing will notice such errors immediately. These errors can confuse your readers or make them lose interest in what they are reading.

    If you are in doubt about the spelling of a word, look it up or ask someone for help. If you are unsure about your grammar, read your writing aloud and listen carefully. Does anything sound wrong? Check with a friend or classmate if you need a second opinion—or refer to a grammar handbook.

    Make sure every group of words is a complete sentence. Are any of your sentences run-ons? Do proper nouns begin with capital letters? Is the first word of every sentence capitalized? Do all your sentences have the correct end marks? Should you add any other punctuation to your writing to make your ideas even clearer? If your writing includes dialogue, have you used quotation marks correctly?

3. **Make a clean final draft to share.** After you are satisfied with your writing, it is time to share it with your audience. If you are lucky enough to be composing on a computer, you can print out a final copy easily, after running a spell-check. If you are writing your final draft by hand, make sure your handwriting is clear and easy to read. Leave margins on either side of the page. You may want to skip every other line. Make your writing look inviting to your readers. After all, you put a lot of work into this piece. It's important that someone read and enjoy it.

A WRITING CHECKLIST

Ask yourself these questions before beginning a writing assignment:

- Have I chosen a topic that is both interesting and manageable? Should I narrow it so I can cover it in the space that I have?
- Do I have a clear prewriting plan?
- How should I gather my facts and ideas? Be reading? interviewing? observing?
- How will I organize my ideas? In a list? an outline? a cluster map?
- Do I have an opening sentence or paragraph that will pull my readers in?
- Do I need to add more information? switch the order of paragraphs? take out unnecessary information?

Ask yourself these questions after completing a writing assignment:

- Did I use my prewriting plan?
- Is the organization of my writing clear? Should I move, add, or delete any paragraphs or sentences to make the ideas flow more logically?
- Do all the sentences in one paragraph relate to one idea?
- Have I used active, precise words? Is my language interesting? Do the words say what I mean?
- Are all the words spelled correctly?
- Have I used correct grammar, capitalization, punctuation, and formatting?
- Is my final draft legible, clean, and attractive?

GLOSSARY OF LITERARY TERMS

This glossary includes definitions for important literary terms that are introduced in this book. Boldfaced words within the definitions are other terms that appear in the glossary.

alliteration   the repetition of consonant sounds especially at the beginning of words. Alliteration emphasizes certain words and adds a musical quality. *She sold sea shells by the sea shore* is an example of alliteration.

allusion   a reference to a well-known person, place, thing, or event. The writer expects that the reader will recognize the reference.

aphorism   a concise, polished statement of a thought or principle. An aphorism makes a strong point in a memorable way. *The truth is never pure and rarely simple* is an example of an aphorism.

argument   the reasoning a writer uses to lead the reader to a logical conclusion.

article   a nonfiction work that tries to inform or explain a subject to the reader. Authors of articles usually try to be objective; that is, they try to present facts rather than opinions. Articles are generally found in magazines and newspapers.

author's purpose   the writer's reason for creating a particular work. The purpose may be to inform, to instruct, to entertain, to express an opinion, or to persuade readers to do or believe something. An author may have more than one purpose for writing, but usually one is the most important.

autobiography   the story of a real person's life written by that person.

biography   the story of a real person's life written by someone else.

cause-and-effect analysis   a method of explanation used to show how events and situations are related to one another. Two events are related as cause and effect if one brings about, or causes, the other. The event that happens first is the cause; the one that follows is the effect. Writers often signal cause-and-effect relationships with words and phrases such as *because, next, therefore, since, so that,* and *in order that.*

chronological order   the arrangement of events in the order in which they occur. *See* **developmental order, general-to-specific order, order of importance, spatial order,** and **specific-to-general order.**

comparison   the focus on similarities between two things or ideas. **Comparison** is generally used to cover both **comparison** and **contrast.** *See* **contrast.**

connotation   the emotion that a word arouses or the meaning that it suggests beyond its dictionary meaning. *See* **denotation.**

contrast   the focus on differences between two things or ideas. *See* **comparison.**

deductive reasoning   the process that begins with one or more generalizations and moves to a conclusion that is a specific example of the general statements. If the general statements are true, then logically an individual example of the statements must also be true. *See* **inductive reasoning.**

denotation   the literal, or dictionary, definition of a word. *See* **connotation.**

description   the kind of writing that helps readers picture a person, a place, or an event. The other basic kinds of writing are **narration, exposition,** and **argumentation.**

developmental order   the ordering of facts that highlights the natural relationship of one fact to another.

diction   a writer's choice and arrangement of words. Diction is part of a writer's **style.**

essay   a brief work of nonfiction that expresses a person's opinions or views about a particular subject. The purpose of an essay may be to analyze, to inform, to entertain, or to persuade.

exaggeration   an intentional overstatement of facts or events so that their meanings are intensified.

exposition   the kind of writing that explains a subject by presenting information and analysis. The other basic kinds of writing are **narration, description,** and **argumentation.**

figurative language   words or phrases used in unusual ways to create strong, vivid images. Figurative language focuses attention on certain ideas or compares things that are unlike. Figurative language uses **figures of speech.**

figures of speech   words or phrases that are used in other than their literal sense to create vivid images by comparing unlike things. *See* **simile, metaphor,** and **personification.**

frame of reference   the social and historical conditions in which a writer lives. Every writer is influenced by the attitudes and outlook of the society and the historical period in which he or she lives.

general-to-specific order   the arrangement of information that starts with a general discussion of the main points and then proceeds to specific examples, facts, or other evidence. *See* **chronological order, developmental order, order of importance, spatial order,** and **specific-to-general order.**

generalization   a broad statement or conclusion that is true of *some* or *most* but not *all* examples.

historical analysis   a method of explanation used to show how events and situations are related to one another. Historical analysis puts an idea, an event, or an action in historical perspective.

imagery   the use of words or phrases that appeal to one or more of the senses of sight, sound, taste, smell, and touch.

inductive reasoning   the process of being convinced that a number of examples, all leading toward the same general conclusion, do in fact justify accepting that general conclusion. Another term for inductive reasoning is **generalizing.** *See* **deductive reasoning.**

interpretation   one person's view of the meaning of certain words, events, or actions. Nonfiction writers continually interpret facts by explaining their meaning and evaluating their importance.

lead   the opening paragraph of an article.

metaphor   a figure of speech that compares two unlike things without using a word of comparison such as *like* or *as*. A metaphor suggests that one thing *is* another. The purpose of a metaphor is to give readers an unusual way of looking at one of the things.

motif   a recurrent theme in a piece of writing.

narration   the kind of writing that gives the events and actions of a story. The other basic kinds of writing are **description, exposition,** and **argumentation.**

order of importance   the arrangement of topics and events based on the significance the writer places on each. *See* **chronological order, general-to-specific order, spatial order,** and **specific-to-general order.**

parallelism   the repetition of forms, words, phrases, or clauses that are similar in structure. Such repetitions add to the continuity within a paragraph as well as highlight the connections between ideas.

personification   a figure of speech in which an animal, an object, or an idea is given the characteristics of a person. Personification can be used to add humor to a work or to describe abstract ideas such as freedom, truth, and beauty.

persuasion   the kind of writing that uses reasons, arguments, and logic to make a point. Essayists, for example, often use persuasion to convince readers that the essayists' opinions are correct. The other basic kinds of writing are **narration, description,** and **exposition.**

primary source   information that comes directly from the time a subject lived or an event occurred. *See* **secondary sources.**

proposition   a belief or action that the writer wants the audience to support.

secondary source   information that comes from a later time than a subject lived or an event occurred. *See* **primary source.**

simile   a direct comparison between two basically unlike things that have some quality in common. Similes connect the two things by using the words *like, as,* or *than,* or the verbs *appears* or *seems* to make the comparison. The purpose of a simile is to give the reader a vivid new way of looking at one of the things.

spatial order   the arrangement of information in the order in which objects are arranged in space. *See* **chronological order, developmental order, general-to-specific order, order of importance,** and **specific-to-general order.**

specific-to-general order   the arrangement of information that starts with specific examples, facts, or other evidence and then proceeds to a general discussion of the main points. *See* **chronological order, developmental order, general-to-specific order, order of importance,** and **spatial order.**

structure   the writer's arrangement and overall design of a work. Structure refers to the way words, sentences, and paragraphs are organized to create a complete work.

style   the way writers express themselves in their writing. Style is a particular way of writing. It involves *how* the writer says what or he or she says. The writer's choice of sentence structure and choice of words are two elements of style.

subject   the person whose life story is being told in a **biography** or **autobiography.**

theme   the underlying message, or central idea, of a piece of writing.

thesis   the directly-stated prupose or main idea of an article or essay.

tone   a writer's attitude toward his or her subject or audience.

topic sentence   a sentence that states the main idea of a paragraph.

viewpoint   the feelings, opinions, and experiences that affect a writer's outlook on life. Viewpoint affects not only how the writer understands the facts he or she presents but also which facts he or she includes in a piece of writing.